MW00804135

Applied Hypnosis
and
Hyperempiria

Applied Hypnosis
and
Hyperempiria

Don E. Gibbons
West Georgia College
Carrollton, Georgia

PLENUM PRESS · NEW YORK AND LONDON

Library of Congress Cataloging in Publication Data

Gibbons, Don E
  Applied hypnosis and hyperempiria.

  Bibliography: p.
  Includes index.
  1. Hypnotism—Therapeutic use. I. Title
RC495.G46   615'.8512   79-20879
ISBN 0-306-40271-8

© 1979 Plenum Press, New York
A Division of Plenum Publishing Corporation
227 West 17th Street, New York, N.Y. 10011

All rights reserved

No part of this book may be reproduced, stored in a retrieval system, or transmitted,
in any form or by any means, electronic, mechanical, photocopying, microfilming,
recording, or otherwise, without written permission from the Publisher

Printed in the United States of America

To Patsy and Kathleen

Foreword

Professionals who are well-trained in hypnotherapeutic procedures are able to utilize a variety of suggestions—suggestions for age regression, cessation of smoking, weight control, relaxation, reduction of pain, etc. In fact, the art of "hypnosis" can be conceptualized as the art of administering suggestions in an effective and useful way. In the teaching of hypnosuggestive methods, the need has long been apparent for a manual that could provide examples of suggestions that would be serviceable in applied settings. Now we are fortunate to have this text by Don E. Gibbons, which offers many different kinds of suggestions that can serve as models for both the novice and the experienced practitioner. Students who are training in this area can use the text to learn how to formulate their own suggestions in professional settings. Experienced hypnotherapists will also find the text helpful in expanding their repertoire.

In addition to presenting useful models of suggestions, Dr. Gibbons's text also meets the need for a clearly written manual that explains hypnosis in accordance with the results of modern research. During the past 25 years, more research has been conducted on hypnosis than in all the preceding years since Mesmer. These investigations have led to a view of hypnosis which differs markedly from the traditional view of the passive subject who is hypnotized by and is subservient to the dominant hypnotist. From such a modern viewpoint, one sees good hypnotic subjects as *actively doing,* as actively becoming involved in the situation, and as actively thinking with and imagining those things that are suggested.

Responsiveness in a hypnotic situation is much more closely related to the subjects' readiness to accept suggestions and to their
capabilities of responding to the specific suggestions they are given
rather than to the special characteristics of the hypnotist or of the
hypnotic induction procedure. The main tasks of the hypnotist are to
remove the subjects' misconceptions and negative attitudes, to elicit
their maximum cooperation, and to release and guide their capabilities for imagining and fantasizing. The use of a formal hypnotic induction procedure is only one of many possible methods for eliciting
the subjects' capabilities. Other methods for evoking maximal
responsiveness include, for example, asking the subjects straight-
forwardly to think of and imagine those things that will be suggested,
or implementing one of the various hyperempiric procedures developed by Dr. Gibbons, which are worded in terms of mind expansion and heightened awareness, and which are in harmony with our
present-day culture.

Dr. Gibbons appropriately notes in the text that base-level or
"normal" responsiveness to test suggestions—for example, suggestions for arm rigidity, hand levitation, age regression, and amnesia—is
much higher than is commonly believed. Uninformed individuals
incorrectly assume that, when test suggestions are given under a
control condition (without an attempt to hypnotize the subjects), very
few individuals respond positively to the suggestions. The truth is
that, under base-level conditions, most individuals are responsive to
some test suggestions, and approximately 10% of experimental subjects (typically, college students) respond positively to practically all
the test suggestions. Responsiveness to suggestions is simply *not* an
uncommon phenomenon. Hypnotic induction procedures aim to enhance this base-level responsiveness by removing fears and misconceptions and by helping subjects to think and imagine with the suggestions that are given. Without the underlying base-level responsiveness
to suggestions, which is found in most individuals to a moderate
degree and in some individuals to a marked degree, hypnotic induction procedures could by themselves do very little. These procedures
aim to elicit the subjects' maximal level of responsiveness to suggestions; they do not produce responsiveness *de novo*.

The importance of imagining and fantasizing is commendably
emphasized in Dr. Gibbons's presentation. Individuals who respond
well to the types of suggestions employed in hypnotic settings typically have a lifetime history of involvement in imagining and fantasiz-

ing. Furthermore, many of the suggestions given in hypnotic situations summon forth directly the capability to visualize, to imagine, and to fantasize—for example, to imagine oneself at a future time (age progression) or at a prenatal time ("past life regression"), to visualize vividly objects that are not present (visual hallucinations), or to experience a dreamlike fantasy (suggested dreaming). Dr. Gibbons succinctly summarizes this very important feature of hypnosis in a striking statement: "An 'induction procedure,' then, is . . . a method of providing both the opportunity and the rationale for those who are able and willing to utilize their imagination in an 'Alice-in-Wonderland' fashion to go ahead and do so" (pp. 16–17).

Dr. Gibbons's text also clearly underscores many other important points. For example, it dispels some of the confusion surrounding the question "Is hypnosis an altered state?" by noting that there is no end to the number of altered states that can be produced by suggestions in a receptive subject. I have likewise noted elsewhere that it can be suggested to responsive subjects that they are entering a drowsy-sleepy state, a superawake state, an absolutely normal awake state, a state of mental calm, a state identical to alcoholic inebriation, a state similar to the marijuana or LSD "high," or any other state that can be clearly conceived by both the suggestor and the subject. Similarly, Dr. Gibbons has interesting and practical things to say about methods which are said to "deepen hypnosis." He forcefully notes that so-called *deepening procedures* are categorized in a misleading way because, in reality, they are methods for enhancing the credibility and the degree of the subject's imaginative involvement in the suggested experience.

This text, which contains many useful models of hypnosuggestive procedures and which presents the procedures within the context of recent research findings, should have a long and fruitful life.

THEODORE X. BARBER, PH.D.
Director of Special Projects
Cushing Hospital
Framingham, Massachusetts

Preface

Only a minority of the professionals who have been trained in the use of hypnosis and related techniques routinely employ these procedures after their training has been completed, in spite of the rapid advances being made in this area and the burgeoning interest which these advances have aroused. Much of the difficulty, I am convinced, can be traced to the lack of sufficiently precise instructional material on the use of suggestion in applied settings.

This book was written in response to this need for a practical teaching text stressing concrete applications. It is intended for both the beginning student and for the established professional who wishes to expand his repertoire. Discussion and commentary have been integrated into a functional, "how-to-do-it" approach; and all the techniques and inductions contained herein are set forth in the form of concrete verbalizations which are designed to cover most of the situations for which suggestion-induced trances are commonly employed in psychological and counseling situations, together with a number of applications which are entirely new.

I should like to express my particular appreciation to Leonard R. Pace of Plenum Publishing Corporation for his timely cooperation and assistance, to Dr. T. X. Barber for reading and commenting upon the manuscript and for contributing the foreword to this volume, and to the many students and subjects, too numerous to mention individually, who have provided me with much helpful feedback over the years, thereby teaching me a great deal more than I have taught them.

DON E. GIBBONS

Contents

PART TWO • THERAPEUTIC SUGGESTIONS

PART THREE • SUGGESTION AS AN INSTRUMENT OF PERSONAL GROWTH

PART ONE

INDUCTION TECHNIQUES

"But oh, beamish nephew, beware of the day
If your Snark be a Boojum! For then
You will softly and suddenly vanish away
And never be met with again!"

—Lewis Carroll, *The Hunting of the Snark*

CHAPTER 1

The Nature of the Induction Process

"You are going into a deep, sound sleep," the stage hypnotist intones. "Every word that I utter is putting you faster and faster into a deep, sound sleep. . . ." After a few moments, the subject is handed a raw onion and told that it is an apple, whereupon he proceeds to eat it with evident enjoyment.

In a hospital obstetrical unit, a woman prepares to undergo a Caesarean section by listening to a similar patter. No chemical anesthetic is employed, and the operation is successful with no complications. The surgeon notes, however, that the recorded volume of blood loss is less than would normally be expected.

In the office of a clinical psychologist, a patient listens with his eyes closed while the therapist goes through an induction routine which is quite similar to the one employed by the stage hypnotist and the surgeon. In response to subsequent suggestions, the patient proceeds to act out a supposedly forgotten traumatic event from his childhood, believing as he does so that he is a little child once more, and that the long-forgotten event is taking place at that very moment.

How is it possible to induce such dramatic effects merely by speaking to a person in a repetitive monotone, suggesting that he is "going to sleep," when it is obvious to all concerned—including the subject himself—that people who are *actually* asleep are definitely *not* able to do these things?

There is an old saying that those who do not know history are

3

condemned to repeat it; and nowhere is this more evident than in the history of suggestion-induced trances. Although healing by means of trance induction probably dates back to prehistoric times, the revival of modern interest in such procedures, at least in Western culture, may be traced directly to the work of the Viennese physician, Franz Anton Mesmer (1733–1815). Mesmer was considerably influenced by the teachings of Paracelsus, who had held two centuries earlier that the stars and the planets exert considerable influence over human behavior by means of their magnetic fields. Mesmer decided to investigate the implications of this theory for himself by slowly drawing some small magnets along the bodies of his patients. This was frequently found to induce convulsions, fainting, and the disappearance (at least temporarily) of a host of various symptoms; and thus, magnetic treatment appeared to Mesmer and his followers to constitute an exciting medical breakthrough.

Mesmer soon discovered, however, that he was able to produce the same results without the aid of special magnets, and thereby concluded that the "magnetism" in question was coming from his own body. In order to make the most efficient use of this "animal magnetism," as he began to call it, Mesmer abandoned the use of metal magnets altogether and simply began to make passes in the air with his hands near the bodies of his patients, frequently snapping his fingers in the air as he did so (Sarbin & Coe, 1972). Needless to say, the frequency of his dramatic "cures" remained undiminished.

The Viennese medical establishment began to look askance at such strange goings-on, and Mesmer decided to move his practice to Paris, where he promptly established a large following. His patients would customarily seat themselves around a large wooden tub, or *baquet*, which was filled with a mixture of iron fillings, ground glass, and water, with iron rods protruding from holes in the wooden top of the tub so that the patients could grasp the rods and apply them to the site of their respective afflictions.

Just as a piece of iron will itself become magnetized if it is placed next to a magnet for a period of time, it was soon discovered that objects which were known to have been touched by Mesmer were apparently endowed with the same ability to induce "crises" as a touch from the wand of the master himself, thus creating a considerable demand for such objects and enlarging the scope of Mesmer's influence still further.

When the demand had reached its height, Mesmer proceeded to "magnetize" a large elm tree on the estate of his patron, the Marquis de Puységur, a few miles outside of the city of Paris; and great crowds would often gather to stand under the tree, either to derive the benefits of its healing power for themselves or simply to observe the dramatic results which were apparently produced in others.

By this time, the French medical establishment was becoming as concerned as their colleagues in Vienna had been over Mesmer's flamboyant style and his dramatic claims of "cures." In 1784, the French government commissioned a special panel, chaired by Benjamin Franklin, who was the American ambassador to France at the time, to investigate the phenomena of "mesmerism" from a scientific point of view. The conclusion of this committee was that all the phenomena attributed to mesmerism could be explained as the result of imitation and the workings of the subject's own imagination.

Events were to take yet another turn when a retarded peasant lad of twenty-three named Victor Emmanuel was brought to stand under the now-famous elm tree of the Marquis de Puységur in the hope that the "magnetic rays" which were supposedly emanating from the tree might also be of some benefit to him. As many retardates are apt to do when they are placed in a situation in which they are not quite certain what is expected of them, Victor, though he remained standing, promptly utilized the occasion to avail himself of a quick nap. Other patients standing under the tree, seeing Victor asleep on his feet, apparently perceived this event as merely another result of the strange mesmeric rays emanating from the tree; for they promptly began to feel drowsy and to "fall asleep" themselves, thereby initiating a change in the form of suggestion-induced trances which heralded the death of mesmerism and the birth of hypnotism as it exists today. Additional accounts of these developments are to be found in Hull (1933) and Rosen (1963).

By now the role of suggestion in determining the outward form of trance behavior should be fairly obvious. The mesmeric "crises" were brought about by implicit suggestions or expectations arising from the eccentric astrological notions of Paracelsus, whereas the "sleeping" or hypnotic trance was first manifested by people who were imitating the behavior of a retardate, who was *too stupid* to realize that he was supposed to go into convulsions and went to sleep instead!

This is essentially the same interpretation as that provided by

Franklin's report, which attributed such phenomena to imitation and the workings of the subject's imagination. However, the unintended effect of Franklin's impartial investigation was to discredit the systematic use of suggestion by responsible professionals and to relegate such procedures for many decades to the virtually exclusive province of charlatans and stage entertainers. The reason for this unfortunate outcome is rooted in our Western habit of describing things as being *either* real *or* imaginary, with the attendant implication that the word "imaginary" is synonymous with "nonexistent." Thus, if mesmerism and hypnosis are due to the workings of the imagination, then to many people this implied that such phenomena simply do not exist; for nothing which has imaginary (and therefore nonexistent) causes can produce "real" effects.

It was not until 1958 that the Council on Mental Health of the American Medical Association became sufficiently aware of the multiplicity of "real" effects produced by trance suggestion that it endorsed hypnosis as a valid therapeutic modality. But the implicit semantic assumptions remained unchallenged; for now that the *effects* of suggestion had been found to be real, a lively search was undertaken to find the "real," that is, *physiological*, correlates of the hypnotic trance—a search which continues even today, with little apparent success.

It has been found, for example, that more responsive subjects tend to look in one direction when pondering the answer to a question, and less responsive subjects tend to look in the opposite direction (Bakan, 1969); and Paskewitz (1977) has concluded that the relationship between alpha brain-wave patterns and suggestibility is "encouraging" but far from definite—which should not be surprising, in view of the degree to which he admits it is possible to regulate one's own alpha rhythm, and the degree to which it is possible to regulate one's responsiveness to test suggestions (Barber, 1975; Katz, 1975). However, such findings, although extremely interesting in themselves, do not demonstrate the suggestion-induced trance experience is a separately identifiable physiological state of the organism, in the same sense that sleep, coma, fainting, and shock can be shown to be separately identifiable physiological states. Indeed, the findings to date seem to indicate at best that people who are highly responsive to suggestion may be somewhat different from those who are not. But that, of course, has been apparent from the beginning.

In the course of such investigations, several previously held notions concerning the nature of trance experience have come to be reevaluated. For example, although some writers such as Gibson (1977) are still convinced that there is such a thing as "animal hypnosis," the majority appear to be convinced that such a phenomenon does not exist. "Animal hypnosis" appears to be a catch-all term for various species-specific cataleptic states which are as unrelated to "hypnosis" as they are to each other (Gibbons, 1973). For example, a reclining cat will tend to remain in the same position for a time if it is gently stroked under the chin, and a chicken will frequently remain immobile for a few moments if its beak is held to the ground and a line is slowly drawn straight away from the beak with a piece of chalk. Yet, there are so many ways to "hypnotize" a human being—from gently stroking his outstretched arm, to gazing intently into his eyes, to almost any other routine one can think of—that the only thing such methods seem to have in common is that they all provide ways of credibly communicating the suggestion that one is being hypnotized, which is clearly impossible with animals.

Many purported demonstrations of enhanced abilities in response to trance suggestion, long a staple of stage demonstrations, have also been found to be inaccurate. For instance, one classic demonstration involves placing a subject between two chairs, supporting the back of his neck by one chair and his heels by the other, and removing all other sources of support after telling him that his body has become as stiff and as rigid as a bar of iron. What most people do not realize, however, is that the muscle groups involved in a maneuver such as this are indeed quite strong; and virtually anyone who is in reasonably good physical condition is able to perform such a feat with or without an induction.

The ability of some patients to undergo surgical operations with hypnotic suggestion as the sole anesthetic has long been known, having first been used by James Braid and James Esdaile before the introduction of ether as a general anesthetic (Marks, 1947). But as we shall see in the following discussion of the leading theories of hypnosis, many investigators are inclined to view this phenomenon as owing to something other than a property of the hypnotic trance.

Decreased bleeding is also commonly reported in operations using hypnotic suggestion as the sole anesthetic; and some writers (e.g., Hartland, 1971b) have claimed that it is possible virtually to eliminate bleeding in dental extractions by means of strong hypnotic suggestion. Of course, unlike many chemical anesthetics, a trance induction does not in itself function as a depressant to the nervous system. Thus, when suggestion alone is employed for the relief of pain, the normal operation of the capillary reflex in reducing the flow of blood is not interfered with.

Perhaps the most intriguing argument to date supporting the notion that hypnosis is an objectively "real" phenomenon has been provided by Martin T. Orne (1972), and replicated by McDonald and Smith (1975). Using one group of subjects who were administered a hypnotic induction, and another group who were merely instructed to pretend that they were hypnotized, Orne found that both the hypnotized subjects and the simulators would respond convincingly to the suggestion that they would "see" a man sitting in a chair which was actually empty; but the two groups responded quite differently when they were then requested to describe the back of the chair in which the hallucinated individual was supposedly sitting. The hypnotized subjects would occasionally comply with this request, whereas the simulators all responded in quite logical fashion that they could not see the back of the chair because there was a man sitting in it. The genuinely hypnotized subjects, in other words, were able to make use of what Orne (1972) has termed *trance logic*—the tendency to comply with suggestions with little or no concern for their logical implications, in a manner which resembled the "logic" often found in dreams. However, Orne's conclusions have subsequently been challenged (Johnson, Maher, & Barber, 1972), and Orne himself has recently admitted that his view of hypnosis is not incompatible with a notion of trance experience as "believed-in imaginings" (Sarbin & Coe, 1972), as long as such imaginings *are* actually believed in and therefore experienced as real by the subject (Orne, 1977).

Several other intriguing speculations have arisen regarding the nature of trance experience. Among the most prominent of these is Ernest R. Hilgard's "neo-dissociation" theory (Hilgard, 1973, 1974, 1977a,b; Knox, Morgan, & Hilgard, 1974), which characterizes the hypnotic trance as an altered or dissociated state of consciousness. Dissociation itself, of course, is experienced in varying degrees by virtually everyone at one time or another, as illustrated by the common tendency to drive along a familiar thoroughfare with one's conscious attention largely preoccupied with other matters, or the ability to answer a question while one is engaged in reading a book without subsequently being able to recall that one has done so. More extreme forms of dissociation include sleepwalking, amnesia, fugue, and multiple personality.

The ability of mediums to behave as though they were possessed by the personalities of others, and the use of the Ouija board to answer fortune-telling questions, believing as one does so that one's fingers are being guided across the board by some unseen force, may also be viewed as examples of dissociaton. In addition, dissociative behaviors include those which are subsumed under the heading of conversion hysteria, or loss of physical function for psychological reasons. Since normal individuals also respond to hypnotic inductions, however, the theory originally propounded by the French neurologist and anatomist Jean Martin Charcot that hypnosis itself is merely a form of hysteria—and therefore limited to hysterics—has long since been discarded.

Most of the phenomena collectively referred to as "hypnotic," however, do appear to be capable of being included under the general category of dissociation, at least as such phenomena have *traditionally* been conceived and measured; and even hypnotically induced surgical anesthesia may be viewed as merely a manifestation of the ability of many persons not to respond to pain stimuli when their attention is appropriately directed elsewhere (Hilgard & Hilgard, 1975).

For example, news accounts occasionally tell of an athlete who has suffered substantial injuries in the course of a game, but who did not become aware of them until the competition was at an end—presumably because his attention was so completely focused on the game itself. Similarly, many people who have been injured in automobile accidents have reported that they did not become aware of most of the pain until they were safely on the way to the hospital and the emergency was over, even though they did not go into shock.

Other theorists have been less willing to posit the existence of a separate state of awareness termed hypnosis. According to T. R. Sarbin, for example (Coe & Sarbin, 1977; Sarbin, 1950; Sarbin & Andersen, 1967; Sarbin & Coe, 1972), the subject who is regarded as hypnotized is merely behaving in accordance with a social role which is defined for him by prevailing cultural attitudes concerning the nature of the hypnotic trance and by the specific suggestions of the hypnotist. In other words, when it was believed that the mesmerists had the ability to induce "crises" in their patients, the convulsions and swooning which purportedly constituted the outward manifestations of a "readjustment of the balance of magnetic fluids" within the body were induced with relative ease; but when people ceased to believe in mesmerism, mesmerism ceased to exist. And so it is with hypnosis; for hypnosis, like mesmerism, possesses no unique, objective characteristics which are independent of the attitudes and expectations which people hold about it.

It should not be assumed, however, that the use of the term *role* by Sarbin and others implies any deliberate acting or simulation on the part of the person who is hypnotized; for the degree of organismic involvement in role taking can be very great. In fact, such phenomena as voodoo killings may be viewed as a form of "role taking to the death." The victim, knowing that he has been "hexed" and believing that he is going to die, is cast out of his village and left to wander alone in the jungle, bereft of family and friends; for it is assumed that anyone who attempts to aid such a person will suffer a similar fate. Eventually, of course, the victim dies—primarily from the stress induced by his having been cast in the role of victim in the first place. Other examples of roles in which there is usually a high degree of organismic involvement include the role of bride and groom at a wedding ceremony, and the role of one who is judged by those around him to be mentally ill.

According to a role-theoretic interpretation of hypnosis, the ability of some people to ignore surgical pain in response to suggestions of anesthesia is seen as a result of their high capacity for organismic involvement in the role of subject, hypnotizability itself being defined as "role-taking aptitude."

Perhaps the most skeptical of all the investigators of "so-called 'hypnotic' phenomena," as he terms them, is T. X. Barber (1969, 1972; Barber & De Moor, 1972; Barber & Wilson, 1977). For Barber, "hypnosis" is a construct which has been invoked to explain the apparent changes in thinking and behavior which distinguish the person who is "hypnotized" from one who is not. Constructs are not to be "believed in," however; they are either useful or not useful, and for Barber, the construct of the "hypnotic trance" is not useful and ought to be discarded.

Barber prefers to account for the behaviors which are currently referred to as "hypnotic phenomena" in terms of general social psychological variables operating within the situation, plus the subject's ability to think along with and vividly imagine the suggestions he is given; and, in particular, his tendency to make use of what Barber refers to as "goal directed imagery," or to picture in his mind certain conditions which would act to bring about the suggested responses if they were true. For instance, when it is suggested to a subject that his arm is becoming lighter and that it is rising into the air, the subject may later report that he visualized his arm as a hollow sausage which was slowly being filled with helium. If one is predisposed to employ such imagery, his arm *is* likely to rise into the air in response to the suggestion that it is becoming lighter; but if one is not, then the arm is likely to remain inert regardless of whether or not a "trance induction" has been presented before the suggestion was given.

The ability of some persons to behave as if they felt no pain in response to suggestions of surgical anesthesia is regarded by Barber as a result of the patient having learned to pay attention to other things while the operation is going on, combined with the fact that pain is not sensed as readily in the organs as it is in the skin; and, therefore, the task of not attending to it is not really as difficult as one might at first surmise.

Such an explanation of suggested surgical anesthesia becomes even more plausible, Barber points out, when it is recognized that the claims of acupuncturists to induce surgical anesthesia by inserting small needles into the proper "meridians" of the body are neurologically impossible; and that any decreased responsiveness obtained by such methods must therefore be the result of other factors, such as the ability of the procedure to divert the patient's attention.

Which theory is the "correct" one? It is currently becoming fashionable to speak of *models* rather than *theories*, because use of the former term implies no concern with whether or not a particular explanation happens to be "true," but merely addresses itself to the degree to which such an explanation happens to be "useful." This usefulness may be either *expository*, in the ability of a particular model to deal simply and elegantly with all the phenomena with which it is purportedly concerned, and to "make sense" out of a great deal of information which would otherwise be merely a collection of disjointed facts, or it may be *heuristic*, in the degree to which a particular model is able to serve as a source of testable hypotheses for future laboratory investigation. Of course, individual models may vary to a considerable extent in regard to these two criteria of usefulness; and for this reason, some models or paradigms are to be preferred more than others. Moreover, if *usefulness* rather than "truth" becomes the criterion by which various models are to be evaluated, it follows that models which initially appear to be quite different from one another need not be considered as mutually exclusive.

All three of the models presented here have shown themselves to be highly useful in terms of their expository and heuristic value, which accounts in large measure for the fact that they are the three leading contenders in popularity among investigators in the area of sugges-tion-related cognitive processes. In order to examine the relative usefulness of these models in enabling one to arrive at satisfactory conclusions concerning the ultimate nature of such phenomena, how-ever, it may be helpful to adopt an existential level of discourse and to turn to a closer examination of trance induction procedures them-selves.

Most induction procedures currently in use are organized in such a manner as to facilitate the acceptance of later, more difficult sugges-tions by presenting easier or more credible ones at the beginning. It is rather difficult to suggest credibly that a subject is entering a hypnotic trance merely by staring into his eyes and commanding him to "Sleep!" for example, although the Abbé Faria is reported to have used such a procedure in the early days of hypnotism, and some stage hypnotists still employ this technique occasionally for its dramatic effects. The induction technique originated by James Braid (1795–1860), however, soon gained widespread acceptance and has remained the most commonly used approach until comparatively recently.

For purposes of illustration, the Braid technique will be described in detail. The subject is first requested to stare fixedly at some bright, shiny object which is held a few inches in front of his eyes and slightly above his normal level of vision, in such a manner as to induce some degree of eyestrain. He is then asked to continue to focus on the object while the suggestor swings it slowly back and forth. During this time, the subject is given a steady stream of suggestions to the effect that his eyes are becoming heavy and tired, that they will soon be so tired that he will want to close them, and that they will eventually tend to close of themselves.

Since the subject is focusing his eyes in such a manner as to produce strain and fatigue, he is inevitably going to experience such feelings sooner or later, regardless of how suggestible he happens to be. But because the situation has been arranged in such a manner as to capitalize on this naturally occurring fatigue, the subject is led to believe that the feelings he is experiencing are the result of the induction—thus enhancing the credibility of the entire procedure and predisposing him to accept the suggestions which follow.

After the subject's eyes have closed, he is given suggestions of progressively increasing relaxation: "You can feel yourself relaxing more and more now. You can feel a heavy, relaxed feeling coming over your entire body." Of course, the subject is relaxing voluntarily because he wishes to cooperate; but in the context of the situation and the suggestion being administered, this relaxation is likely to be experienced by the subject as additional evidence that the induction is indeed "working."

After the subject has been cognitively prepared in such a manner, it is a great deal easier for him to accept subsequent suggestions that he is "going into a deep, sound sleep"; and, finally, the suggestion that he *is* asleep—even though, as previously indicated, no measurable physiological changes such as those which characterize actual sleep have ever been reliably associated with the induction of hypnosis.

When the subject has begun to respond successfully to the suggestion that he is now in a state of hypnosis, virtually any other suggestion with which he is able and willing to comply may be presented as yet one more manifestation of the processes which have purportedly been brought about within him. Those who are not sufficiently suggestible to "feel any different" after the induction is completed are frequently encouraged to think of hypnosis as merely the ability to focus and to concentrate one's attention. Since the base line of suggestibility in the general population is much higher than is commonly assumed (Barber & Calverley, 1963), simple phenomena such as eyelid catalepsy or arm levitation are often used to convince the subject that he is indeed hpnotized, regardless of how he may actually feel, thus providing the necessary framework of plausibility for the presentation of whatever additional suggestions the subject may be able and willing to accept. In other words, the "heightened state of suggestibility" which may cause a person to think and behave differently after an induction has been administered may be seen as a necessary implication of accepting the suggestion that one is in a trance.

It is not always necessary to employ the words "sleep" or "hypnosis," however, to communicate the suggestion that one is about to undergo an alteration in the perception of one's own awareness; for as we have seen in the discussion of the development of both the mesmeric-convulsive and the hypnotic-sleeping forms of trance behavior, suggestions may be easily communicated to the subject in an implicit manner. It is perfectly possible to substitute other terms for the term "hypnosis," or even to eliminate the use of overall descriptive labels altogether, as long as the procedure which is employed effectively communicates the suggestion that one's mental processes are beginning to function differently, thus providing an appropriate set for the subsequent uncritical acceptance of suggestions which may be at variance with everyday experience.

Spanos and Barber (1974) have pointed out that an induction procedure tends to heighten the subject's involvement in "suggestion-related imaginings." That is, it provides a point of transition from a rational to a nonrational mode of discourse, wherein a person is able to suspend his customary patterns of critical thought temporarily to allow himself an opportunity to identify more closely with what is about to be expressed. This suspension of critical thinking is facilitated by the vocal inflections and style of delivery which are employed; by the rhythm and cadence of the induction itself; by the setting in which the induction takes place and the use of various types of props or background effects, such as soft lights, music, and the presence of visual fixation objects or other forms of distraction; and by the employment of specific imagery which will evoke modes of nonrational involvement with which the subject is already familiar or which he can easily imagine—going to sleep, relaxing on the beach, entering a cathedral, or becoming absorbed in an adventure story or a fairy tale, to name but a few.

It is this shift from an active-rational to a receptive-imaginative orientation, legitimized by the acceptance of explicitly or implicitly communicated suggestions to the effect that one is now in an "altered state of consciousness," which is responsible for both the development of incongruous thought patterns (Sheehan, 1977), and the phenomenon of *rapport*, or the tendency of the subject to focus his attention on the voice of the suggestor and on the phenomena he describes, often to the exclusion of other stimuli—including pain, if anesthesia is suggested or implied. If a dentist were merely to suggest to a patient that he would not experience any pain during a tooth extraction, for instance, with no induction administered beforehand, it is not likely that such a suggestion would be effective by itself, regardless of how responsive to suggestion the patient happened to be. But if the dentist were first to suggest that the patient was "entering a trance," and *then* he suggested that the patient would feel no pain, the latter suggestion could be actualized much more easily because it would then be much more credible (Gibbons, 1974).

In addition to an increased responsiveness to suggestion, the purported existence of "trance logic," and the phenomenon of *rapport*, other effects, such as transference, or the tendency to respond to the suggestor with emotions similar to those with which one formerly regarded one's parents, and various other regressed or childlike thought patterns, may occur in certain individuals at least part of the time during or subsequent to an induction; and various authorities have seized upon all these at one time or another as the ultimate explanation of "hypnosis" (Gill & Brenman, 1959; Sheehan & Perry, 1976). But by now it should be clear that all such phenomena, like the various forms of dissociation which may occur in response to suggestion, are by-products of the suggestion that one is experiencing a trance rather than the essence of the trance itself.

In order to conclude our discussion of the alterations in conscious experience which may be induced by suggestion, it is necessary to examine just what it means to be aware of oneself as conscious in the first place; and this examination can perhaps best be accomplished by turning once more to a historical illustration. In the early years of this century, adherents of the school of psychology known as *structuralism* were attempting to discover the basic elements of consciousness by employing a method called *introspection*. This "looking inward" to identify the basic components of one's own thoughts and feelings led to widespread disagreement among various investigators regarding just how many such elements of consciousness there actually were (Boring, 1950). The difficulty, of course, lay in the fact that consciousness, like a mirror, tends to reflect back what is put into it; and if one's reading and speculation have led a person to surmise that a particular element exists in consciousness, as soon as one begins musingly to "look inward" to discover such an element, that element is likely to appear. The process is somewhat reminiscent of the game which Tolstoy and his brother used to play when they were children, which involved seeing how long they both could go *without* thinking of a white bear.

Since the perception of one's own awareness is, by definition, a subjective phenomenon, what is true regarding the elements of consciousness is also true regarding the experience of one's consciousness as a whole. In other words, the number of "altered states" (or more accurately, altered *experiences*) of consciousness which may be induced by suggestion is probably equal to the number of such states or experiences which it is possible to conceive or to imagine; for each of these imagined definitions may be presented in the form of an induction procedure or similar ritual containing explicit or implicit suggestions which will bring about such an experience in subjects who are sufficiently responsive and willing to comply. Thus, the suggestor is free to define the dimensions and experiential properties of a suggestion-induced "trance state" *in virtually any manner he desires* (Gibbons, 1973).

Today, for example, we frequently hear of meditation, mind control, autogenic training, suggestology, dianetics, and a host of other techniques too numerous to mention. Rather than concluding that these techniques are all variations of "hypnosis," it is more accurate to describe them as changes in perceived awareness which are brought about by means of suggestion, and which differ from hypnosis in the same way that they differ from each other: in the specific phenomenological content of the changes in perceived awareness which are either directly suggested or implied by the procedure which is utilized to bring about such changes, and, hence, in the "feel" of the resulting subjective experience of trance, and in the effect of that experience upon the subsequent thought and behavior of the subject who undergoes it (Gibbons, 1974). A highly responsive hypnotic subject *may feel* as if he has been unconscious, for example, and report that he remembers nothing of the events which transpired while he was supposedly under the influence of the "trance" (unless he has been previously told that he is not *supposed* to feel that way in hypnosis, or it has been specifically suggested to him that he will remember everything), whereas a student undergoing an advanced form of yogic training may feel as if he is merging with infinite reality!

An "induction procedure," then, is not some sort of mechanical process which one person "uses on" another to render the subject more compliant with the will of the suggestor, as laymen occasionally tend to perceive it; and neither does it operate in some mysterious manner to open up a direct channel of communication with the "unconscious mind." It is, rather, a method of providing both the opportunity and the rationale for those who are able and willing to utilize their imagination in an "Alice-in-Wonderland" fashion to go ahead and do so. In terms of the opening quotation to this section, the "Snark" of trance induction has turned out to be nothing more than a "Boojum" of the active imagination; and the "skeptical" positions of Sarbin and Coe (1972) and Barber and Wilson (1977) appear to be vindicated. But far from "vanishing away," as the quotation would have it (and as some state theorists seem to fear), modern-day practitioners of the ancient art of suggestion are finding an ever-growing range of application for such techniques—in part, because their essential nature is now more clearly understood. If imagination is responsible for what is often referred to as "hypnotic" phenomena, then it is clear to all that the true potential of the human imagination has scarcely been tapped.

Rather than inquiring *how many* alterations in perceived awareness it is possible to induce by means of suggestion (de Ropp, 1968; Fischer, 1971), or how one might go about measuring their purported "depth" (Hilgard, 1965; Spiegel, 1977)—which is, after all, pointless when one is dealing with subjective experiences for which new phenomenological dimensions can be invented, suggested, and consequently experienced by sufficiently responsive subjects virtually at will (Gibbons, 1973, 1974)—it is more appropriate to inquire how such experiences may best be defined and guided to fulfill their primary purpose, which is to assist the subject in achieving an increased measure of self-awareness and self-control.

It is to the fulfillment of this latter purpose that the remainder of this volume is dedicated.

CHAPTER 2

Preliminary Tests of Suggestibility

Suggestion may be defined as the presentation of an idea in nonlogical fashion in such a manner that it is likely to be accepted as literally true, and therefore "real"—as illustrated in everyday life by the parent who kisses a child's scraped knee to "make it stop hurting," or by the athletic coach who convinces his apprehensive team that they "can't lose."

Generally, the supposition was that responsiveness to suggestion tends to be distributed in accordance with the normal probability curve, with roughly one person in five being relatively unresponsive, about one in five being fairly high in responsiveness, and the remaining three falling somewhere in between (Hilgard, 1965)—although these proportions may vary somewhat between clinical and laboratory settings (Pearson, Thompson, & Edmonston, 1970), and between one subgroup and another within the general population (Hilgard, 1970, 1974). For instance, suggestibility has long been known to be higher among people of greater intelligence, among females, and among older children and adolescents of both sexes (Hull, 1933). Contrary to popular opinion, however, suggestibility seems to be *unrelated* to gullibility or naiveté (Hull, 1929), perhaps because imagination and the willingness to "think along" are so important in determining one's responsiveness (Barber & Wilson, 1977).

Whatever the ultimate nature of suggestibility may be, none of the obtained correlations between responsiveness to suggestion and other traits is sufficiently strong, either singly or in combination with others, to permit the use of a practical rule of thumb for determining just who is a good candidate for a trance induction format and who is not; nor are the obtained correlations of sufficient magnitude to provide a satisfactory explanation for the dramatic differences between the responsiveness of subjects who are high in suggestibility and those who are low. In other words, suggestibility appears at present to be *usefully* correlated only with itself!

Apparently substantial individual differences in responsiveness to suggestion do exist; and at present, no reliable method is available for turning a previously poor trance subject into a good one, although a breakthrough in this area may be imminent (Barber & Wilson, 1977; Diamond, 1977; Wickramasekera, 1977; Wilson & Barber, 1978).

Although it may be possible in the near future to elicit trancelike behavior in virtually everyone, and subjects may now occasionally respond to one approach or to one suggestor more easily than to another, in practice it is usually not worth the effort to continue to use a trance format with subjects who are extremely low in responsiveness, as long as no misconception or undue apprehension is preventing the subject from responding to the best of his ability and he is genuinely willing to try. Thus, many suggestors prefer to administer a quick, single-item test of responsiveness or one of the more elaborate susceptibility scales before proceeding further. Others, however, realizing that no test is a perfect predictor of subsequent performance, and that a single-item screening device is particularly prone to error, may prefer to go ahead and take their chances with an induction, since most such procedures can be accomplished in a matter of minutes.

I have found it most convenient to simply *tell* the subject that trance induction techniques do not work with everyone, but that such an approach is certainly well worth trying, since if it does work it will be very useful indeed. Such statements do not seem to act as prejudicial suggestions in themselves, arousing expectations of the possibility of failure in such a manner as to increase the likelihood of failure actually occurring; for most subjects respond with apparent interest and curiosity to see whether or not the induction will be effective, and perhaps with some eagerness to accept what they perceive to be a slight challenge. The following directions for administering the two most commonly employed single-item tests of suggestibility have been included, however, for those who may wish to use them.

The handclasp test of suggestibility is particularly useful with groups, and may be given in the following manner:

First of all, I would like to ask you to interlock the fingers of your hands together, palms facing inward. And as soon as you have done this, please place your interlocked fingers on top of your head, with the palms down, and close your eyes. Hands interlocked and resting on top of your head, with the palms down; and eyes closed.

As soon as everyone who wishes to participate in the demonstration has placed his clasped hands above his head and closed his eyes, I'm going to count to five; and as I do, you will begin to notice your fingers becoming stuck together, tighter and tighter, until by the time I get to five, most of you will not be able to take your clasped hands apart until I touch them. But as soon as I touch your hands, they will fall apart easily. So just keep your eyes closed, and listen to my voice as I begin the count from one to five.

One. As I begin the count, you can feel your hands becoming stuck together, tighter and tighter above your head. And by the time I get to the count of five, your hands will be stuck together so very tightly that you will not be able to take them apart until I touch them, no matter how hard you try. In fact, the harder that you try to do so, the harder to do so it will actually become.

Two. Your hands are becoming stuck together now; stuck together, clasped together, clenched together, tighter and tighter, all of the time.

Three. You can feel your hands becoming tightly stuck together now, and by the time I get to the count of five, you will not be able to take your clasped hands apart, no matter how hard you try. The harder you try, the harder to take them apart it will actually become.

Four. Now your hands are becoming so tightly stuck together that it is becoming impossible to take them apart. Soon you will not be able to take your hands apart until I touch them; and the harder you try, the harder it will be.

Now it is completely impossible. The harder you try, the harder it is. Five. Open your eyes and try, but you cannot take your hands apart until I touch them.

(*Moving quickly around the room, touching each subject's hands in turn:*)
But now, as I touch your hands, they will fall apart easily.

The *postural sway test* involves suggesting to a subject who is standing with his eyes closed and his heels together that he is gradually losing his balance. Unlike the handclasp test just described, the postural sway test must be employed with only one subject at a time, since the suggestions of losing one's balance must be timed to accentuate the normal swaying motions of the body to be effective. When used as part of a group lecture–demonstration with a sufficiently responsive subject as a volunteer (perhaps one who has already re-

sponded well to the handclasp test), the postural sway test provides a
very convincing example of the efficacy of suggestion.

The subject is asked to stand facing away from the suggestor, with
his eyes closed and his head tilted slightly upward. He is also requested to place his feet at about a forty-five degree angle, with his
heels touching. The suggestor, meanwhile, places himself approximately two feet behind the subject, ready to catch him when he begins
to fall. Varying the pace and the specific content of his suggestions to
coincide with the subject's normal postural sway, the suggestor begins:

Now you will begin to notice your body beginning to sway back and forth,
and back and forth; swaying more and more, back and forth, and back and
forth, until you begin to feel as if you are falling—falling forward, falling
backward, falling, falling, etc.

CHAPTER 3

Preparing the Subject for Induction

A comfortable place should be provided for the subject to sit or to recline during the trance session, and the environment in which the induction is to be carried out should be as free as possible from distracting noises and interruptions. Subjects wearing contact lenses may wish to remove them if it would make them uncomfortable to keep their eyes closed for a prolonged period without doing so. It is generally desirable to avoid complete privacy during the trance session, particularly if the subject is female.

Before beginning the induction itself, it is desirable to spend a few moments with each beginning subject helping him clarify his expectations regarding what he is about to experience and answering any questions he may have concerning the procedure. If a subject has never undergone an induction before, I explain that what I am about to do is simply show him how to use his own mental abilities more effectively. I tell the subject that he will remain fully conscious during the entire procedure, and that he will remember everything that occurs. If a *hyperempiric* or alertness induction is to be employed, I tell the subject that hyperempiria may be regarded as the *opposite* of traditional hypnosis, in the sense that I will be helping him to realize an expanded sense of awareness instead of his undergoing an experience which outwardly resembles sleep (Gibbons, 1973, 1974).

I also explain that the "best" trance subjects tend to be normal, well-adjusted individuals who are easily able to lose themselves in sports, music, and nature, or in reading a good novel or watching a motion picture; and that those who are not able to derive at least some benefit from a trance induction generally tend to be uptight, rigid, or compulsive personalities who find it virtually impossible to "let go." I tell the subject that his responsivness to the induction procedure and his subsequent trance performance depend entirely upon his own ability and willingness to comply with the instructions and suggestions he is given.

Finally, I ask the subject if he has any additional questions before we begin. Many people need to be reassured, for example, that they will not "babble" or reveal any private information, as they might do under a chemical anesthetic; that a trance experience does not "weaken the will," foster dependency, or make it possible for a subject to do anything he does not actually want to do; and that there is absolutely no danger of his failing to "come out of it" when the session is over as long as he is willing to do so. It is usually sufficient to respond to such queries by assuring the subject that he still retains his own personality when the induction is concluded; and since he is just as much himself as he was before, he still retains a "veto power" over any suggestion he does not wish to carry out, and still retains his capacity for independent action—including the ability to come out of the trance himself if he should wish to or if an emergency should arise.

If a subject should remain skeptical as to whether or not an induction is actually going to work after an appropriate discussion of the nature of a suggested trance experience has been concluded, he should be encouraged to try it anyway. Many excellent subjects are skeptical at first; but after the induction has begun, their inherent responsiveness to suggestion causes them to perform just as well as if they had been convinced of the efficacy of the procedure all along.

CHAPTER 4

Trance Induction Procedures

HYPEREMPIRIC TECHNIQUE

Just as a new subject may tend to be somewhat nervous until he has been sufficiently informed concerning the nature of the experience he is about to undergo, many people also tend to be unduly apprehensive when they are *conducting* an induction procedure for the first time. However, if a subject's ability to experience a trance is primarily a function of his ability to think along with and vividly imagine the suggestions he is given, as Barber and De Moor (1972) have stated, then the principal function of the suggestor is merely to present the induction in a sufficiently plausible manner; and beyond this, no special talent, ability, or charisma are required. In other words, one should not be led to feel that one has somehow "failed" if a subject has not responded appropriately to an induction procedure; for such an outcome is usually much more the "fault" of the subject than of the suggestor.

Certain nuances of style and delivery may be helpful in communicating suggestions, however, in much the same way that the effectiveness of poetry may be enhanced when it is read with the proper inflections. Inductions should be presented slowly and rhythmically, in an even tone of voice, with a considerable amount of repetition and redundancy in the way they are worded. It is also often desirable to match the cadence of one's spoken suggestions with the rhythm of the subject's breathing and to vary the speed and length of the induction to match the ease with which he appears to be responding, as revealed by his posture or facial expression and the degree to which he appears to be physically relaxed. However, mere repetition and fixation of attention in themselves, without the addition of specific or implied suggestions to the effect that the subject is about to experience a trance, are clearly insufficient to induce anything but boredom and natural sleep. If this were not the case, induction techniques based solely on such principles would be known and practiced in every culture, and independently rediscovered in each new generation by children at their play.[1]

Virtually any type of prop or mechanical aid may be employed to facilitate an induction, as long as it serves to enhance the credibility of the suggestions that are given and/or to facilitate the subject's imaginative involvement. However, sometimes the aids which are used may be individually tailored to the needs of the particular subject. For example, I was once told of a subject who had initially failed to respond to a hypnotic induction even though she had performed very well on preliminary tests of suggestibility. When asked why she had not responded to the induction, she replied, "You can't be a hypnotist. You don't have a cape!" Rather than choosing to argue the point, the suggestor entered the adjacent room and removed a long, dark-colored drape from a window and placed it around his shoulders. Striding firmly back into the room where the subject was seated, he proceeded to administer the induction as before—this time with excellent results.

Tranquilizers or small amounts of a sedative preparation, sufficient to induce drowsiness and relaxation without the subject actually losing consciousness, have been used in conjunction with trance inductions, but the results are often unpredictable or equivocal (Hartland, 1971; Kroger, 1977). For this reason, the majority of suggestors seem to prefer a purely verbal approach.

The term *rapport* refers to the inclination of many subjects to concentrate on the voice of the suggestor, often to the exclusion of most other stimuli. At the conclusion of a trance experience, a subject may state, "It seemed like I could hear your voice coming to me from

---

[1]So-called highway hypnosis, or the tendency of overly tired drivers to fall asleep while staring at the borken lines painted along the center of the road on which they are traveling, is clearly a misnomer; for such a tendency has been associated with the onset of *natural* sleep, and subsequent injury or death as one loses control of one's car, but not with a measured increase in suggestibility!

the end of a tunnel, and everything else just seemed to fade away in the distance." Rapport may be facilitated by means of specific suggestions which are aimed at augmenting and strengthening it, such as those provided on page 38; but in highly responsive subjects it often tends to occur spontaneously, as a result of implicit expectations generated by the relationship with the suggestor or by the nature of the induction procedure.

Because of these implicit cues, it is particularly essential for the suggestor to assume a relaxed and confident manner and to take care that his voice and demeanor at no time communicate any trace of uncertainty. In fact, it is usually helpful for the suggestor to allow himself to "flow along" with the words of the induction as they are spoken—letting his own body slump and allowing a note of drowsiness to creep into his own voice during a hypnotic induction, and allowing himself to feel progressively more energetic and alert during the course of a hyperempiric induction.

Prerecorded cassette tapes are currently available containing both hypnotic and hyperempiric inductions, accompanied by appropriate background music and other sounds. Such recordings may be used in place of a live induction, as long as the suggestor is careful not to dilute the quality of the personal interaction between himself and the subject, which constitutes a vital ingredient of any helping relationship.

It is occasionally useful to record a trance session in its entirety, to allow the subject to obtain repeated, *ad libitum* exposure to the suggestions contained therein. These tapes or cassettes are particularly useful when the suggestions are aimed at such objectives as improving study habits or alleviating situational insomnia, inasmuch as the use of such tapes allows these suggestions to be presented precisely when they are most useful. In addition to an induction and specific suggestions designed to assist the subject in the attainment of his particular objectives, the tape should contain additional suggestions that the subject will continue to be aware of and responsive to outside stimuli while he is listening, and that he will easily and rapidly be able to open his eyes and return to an everyday sense of awareness if the need should arise before the tape is concluded. Such tapes may also be employed in conjunction with self-induced trances, which are described on page 49.

As the induction proceeds, if it is done live, corrective suggestions may be provided to define the subject's ongoing experience in such a manner as to insure that he is comfortable. For example, he may be told, "It will not disturb you to shift your position and make yourself comfortable if you wish to do so," or, "You don't have to slump so much. Just sit naturally, and you will be able to follow along with what I am saying." Similarly, it may be suggested that the subject will not be distracted by background noises, such as the sound of traffic in the street, or footsteps or laughter outside the room in which the suggestions are being given.

If the subject should manifest any signs of discomfort or distress which cannot be alleviated in the manner just described, the proceedings should be smoothly terminated by suggesting that the subject's eyes will be open by the count of three, and that he will be fully restored to an everyday experience of consciousness by that time. When the count has been completed, the subject may be asked what seemed to be bothering him. Occasionally, for example, hypnotic or sleeping suggestions will tend to remind a subject of going under an anesthetic, perhaps when he had his tonsils removed as a child; and this association may cause some of the previously felt discomfort and anxiety to return (Hilgard, Hilgard, & Newman, 1961). However, once the subject realizes the true source of his discomfort and is able to see how different the present situation actually is, he should experience no further distress.

Should a subject be unable to come up with a reasonable explanation for his difficulty, and if he seems to possess an adequate understanding of how he is *supposed* to feel while he is experiencing a trance, his uneasiness may be a reflection of some underlying personality problem, such as a neurotic need to feel as if he were always in complete control of every situation. It may therefore be advisable to postpone further induction attempts until the subject's attitudes have been appropriately modified in the course of therapy.

Occasionally, a subject may be inclined to "get the giggles" during an induction and be unable to continue without bursting out with laughter. This reaction is much more common in female than in male subjects, and is best regarded as a form of resistance to the induction itself. If a subject is unable to acknowledge any lingering doubts or uncertainties which may be interfering with the successful completion of the induction, it may be helpful to state specifically that the suggestor considers such giggling to be merely a form of resistance—albeit an unconscious one—and that, if the subject truly wishes to continue, it will be up to him to overcome it.

Even more rarely, a subject may actually go to sleep in the course of being administered an induction. When this occurs, it may be verified by observing the bulge of the cornea beneath his closed eyelids. In natural sleep, the eyes will tend to move slowly back and forth, once every 20 seconds or so, unless the subject happens to be dreaming—in which case, he will tend to produce rapid eye movements similar to those which would occur if he were actually watching the events taking place in his dream. Should a subject go to sleep, he may either be awakened or left to sleep it off as circumstances warrant.

If a different person is to administer suggestions at the conclusion of an induction, it is helpful to suggest to the subject, "Now you will be able to respond to another voice, just as easily as you do to mine."

After the induction has been completed, one may proceed with suggestions for increasing rapport and for facilitating the trance experience ("heightening" or "deepening" the trance), followed by suggestions of time expansion as a means of intensifying the experiential qualities or subsequently administered suggestions. Heightening or deepening suggestions may also be administered on occasion during the remainder of the session, particularly if it is to be a long one. It is generally not worthwhile to spend a great deal of time and effort on such procedures, however; for as stated previously, the degree of subjective involvement with trance suggestions is primarily a function of the subject's own ability and willingness to comply with them. Responsiveness tends to stabilize fairly rapidly, whether it be high, medium, or low; and with rare exceptions, little in the course of subsequent change may be expected with methods presently available, although recent research seems to indicate that a breakthrough in this area may be immanent (Diamond, 1977; Wickramasekera, 1977; Barber & Wilson, 1977).

Since the purpose of an induction is to facilitate or to enhance the credibility of the suggestions which are subsequently provided to the subject, many of the following inductions are referred to as "hyperempiric" procedures. The term *hyperempiria* is derived from the Greek *empeiria*, or "experience," with the prefix *hyper-* added to denote a greater or an enhanced quality, whereas the term *hypnosis* is derived from the Greek *hypnos*, meaning "sleep." Thus, it is etymologically correct to refer to inductions based on suggestions of alertness as *hyperempiric* procedures, reserving the term *hypnotic* for inductions which are based on implied or explicit suggestions of sleep. Hyperempiria appears to be equally as effective as hypnosis in providing a plausible rationale to enhance the credibility of subsequently administered suggestions (Gibbons, 1973, 1976; Gibbons & Glenn, 1978; Katz, 1975; Severson & Hurlbut, 1977), particularly in those situations wherein a subject may express a preference for a "mind expanding" approach.

It is often said that a trance experience is a common, everyday phenomenon which takes place whenever a person's attention is captured by whatever is going on around him, as is the case when one becomes so absorbed in watching a motion picture or reading a novel that all awareness of self is temporarily lost. However, this is much too broad a definition of the term; for the increase in suggestibility which constitutes the essential function of any induction procedure is only present if trance is either directly suggested or implied by the procedure itself. If one should be inclined to doubt this, let him attempt to administer a test of suggestibility, such as eyelid catalepsy or glove anesthesia, to a person who *is* engrossed in watching a motion picture or his favorite television program!

The actual decision regarding which induction to use depends to a considerable extent on the preference and background of the individual subject or group. The "cathedral" induction which follows may sometimes be preferred by persons with a strong Roman Catholic or Eastern Orthodox background, whereas the "lotus" induction may be desired by those who are currently "into meditation." Since subjects vary to a considerable extent in both their preferences for various types of imagery and in their ability to visualize specific types of situations, it is generally desirable, before beginning a particular induction, to ask the subject whether or not he would be able to respond appropriately: "Would you have any trouble picturing yourself relaxing on the beach at night as you follow the induction?" (If the subject happens to have an intense fear of water, or a close relative who drowned while at the beach, he might indeed.)

Finally, a few words of caution are in order. As we have seen in discussing the history of suggestion-induced trance experiences, imitation may occasionally play a major role in determining the nature and extent of a subject's behavior in responding to trance suggestions.

In fact, some nineteenth-century hypnotists would often keep a subject hypnotized in their waiting rooms, just so their new patients would be sufficiently impressed to respond more easily themselves. As a further illustration of the effectiveness of imitation, it is not uncommon to find that, even though an induction has been unsuccessful with one subject, a friend who merely came along as an observer to watch the proceedings is "out like a light!" Such a situation may be easily handled by addressing the "surprise" subject directly and terminating the trance in the usual manner. If both subjects have responded to the induction, one may say to the unintended respondent, "All right, Steve, you can just rest quietly by yourself for a moment while I go ahead and give some suggestions to Jerry, and then I'll bring you both out of the trance together. But the suggestions which I am about to give will only be effective for Jerry, and not for you, until I start to terminate the trance, and then you will both come out of it together."

A similar procedure may be employed when dealing with an occasional surprise subject during a group demonstration. If one is conducting a series of repeated individual inductions during a group lecture or demonstration, one will occasionally encounter subjects who are "repeaters"; that is, they will spontaneously respond to each induction as though it were specifically intended for them. Such tendencies may easily be eliminated in most instances by saying to the group, "Anyone who feels himself responding to the induction, or who thinks that he might respond to it, will only need to silently tell himself, 'I will not go into a trance this time,' and this will be effective in enabling all those who are supposed to be merely watching to go ahead and observe the induction without responding to it themselves."

Because of the tendency of an occasional spectator or listener to respond to an induction as though he were a subject, inductions should *never* be broadcast over the radio or television; and in many localities this is already prohibited. Neither should one permit an induction to be recorded, filmed, or videotaped unless such recording is undertaken with proper safeguards against its careless use.

Provided that one is able to read aloud without conveying the impression that he is merely reading, the following inductions may be administered verbatim, much as one would read from a script in a play. However, once the reader has become sufficiently familiar with their content, he should feel free to ad-lib as conditions warrant and eventually to improvise hypnotic and hyperempiric inductions of his own.

Considering the wide variety of induction procedures currently in use, such improvisations should not be difficult; for the only thing which such procedures seem to have in common is that they provide a means of credibly communicating the suggestion that the subject is entering a trance.

Although it is not strictly necessary, the degree of imaginative involvement with the procedure may often be enhanced by the use of an appropriate background sound effect, such as a recording of soft music or the sound of ocean waves, or a wind harp, or other sounds appropriate to the particular verbal imagery which is being employed. Such background effects are particularly helpful when one is working with groups.

Hyperempiric Inductions for Adults

ON THE BEACH AT NIGHT

Just relax now and close your eyes. Imagine that it is late at night, and that you are sitting or lying on a sandy beach by the side of the ocean. If you accept each detail of the scene as I describe it, without trying to think critically, your imagination will be free to allow you to experience the situation just as if you were really there. So just keep your eyes closed and let yourself relax completely, on that sandy beach, late on a warm spring evening. Feel the gentle breeze blowing from the direction of the sea and savor the freshness of the pure night air.

As you listen to the sound of the waves gently breaking upon the shore, you can just let go and relax completely, experiencing the full reality of the scene and all its beauty. And as you continue to allow yourself to be guided by my voice, I am going to show you how to release your awareness for its fullest possible functioning.

There is a bright, starlit sky overhead, broken here and there by patches of dark gray clouds and an occasional shaft of moonlight. Now and then a distant splash can be heard above the sound of the waves, as the night continues to pass; but it is too dark to be able to tell what might be the cause of this sound, and you are feeling just too relaxed and too peaceful to get up and investigate. So just let yourself absorb completely the peacefulness which is all around you, as the night slowly passes and the moon begins to set.

Now, as the first probing fingers of the new day begin to lighten the sky over the ocean, and as you continue to be guided by my voice, I am going to show you how to release your awareness, letting it rise to a much higher level than you have known previously. You will find that you experience very pleasant feelings of increased alertness and sensitivity, as your consciousness expands more and more. Just let yourself continue to be guided by my voice now, as your awareness continues to increase.

The sky above you is becoming lighter, as the first rays of sunrise begin to appear on the distant horizon. And as the scene progresses, you can feel yourself becoming more and more alert, as your awareness continues to grow. You are beginning to enter a higher level of consciousness now, one in which your ability to realize your full capacity for experience is greatly enhanced; yet, you are feeling no strain or discomfort. On the contrary, you are beginning to experience a pleasant exaltation in your ability to use your consciousness so much more effectively, as your awareness continues to expand, more and more.

Let yourself continue to drink in the beauty of the scene, as the horizon continues to grow lighter and your awareness continues to increase. The sky over the ocean is becoming flooded with a warm, rosy glow as you watch; but the horizon itself is hidden by a gray mist rising from the surface of the sea. You decide to walk up to the water's edge in order to see more clearly; and as you approach, you discover a row of boulders jutting out into the water like a pointing finger. You approach this crude pier and begin to walk out to the end of it, so that you will be better able to take in the full beauty of all that is happening around you; and with each passing second, your awareness continues to grow, and your consciousness continues to expand. And the more your consciousness expands, the more pleasant and the more beautiful the scene becomes.

Tiny waves are rolling gently past the end of the pier as you watch, breaking beneath the rocks underfoot, and hurling tiny droplets of spray into the puddles which have formed here and there in low depressions in the rock. The waves are creating little eddies of current around the end of the pier, as if they were trying to break it off and pull it away from the shore. And as you continue to watch, you continue to enter into a higher state of consciousness, in which your ability to utilize your full capacity for experience is greatly enhanced. Yet, you feel no sense of strain or overload, but merely a pleasant exaltation, as your consciousness continues to expand, more and more.

As you continue to watch the gray mist rising from the surface of the sea, your ears begin to detect the faint sound of distant rowing. And as you wait for the mysterious boat to appear, you can feel a surge of joy and anticipation as you eagerly await the first glimpse of the boat through the mist.

It's a wonderful feeling of release and liberation which you are experiencing now, as all of your vast, untapped potentials are becoming freed for their fullest possible functioning, and soon your entire capacity for experience will be fully realized. Your perceptions of the world around you will take on new and deeper qualities, and they will contain a greater depth of reality than anything you have experienced previously.

The beauty and the joy of the scene before you continues to increase, as your consciousness expands more and more. Suddenly, as you peer into the mist, you notice the outline of a small boat coming toward you, with an old man seated at the oars. He smiles as he pulls up to the end of the pier, motioning for you to take a seat in the boat beside him. You leap in without hesitation and do as he suggests, while he begins to row away with rapid, steady strokes.

As you feel yourself carried rapidly along, you become ever more aware of the pleasant exaltation you experience as you find yourself able to use your consciousness so much more effectively. And your awareness continues to expand, more and more, multiplying itself over and over again. Until you feel as if you are able to hold within your own mind an awareness of the entire universe, and all its beauty.

It's such a plesant feeling, as the oarsman pulls you gently on and on, and your consciousness continues to expand.

As the horizon continues to grow brighter, you are being drawn irresistibly along in the direction of the sunrise. And the farther you go, the more your consciousness expands, and the more pleasant it all becomes.

Directly in the path of the sunrise, you glimpse the silvery outline of a small island. As you approach, your feelings of joy and exaltation continue to grow; for your capacity for experience is becoming infinitely greater than it could possibly be in any other state.

You pull up and prepare to land. And as you do, you are entering fully into a state of hyperempiria. In just a few seconds now, all of your mental abilities will be tuned to their highest possible pitch, without any sense of strain or overload; and you will be able to concentrate infinitely better than you can in an everyday state of awareness.

Now, as you leap out onto the shore and the boatman begins to row away, all the vast resources within you have been freed for their fullest possible functioning. And while you remain within this state of hyperempiria, the quality of all your experiences will be infinitely keener; and you will be able to discern new and greater levels of reality and of meaning which will enable you to discover new dimensions of experience, greater and more profound than those you have encountered previously.

THE AWAKENING LOTUS BUD

First of all, just sit back or lie down; or assume a lotus position, if you prefer. And when you are ready, close your eyes.

Now with your eyes closed, imagine that it is late on a warm summer night and that you are peacefully and comfortably resting inside a lotus bud which is floating gently on the surface of a large pond of water. If you accept each detail of the scene as I describe it, without trying to think critically, your imagination will be free to allow you to experience the situation just as if you were really there. So just let yourself relax completely now, inside this soft, emerald lotus bud, late on a warm summer night. It's so comfortable resting there, snug and secure and nestled down among the bud's emerald green leaves.

You can feel the soft summer breeze gently caressing the outside of the bud, and the water beneath you gently causing the bud to rise and fall. Just listen to the water gently lapping and contir ue to focus on the beauty and the peacefulness which is all around you. And as you continue to allow yourself to be guided by my voice, I am going to show you how to release your awareness for its fullest possible functioning.

There is a sudden rush of wind through the reeds and lotus leaves in the pond; and as the soft, emerald green leaves of the bud around you gently begin to stir, you can feel the breeze beginning to filter through the cracks which are appearing all around you as the bud prepares to open. Let yourself breathe slowly and deeply now, as you inhale the warm night air and your consciousness commences to expand and to unfold along with the bud.

The late night air is so pure, so fresh, and so crystal clear. Feel it entering your lungs, and feel the warmth of it entering your body as your awareness continues to grow. In. Out. In. Out.

The sky is strewn with hundreds of blinking, bluish-white stars. As the bud continues to open and your awareness continues to unfold along with it, you are breathing slowly, in and out, carrying this expanded awareness to every part of your body.

The lotus petals are releasing a delicate perfume as the bud continues to open. Breathe in this joyous nectar, and follow its passage from your nostrils through your nasal passages, down your throat, and on into your lungs. Let yourself become ever more aware of the rhythm of your breathing, as it carries you on to ever-increasing sensations of awareness. In. Out. In. Out. Breathe out tension. Breathe in calm. Breathe out worry. Breathe in awareness.

With every breath you take, your consciousness drifts higher. With every breath you take, all the vast, untapped resources within you are being freed for their fullest possible functioning.

The lotus leaves are unfolding more rapidly now, and the bud is nearly open. And as the bud continues to unfold, your feelings of joy and exaltation continue to increase also. You can feel your awareness and your capacity for experience becoming greater than it could possibly be in any other state. And soon your entire potential for experience will be fully realized. Your perceptions of the world around you will take on new and deeper qualities, and they will contain a greater depth of reality than anything you have experienced previously.

The petals are trembling slightly as they continue to reach out to the fresh night air. In just a short while the blossom will be fully open, and in just a short while, all of your mental abilities will be tuned to their highest possible pitch without any sense of strain or overload, and you will be able to concentrate infinitely better than you can in the everyday modes of awareness in which we spend most of our waking lives.

Now the blossom is fully open, and the petals are extended as far as they will go. And as the fresh, warm air gently caresses the flower around you, all of your own vast resources have been freed for their fullest possible functioning.

And while you remain within this state of hyperempiria, the quality of all your perceptions will be infinitely keener, and you will be able to discern new realms of meaning, and new dimensions of experience, greater and more profound than you have encountered previously.

THE CATHEDRAL

Just make yourself comfortable and close your eyes; and I am going to show you how to release your consciousness, so that it may rise to a higher level than you have known previously. First of all, I would like you to picture yourself standing in front of two large wooden doors, which are the doors to a great cathedral. If you accept each detail of the scene as I describe it, without trying to think critically, your imagination will be free to allow you to experience the situation just as if you were really there. Just let yourself stand there a few seconds, gazing at the carved wooden panels of the door as you prepare to enter.

Soon the doors will open and you will go inside, as I guide you into a higher state of awareness called hyperempiria. You will begin to experience very pleasant feelings of increased alertness and sensitivity as your consciousness commences to expand.

As the doors swing open and you enter the cathedral, you first traverse a small area paved with stone and stop at the font, if you desire. Then you pause before a second pair of doors which leads to the interior. You are beginning to enter a higher level of consciousness now, for it's as if this cathedral were providing you with an image which will allow your consciousness to encompass all the vast reservoirs of strength and spiritual power contained within your own being, and within the universe as well. And as you enter, you can begin to feel all these vast resources flowing into your awareness.

As you pass through the second pair of doors and into the dimly lit interior, you can hear gentle tones of music floating on the quiet air. Let yourself breathe slowly and deeply now, as you inhale the faint aroma of incense, and your consciousness drifts higher.

Breathe slowly and deeply, as you inhale the incense and listen to the music. Feel it flowing through you, and filling the very core of your being. Let your mind flow with it. Let the music merge completely with your own awareness and carry it along. And soon you will feel as if you were able to hold within your consciousness an awareness of the entire universe and all its beauty.

You are entering into a much higher level of consciousness now, one in which your ability to utilize your full capacity for experience is greatly enhanced. You can feel a pleasant exaltation in your ability to use your imagination so much more effectively, as your awareness continues to expand, more, and more, and more.

Your perceptual abilities are becoming infinitely keener, as the music swells within you; yet, you can still direct your attention, as you would normally, to anything you wish. It's such a pleasant feeling, as your awareness expands, more and more, multiplying itself over and over again.

It's a wonderful feeling of release and liberation which you are experiencing now, as all of your vast, untapped potentials are being freed for their fullest possible functioning; and in just a short while, your entire potential for awareness and for experience will be fully realized. Your perceptions of the world around you will take on new and deeper qualities, and they will contain a greater depth of reality than anything you could have possibly experienced previously.

Some distance away from you stands the High Altar, bordered by banks of softly glowing candles. As the music continues, and your awareness continues to grow, you can feel yourself being drawn irresistibly toward it. And as you begin to approach, the closer you get, the more your awareness expands, and the more pleasant it becomes.

As you feel your consciousness expanding more and more, you can feel an ever-growing sense of joy as all of your abilities are being tuned to their highest possible pitch, and it's not fatiguing or tiring in the least.

As you approach nearer and nearer to the High Altar, you can feel your awareness and your capacity for experience becoming infinitely greater than it could possibly be in any other state. In just a few seconds now, all your mental abilities will be tuned to their highest possible pitch; and you will be able to concentrate infinitely better than you can in an ordinary state of consciousness.

Now, you are ready. All the vast resources within you have been freed for their fullest possible functioning; and while you remain within this state of hyperempiria, you will be able to discern new and greater levels of reality, new realms of meaning, and new dimensions of experience, greater and more profound than anything you have encountered previously.

The following hyperempiric induction is particularly rich in affective imagery, for use with subjects who are so inclined:

RIDING THROUGH A RAINBOW

Now, with your eyes closed, picture yourself floating high above the earth, drifting, and dreaming, and floating through patches of fleecy white clouds, just after a sudden spring shower. If you accept each detail of the scene as I describe it, without trying to think critically, your imagination will be free to allow you to experience the situation just as if you were really there.

Feel yourself drifting on now, as you continue to listen to my voice— drifting slowly and gently, on and on, until you come to a beautiful rainbow, shimmering brightly before you, with shades of hearty red, creamy peach, golden yellow, cool mint green, aqua blue, and dusky violet.

You think how pleasant it would be to drift on through the rainbow, experiencing the colors one by one—and changing direction ever so slightly. You prepare to do just that, starting first with the band of hearty red.

Feel the band of red beginning to enter the soles of your feet now, carrying with it a warm glow of strength and power which spreads quickly up through the calves of your legs, and on up through the rest of your body, flooding every fiber and nerve with a warm, rosy glow of energy and strength and power. Breathe deeply and slowly, as you continue on through the band of red, and inhale the color and the feelings that go with it. Let yourself experience them fully and completely, as you breathe them in and saturate yourself in their warmth.

Now, as you continue slowly drifting on, the band of creamy peach begins to penetrate the soles of your feet and spreads itself throughout your body in just the same way as did the red, bringing with it an indescribably beautiful sensation of complete and perfect peace. And as this peacefulness progresses on throughout your body, it blends with the energy which you already feel, making you serenely more aware of everything you experience.

Next, the golden yellow band begins to spread itself throughout your being, filling and flooding you with its delicious golden glow, and bringing to your consciousness an ever-increasing sense of happiness and well-being. Flow with it and breathe it in, as you allow yourself to merge completely with this wave of radiant happiness—blending with it so completely that you begin to radiate back an answering happiness of your own.

You are entering the green band now, as you begin to experience a wave of pure, refreshing joy, carrying you ever higher, as you feel yourself being inundated by endless sensations of indescribable joy and bliss. Rapture and ecstasy, wonder and delight—breathe it in, blend with it, and savor the delicious emotions which are being added now to all of the other feelings you have gathered in your journey through the rainbow, and which you still retain.

Now you are beginning to draw in the color of aqua blue, which causes you to feel as free and as fluid as the aqua waters themselves. Feel yourself blending, in your imagination, with all the water everywhere on the planet, rushing over the surface of the earth as her banks caress you, moving over rocks and soft river beds, plunging down cliffs to form waterfalls in a headlong rush to the sea, where you are again drawn up to the sky and back to the rainbow and the blue band once more, ready to enter the next band of light, but retaining this sensation of freedom which becomes blended with all the others.

Finally, you enter the violet band on the inner side of the rainbow. It fills you silently as nightfall, extending your previous feelings of freedom to an almost infinite degree; for you now feel able to step behind all your everyday thoughts and all your customary social roles. You slowly drift to a stop within this violet band, and you are filled with the stillness and peace of a warm, mimosa-scented summer night. You can feel within your own being the beautiful, tranquil color of the violet sky, long after the sun has slipped down behind the horizon. And while you remain here within this violet band of light, in the hyperempiric trance which you have entered, the suggestions which you receive will help to guide you into new paths of awareness and new dimensions of being, richer and more rewarding than those you have known before.

Heightening Rapport in Hyperempiria

The term *rapport* refers to the relationship which exists between suggestor and subject, particularly during the course of a trance session. Since this relationship may do much to determine the experiential qualities of the suggested trance and vice-versa, specific suggestions for heightening rapport and for optimally defining the ongoing trance experience may be administered at the conclusion of an induction as a means of maximizing responsiveness to subsequently administered suggestions. At the conclusion of a hyperempiric induction, one may proceed as follows:

You are continuing to go higher and higher into hyperempiria with every word I utter. And as you feel yourself carried on to ever greater heights, the higher you go, the stronger and the more pronounced the effects of my words become. The higher you go, the more easily you are able to respond to everything I say, and the clearer and sharper are the results.

As you continue to be guided ever higher by my voice, you can experience everything I describe to you just as if it is actually happening—without having to infer it from your senses, and without the confining thought patterns which have been imposed upon you by the culture in which you live.

As you continue soaring higher and higher into hyperempiria, your ability to experience directly the reality of whatever is suggested to you will be a never ending source of wonder and delight, wonder and delight.

The communication between us is perfect, and it will remain perfect throughout the remainder of your trance experience, for we both feel as if we are a part of each other and part of a larger whole.

With appropriate modifications in wording, the foregoing suggestions may be easily adapted for use with a hypnotic induction: "You are continuing to go *deeper* and *deeper* into *hypnosis* with every word that I utter," etc.

Because an important key to effective group functioning is the mutual support and encouragement which the members derive from each other as well as from the leader, the following suggestions may be added in group settings:

As the group continues to function, you will find yourself communicating more and more easily with those around you. As the group continues to function, you will become more aware of a growing sense of fellowship, good will, and mutual understanding as communication continues to flow more freely. And as the group continues to function, you will feel ever more free to communicate your own feelings of warmth and fellowship in return.

As the group continues to function, you will become ever more involved, and ever more responsive to the needs of the others. And you will be responding in a manner which will meet your own needs as well. You will gain new insights, new knowledge, and new experience, which will be of great help to you in your own personal growth and in facilitating the growth of those around you.

Intensifying the Trance Experience

Time Expansion

All too frequently, pleasant experiences seem to be over in just a short while, regardless of how long they have actually lasted, and events which are perceived as dull or boring find us with time hanging on our hands. However, the subjective sense of the passage of time may easily be altered by means of suggestion (Cooper, 1956; Cooper & Erickson, 1954), thus permitting this effect to be nullified or even reversed. For example, suggestions of time expansion may be utilized in conjunction with a trance-induction technique in order to enhance the experiential qualities of fantasy trips and other trance suggestions, thereby perhaps also enhancing both their desirability and their effectiveness. At the conclusion of a hyperempiric or a hypnotic induction, suggestions may be provided as follows:

> During the remainder of your trance experience, time will seem to be passing very, very slowly for you. It's going to seem as if your trance experience will be going on for a much, much longer time than it actually is. And because time will seem to be passing so slowly, your enjoyment of the experience, and all of the other benefits which you will derive from it, will be correspondingly increased. And when the trance is over, your normal sense of the passage of time will be restored also.

Hyperempiria for Children

It is often said that young children are difficult to hypnotize because of their short attention span. But as every parent knows, children who are well below kindergarten age are able to sit enraptured for long periods, listening to one fairy tale after another, for as long as the reader's voice holds out. Perhaps their "short attention span" may occasionally have more to do with what they are supposed to be paying attention to rather than with their chronological age or their level of maturity.

A second reason why very young children are often difficult to hypnotize has to do with their tendency to take the sleeping suggestions of a traditional hypnotic induction too literally. But if you omit the word "sleep" from the induction and merely try to explain to a very young child just what it is that he is supposed to do and to feel during the course of a trance session, then the description becomes equally difficult to grasp because it is too abstract.

To avoid these difficulties, the following hyperempiric induction has been based on a fairy-tale format rather than the usual hypnotic or sleeping paradigm. With appropriate modifications in vocabulary, my students report having used this procedure successfully with children as young as two-and-one-half years:

Lie back now and close your eyes, and I am going to tell you a magic story. It is a story about a very special place, deep in an enchanted forest, where everything I tell you will come true. And it is a magic story because, if you listen carefully and believe hard enough, it will really take us there. So listen carefully, and soon we will be on our way to that very special place, deep in the magic forest, where everything I tell you will come true.

Imagine now that we are walking together down a long, winding path which runs through the middle of a large woods. We are walking along hand in hand, early on a bright spring morning. Birds are singing in the trees, and here and there a flower is poking its head out of the soft, green grass which grows beside the path. And because this is a magic story, the farther we go along the path, the more real everything around us becomes.

Now and then a ray of sunlight makes its way down through the branches of the trees and falls upon the dewdrops in the grass, causing them to sparkle like a million tiny diamonds. The air is fresh and cool, with gentle breezes blowing now and then, causing the trees, and the grass, and the flowers to move ever so slightly, as if everything in the world were feeling so happy on this bright spring morning that nothing could keep still for very long.

And because this is a magic story, the farther we go along the path, the more real everything becomes.

As we continue on our walk, we can begin to be aware of the sound of rushing water. With each passing second, the sound is becoming clearer and clearer still. And now we are standing beside the bank of a forest stream, which is the source of the sound we have been hearing.

The water is flowing past us swift and clear, for it has come tumbling down from a magic spring many miles away in the hills. And because the water from the magic spring is enchanted, anyone who drinks it will be enchanted, too. And he will easily be able to find that special place, deep in the magic forest, where everything I tell him will come true.

We dip our hands eagerly into the bubbling stream and cup them together, bringing the cool, fresh water up to our lips again and again, until we have taken all we want.

Now it is time to hurry on our way once more; for the water from the magic spring has made it certain that we will soon find that very special place in the enchanted forest, where everything I tell you will come true; and we know now that it cannot be far away.

As we continue on our journey, we notice a tiny path leading off to one side, and we decide to go up this path to see where it leads. Before very long, we notice that the woods are beginning to thin out, and that we are about to enter a clearing. And as we approach nearer and nearer to the edge of the clearing, we can see that the path we have been following leads right up to a small cottage.

This is that very special place I have been telling you about, where everything will come true. For as long as we stay here, in this enchanted cottage, in the enchanted forest, even my words will be enchanted, and everything I tell you will really happen exactly as I say it will.

The door to the cottage is standing slightly open as we hurry up the path, and as soon as we reach the entrance we hurry on inside in order to lose no more time. We have arrived now, at that very special enchanted place in the enchanted forest which we have traveled so far to reach. And as long as we remain here, in this enchanted cottage, everything I say and everything I describe to you will come true as soon as I have said it. For as long as we remain here, in this enchanted place, even my words will be enchanted.

HYPNOTIC TECHNIQUES

Hypnotic Induction Procedures

Standard Hypnotic Induction Technique

As is the case with the foregoing hyperempiric techniques, if a subject should express any particular preferences or reservations concerning the use of specific induction imagery—for example, if it is difficult for a subject to relax while imagining himself floating on a rubber raft, because he happens to have a fear of water or because he is a nonswimmer—other imagery may easily be substituted, such as relaxing on a grassy bank beside a mountain stream, or sinking down in a soft feather bed. If, on the other hand, the subject indicates that he would have no difficulty in utilizing such imagery, one may proceed as follows:

First of all, just close your eyes and imagine that it's a warm summer's day, and that you're floating around on a soft rubber raft at the beach, just beyond the breakers and a couple of hundred feet from shore. Just picture the scene and imagine yourself resting there on that soft, rubber raft, with the water gently rocking you back and forth, as you enjoy the sunlight and the cool ocean breeze. It's so calm and so peaceful out there, with the sound of the waves breaking nearby, that all you want to do is to just keep drifting and dreaming, and floating on, and on, and on into a deep, peaceful, and refreshing sleep. Just continue to picture the scene as I describe it, while I count slowly from one to ten; and by the time I get to the count of ten, you will be resting comfortably in a deep, sound sleep.

One. You can feel yourself relaxing now, relaxing so very, very deeply, as you continue floating on and on, with the water gently rocking you, and the sunlight flooding your body with its soft, golden warmth.

Two. You can feel a heavy, relaxed feeling coming over you as you continue to listen to my voice. You can feel your arms relaxing, and your legs relaxing, and your entire body relaxing completely, as you continue floating, on and on, into a deep, peaceful and relaxing sleep.

Three. You can feel yourself relaxing even more deeply now, as that heavy, relaxed feeling continues to grow. You are relaxing deeper and deeper all the time, as you continue to drift and to float, slowly and aimlessly, on, and on, and on.

Four. You can feel that heavy, relaxed feeling growing stronger and stronger. And as I continue the count on up to ten, that heavy, relaxed feeling is going to continue growing stronger with every passing second, until it causes you to drift into a deep, sound sleep.

Five. Every word that I utter is putting you into a deep, sound sleep, as I continue to count and that heavy, relaxed feeling continues to grow. You are relaxing so very, very deeply now, relaxing so deeply that you can just let yourself go completely and begin to drift even faster into a deep, sound sleep.

Six. Just listen to my voice, as I continue to count, and by the time I get to the count of ten, you will be resting comfortably in a deep, sound sleep.

Seven. You are drifting even faster now, drifting faster and faster into a deep, sound sleep; and by the time I get to the count of ten, you will be resting comfortably in a deep, sound sleep.

Eight. Every word that I utter is putting you faster and faster into a deep, sound sleep, deeper and faster, and deeper and faster, all the time. You are drifting very, very rapidly now into a deep, sound sleep, a deep, sound sleep.

Nine. Into a deep, sound sleep now, a deep, sound sleep.

Ten. Very deeply drifting, in a deep, sound sleep. Very deeply drifting, in a deep, sound sleep. Continuing to drift deeper, with each passing second, drifting deeper and deeper, down, and down, and down.

Hypnosis with Visual Fixation Objects

The James Braid Method. Visual fixation objects should be utilized only in a traditional hypnotic or sleeping induction rather than a hyperempiric procedure, since their function as an aid to induce blinking and eye closure is more readily associated with suggestions of sleep than with suggestions of alertness.

Almost anything can be used as a visual fixation object to facilitate the induction of hypnosis: a coin or a ring of keys, the pendulum of a clock, or even a spot on a wall or a dangling Christmas tree ornament suspended by a thread from the ceiling. Metronomes or revolving spiral disks are also employed occasionally to provide additional dimensions of sound, movement, or optical illusion which further enhance the credibility of the procedure.

Regardless of the type of fixation object which is employed, however, its basic purpose remains the same: to facilitate the uncritical acceptance of the suggestions contained in the induction by diverting the subject's attention from their content. In addition, the naturally occurring eye fatigue which results from continuing to stare at the fixation object is interpreted for the subject as part of the induction itself, as indisputable evidence that the process is beginning to work. Once this suggestion has been accepted, it is more plausible (and therefore much easier) to accept the suggestions that follow.

The subject is usually seated with the fixation object directly in front of him and somewhat above his normal level of vision, forcing him to look up as he focuses on it. If the fixation object is small enough, the suggestor may hold it in his hand and slowly swing it back and forth, to further enhance the development of eye fatigue as the subject continues to watch. The induction is then begun with suggestions as the following: "Now, as you continue to listen to my voice, you will soon notice that your eyes are beginning to feel heavy and tired. Your eyes are becoming tired now, so heavy and tired, and soon they will start to close of themselves."

When the subject's eyes begin to blink—as they inevitably will if the routine is continued long enough—this blinking response is amplified by means of suggestion: "Your eyes are blinking, blinking. They are blinking more and more now. Soon they will want to close of themselves." Pacing the suggestions to match the responses of the subject, the suggestor continues: "Your eyelids are getting heavier and heavier, and now they are beginning to droop. You are blinking faster and faster now. Your eyes are closing, closing. Soon your eyes will be completely closed, and remain so." When the subject's eyes have closed, the suggestor then proceeds in a manner similar to other hypnotic procedures, using suggestions of progressively increasing relaxation, drowsiness and sleep.

Hypnosis with Kinesthetic Imagery

The following technique is particularly advantageous for use with subjects who may have difficulty employing visual imagery. It also provides the suggestor with excellent feedback concerning the subject's responsiveness, as indicated by the ease and rapidity with which the latter's arm descends and then rises in response to suggestion, thereby enabling the length of the induction to be adjusted to suit the requirements of the individual subject with relative ease. Highly resistant or negatively suggestible subjects are usually identifiable without difficulty by means of this procedure, as revealed by their inclination to maintain their arm in a relatively stationary position, or even to move it in the opposite direction to that which is suggested. With appropriate allowances for variation in the responsiveness of individual subjects, the induction may be administered as follows:

Just close your eyes now and listen to my voice. I would like you to hold your right (or left) arm straight out in front of you, with the palm facing upward. That's right: arm straight out in the air in front of you, with the palm facing upward. Now, just imagine that you are holding an empty bucket in that hand, and that I'm slowly pouring some sand into the bucket. And as I do, you will feel your arm getting heavier and heavier as the bucket pulls it down more and more—and as it does, it will pull you deeper and deeper into hypnosis. And as soon as your arm touches your lap, or touches the chair in which you are sitting, you will instantly go into a very deep hypnotic sleep.

Now I've poured five pounds of sand into the bucket, and you can feel it pulling your arm down, pulling your arm down, more and more, and pulling you into hypnosis. Your arm is beginning to sink down more and more now, as you feel the weight of the bucket pulling it down, and down. Seven pounds, and your arm is sinking down and down. Your arm is sinking down more and more as I continue pouring sand into the bucket; and as it does, it's pulling you deeper and deeper into hypnosis. Ten pounds. Fifteen pounds. In just a few seconds now, your arm will touch your lap or touch the arm of the chair, and you will instantly go into a deep hypnotic sleep, a much deeper sleep than you have ever been in before. Ready to touch. Ready to touch. Ready to touch. *Now.*

And as you continue drifting down and down into a very deep, hypnotic sleep, I would like you to visualize a large balloon, which is fastened to your other wrist by means of a string. And as I continue to speak, the balloon is going to begin pulling this arm up, until it is extended straight out in the air in front of you. You can feel this arm becoming lighter now, as I continue to speak; and you can feel the balloon beginning to pull on it.

Your arm is beginning to rise up into the air now, rising up and up. It is rising faster and faster now. Continuing to rise, up and up, continuing to go higher. In just a few seconds, your arm will be straight out in front of you, and then I will touch it—and as I do, it will drop down into a normal resting position as I cut the string which holds the balloon, and you will instantly go much deeper into hypnosis. Your arm is almost straight out in front of you. Now your arm is straight out in front of you, and I am going to touch it as I cut the string which is holding it to the balloon; and as soon as I do so, your arm will drop back into a normal resting position, and you will instantly go much deeper into hypnosis than you are right now. Ready? *Now.*

Hypnosis with the Chevreul Pendulum

The Chevreul pendulum consists of a clear, round crystal about twice the size of a marble, suspended by a chain which is several inches in length. A locket or other pendant may occasionally serve as an effective substitute. The pendulum may be utilized as a visual fixation object in the manner previously described, or, more commonly, the subject may be instructed to hold the pendulum himself, placing his elbow on a table or other flat surface to allow the crystal to swing freely back and forth. Suggestions may then be administered as follows: "Now, as I continue speaking, you will soon notice that the pendulum is beginning to move, as if it were moving all by itself. It may start out slowly at first, but soon it will be moving more and more freely. And eventually it will be moving rapidly, back and forth, and back, and forth."

By watching the pendulum and properly timing one's suggestions as it begins to swing in response to the subject's own slight muscular tremor, the suggestor can begin to direct the subject's normal unconscious movements in such a manner as to cause the pendulum to begin to swing in the suggested manner—back and forth, from side to side, or in a circle; and even to reverse itself once it has started, beginning to swing in the opposite direction if desired. Once a sufficient degree of imaginative involvement has been attained by means of this procedure, suggestions of progressive eye closure, relaxation, drowsiness, and sleep may be provided in much the same manner as in other hypnotic techniques.

Deepening the Hypnotic Trance

What is commonly referred to as "taking a person deeper into hypnosis" is actually any method of increasing the credibility and the degree of the subject's imaginative involvement with the suggested trance experience. Thus, in addition to the previously mentioned adaptation of the suggestions for heightening rapport, virtually any hypnotic induction which the subject begins with his eyes closed may be used with only minor changes as a "deepening technique"; and virtually any "deepening technique" may be modified and used as an induction. For example, the "empty bucket" and the "balloon" sequences of the hypnotic induction with kinesthetic imagery are excellent deepeners when used separately. Another procedure is as follows:

> Now I'm going to count from one to twenty; and by the time I get to the count of twenty, you will be much more deeply hypnotized than you are right now. Just imagine that you are at the top of a long staircase which has twenty steps, and picture yourself taking hold of my hand as I begin the count.

At this point, the suggestor may actually take hold of the subject's hand if he wishes.

> With each count, you will descend, one step at a time. And with each step that you descend, you will go one step deeper into hypnosis. One. Going deeper now, just let yourself sink deeper into hypnosis, as you descend the first step on the staircase. Two. Going down another step, and continuing to go deeper as you do. Three. Going deeper yet, as you continue to descend. By the time I get to the count of twenty, you will be deeper than ever before. Four. You descend the fourth step now, and you go still deeper. Five. The fifth step, and you continue going *much deeper* into hypnosis with every step you take.
> Now I'm going to let you continue on down the staircase by yourself, all the way to the twentieth step at the bottom. Just let yourself keep going down the staircase, counting out loud with each step, as you continue to descend all the way to the bottom. Now you can begin to count out loud, and continue counting all the way down.

Some subjects who may be inclined to be rather passive may need to be reminded once or twice to begin to count out loud, or to continue counting all the way up to twenty. As the subject begins to count, it is helpful to intersperse suggestions such as the following at appropriate intervals:

> Going on by yourself now, all the way to the twentieth step at the bottom, and in just a moment or two, you will have reached the bottom of the stairs, and you will be in a *very* deep hypnotic trance. Just continue to count out loud, as you continue to descend the staircase, and in a moment or so, you will have reached the bottom.

The foregoing suggestions may be modified to "heighten" a suggested hyperempiric trance by asking the subject to picture himself at the *foot* of a staircase leading *upward,* and suggesting that with each count the subject will ascend one step, and that as he does, he will go *higher*. Some of my students have occasionally reported a similar intensification of imaginative involvement by using hypnotic and hyperempiric inductions In sequence, taking a subject first "down" into hypnosis and then "up" into hyperempiria, or vice versa.

RAPID METHODS OF TRANCE INDUCTION

Any of the previously presented hyperempiric or hypnotic inductions may be made either briefer or more elaborate to suit the responsiveness of the particular subject. If, by his breathing, posture, and overall demeanor, a subject should appear to be highly responsive to suggestion during the early stages of a trance induction, there is generally no point in unduly prolonging the ritual as long as an appropriate degree of credibility is maintained.

Once subjects have become adapted to the trance format and the degree of their responsiveness to suggestion has been fairly well ascertained, it is usually possible to save a great deal of time during subsequent inductions. Moderately suggestible subjects may be administered an induction in the usual manner, with words and phrases omitted here and there as the induction proceeds, whereas those who are more highly suggestible may simply be requested to close their eyes while the suggestor counts slowly from one to ten, with brief hyperempiric or hypnotic induction phrases interspersed between the numbers. Indeed, individual subjects have occasionally been noted who would seat themselves comfortably in a chair and spontaneously begin to manifest trance behavior without waiting for the induction to be given.

If the suggestor prefers to use a prearranged signal as a cue for trance induction, almost any stimulus can be made to serve this purpose if it is suggested to a sufficiently responsive subject in the course of a trance session. For example, one might say, "Whenever you are willing for me to place you into a trance again from now on, I will simply ask you to close your eyes while I touch you lightly on the forehead, and you will instantly go right back into a trance, just as you are right now." When such methods are employed, however, care should be taken that they are administered in a spirit of mutual cooperation, as in the example just provided, and that they are not used in such a manner as to catch the subject by surprise; for such a procedure may then implicitly communicate a false sense of intrusiveness which may be damaging to the mutual trust and cooperation which constitute the essence of any helping relationship.

TRANCE INDUCTION BY TELEPHONE

Occasionally, it may be desirable to employ an induction by telephone when the subject may be in need of special assistance and not be able to arrange a personal visit, or when the interval between visits must, for some reason, be prolonged. The procedure for trance induction by telephone is not substantially different from that which is employed face to face; for as long as one is dealing with a sufficiently responsive and willing subject, all that is necessary for a successful induction is to credibly communicate the suggestion that the subject is entering a trance.

For example, in the course of a telephone conversation with a former student who had previously shown herself to be an excellent subject, she happened to mention that she had developed a severe headache from studying for two examinations which were to be held the following day. "Would you like me to hypnotize you over the telephone and take away the headache?" I asked. When she replied in the affirmative, I proceeded in the following manner: "All right, just close your eyes and continue listening to my voice. You will be able to continue to comfortably hold the receiver to your ear as I speak, and you will always be able to hear and to respond to my voice, and to answer any questions I may ask you." I then proceeded to administer a hypnotic induction in the usual manner, concluding with the question, "You're very deeply asleep now, aren't you?" to which she replied, "Yes," in a quiet voice. I then suggested that by the time I reached the count of five, her headache would be completely gone. I began to count slowly, interspersing suggestions to the effect that her headache was beginning to go away, that it was going away more and more, that it was almost gone; and finally, that it was completely gone. When she stated in response to my question that her headache had indeed disappeared, I terminated the proceedings in the usual manner.

Other accounts of the use of induction procedures by telephone may be found in Owens (1970), Stanton (1978), and Weitzenhoffer (1972).

SELF-INDUCED TRANCES

The possibility of administering trance suggestions to oneself may occasionally strike some people as being a bit farfetched. Yet, many persons spontaneously discover ways of using autosuggestion in everyday life without actually being aware that they are doing so. It is by no means uncommon, for example, to be able to awaken oneself regularly at the same time each morning without an alarm clock, with due allowance for the changing seasons made without apparent effort, or to change the time during which one regularly does waken, merely by making an appropriate resolution the previous night. Many people are also able to "talk themselves into" carrying out household chores when they are not initially in the proper mood for such activities; or they may have learned how to "cheer themselves up" by thinking pleasant thoughts when they are temporarily depressed.

Provided one is sufficiently responsive to suggestion, the ability to suggest a trance experience to oneself is largely a matter of willingness, practice, and confidence; and the necessary confidence is most easily acquired by having another person administer the initial inductions and turn the responsibility for administering subsequent suggested trance experiences over to the subject in a few successive stages.

After a hypnotic or a hyperempiric induction has been administered in the usual manner, a posttrance suggestion may be provided according to the procedure described in the section on postinduction tests of responsiveness. The suggestor may then proceed as follows:

I'm going to return you now to the normal, everyday state of awareness, and then I'm going to place you in trance again in a few moments to show you how to administer a suggestion to yourself and how to bring yourself back. And because of the practice you have had, you will be able to go into trance more easily and more rapidly next time.

Although earlier studies concluded that responsiveness to an induction procedure is not greatly affected by practice (Barber & Calverley, 1966; Hilgard, 1965), more recent research indicates that this is not the case if an appropriate degree of interest and involvement with the suggestions is maintained throughout the procedure (Barber, Ascher, & Mavroides, 1971). Thus, it is important that the subject continue to approach the situation with as much confidence, interest, and motivation as possible.

If the subject complies with the posttrance suggestion, regardless of the context in which the response occurs or the reasons given for such compliance, it is likely that he will be able to benefit from the use of autosuggestion and self-induced trance experiences, particularly if he is willing to work at it. On the other hand, if the subject has made no move to comply with the suggestion after a reasonable time has elapsed, and if he indicates that he feels no inclination to do so, it may not be worth the time of either the subject or the suggestor to continue.

One possible exception to the aforementioned situation, however, is the individual who may have such strong needs for independence that he is willing to comply with his own suggestions but not with the suggestions of others. Thus, if an apparently unresponsive subject still desires to continue to learn self-induced trance techniques after it has been mentioned to him that perhaps his own needs for independence are impending the effectiveness of the test suggestion, it may be desirable to proceed through the next stage in order to test the subject's response to autosuggestion before giving up the effort completely.

After the induction has been administered a second time, the following suggestion may be given:

A few moments ago, I gave you a suggestion which you were to carry out immediately after the trance was over. Now I'm going to show you how to give yourself a suggestion, and how to terminate the trance by yourself as well. First of all, I'd like you to think of something that you can tell yourself to do right after the trance is over. It might be a suggestion to yourself that you will touch your right ear, or that you will stand up and shake hands, or almost anything else you can think of; but whatever it is, it should be something that you can do within a minute or two after the trance is over.

Then, when you have decided what it is that you are going to do, you will only have to think to yourself the suggestion, "After I come out of the trance, I will do such and such," and you will be able to carry out whatever suggestion you have given yourself just as well and just as effectively as if I had given the suggestion to you.

When you are ready to bring yourself out of the trance, you will be able to do so by silently counting from one to five and telling yourself as you do that you are gradually coming back, more and more, and that by the time you get to the count of five you will be all the way back, feeling wonderful. Of course, you won't have to use my exact words, just whatever words feel right and natural to you as you bring yourself out of the trance by thinking these suggestions silently.

And later on, you will be able to carry out the entire process by yourself: you will be able to place yourself in trance by sitting back and closing your eyes and silently counting from one to ten, using whatever imagery and whatever words you find comfortable and convenient, telling yourself that by the time you get to the count of ten you will be in a trance; and then you can give yourself a posttrance suggestion and bring yourself out in the manner I have just described. You will always be able to hear and to respond to any outside stimuli, and you will be able to bring yourself out of the trance very easily and very rapidly any time the need should arise.

But right now, just go ahead and give yourself a suggestion that you are going to do something right after the trance is over, and then bring yourself out as soon as you are ready.

If the subject appears to be taking an unduly long time, it may occasionally be necessary to prompt him with a few suggestions couched as reassuring observations: "Almost ready to open your eyes now, feeling just fine," or, "Soon your eyes will open and the trance will be over, and you're going to be feeling absolutely wonderful."

If a subject carries out his previously administered autosuggestion within a reasonable time after his eyes have opened, he is then ready to attempt the entire procedure by himself: to suggest a trance, administer additional autosuggestions, and to cancel the trance suggestions himself. Most responsive subjects are eager to try out their newly acquired abilities immediately; and it is usually helpful for them to do so, if they wish, within a few moments after the previous trance experience has been terminated and while the instructor is still present. However, some subjects may prefer to attempt their first autoinduction at home or in some other setting where they will be able to schedule an abundance of time to themselves, free of distractions and outside interference—perhaps just before they go to sleep at night. This latter alternative is especially preferable in those cases in which a subject's initial responses to autosuggestion have been weak or uncertain.

Many instructors like to encourage subjects to word their autosuggestions in the first person: "*My* whole body feels calm and relaxed," etc. Alternatively, the subject may be instructed to address himself in a totally objective manner, as if he were an outside observer completely detached from his own body: "Feel your whole body relaxing now, deeper and deeper." In the absence of any clear-cut experimental evidence demonstrating the superiority of one technique over another, my own inclination is to let the subject decide for himself whether he feels more comfortable wording his autosuggestions in the first or the third person.

Obviously, the more "dramatic" phenomena of suggestion, such as positive and negative hallucinations, should not be attempted in self-induced trances—and indeed, most of the time they *cannot* be; for some degree of awareness and control must be maintained by even the best subjects to guide the course of their own trance experience. In general, all subjects should be cautioned to check with a qualified professional before attempting to employ these skills for any purpose other than that for which they have initially been taught. Occasionally, for example, a subject might be inclined to use autosuggestion to block out recurring sensations of pain after aspirin and other over-the-counter analgesics have proved ineffective, only to discover—perhaps when it is too late—that he should have consulted a physician as soon as the discomfort began.

It is also desirable to discourage the use of self-induced trance techniques by cultists who wish to "reexperience past lifetimes" or perhaps "learn astral projection." Such people are often unable to comprehend that a suggestion-induced hallucination which happens to coincide with one's occult beliefs is still an hallucination—and one which carries a potential for future mischief if the subject persists in confusing such hallucinations with reality.

Although there is little likelihood of individuals with psychotic tendencies using self-induced trance experiences to develop a Jekyll-and-Hyde personality, it is probably not advisable to encourage the use of autosuggestion by those who are obviously psychotic or pre-psychotic, since such people are generally not able to use these techniques appropriately. However, trance sessions conducted by persons other than the subject himself have been successfully employed in such instances.

MUTUAL TRANCE INDUCTION

It is often helpful for the suggestor to allow himself to experience as much imaginative involvement as possible with an induction he is administering to another. If a hypnotic induction is being employed, the suggestor can close his own eyes and allow his body to become limp, while a note of lethargy creeps into his voice and his pronunciation becomes slower and somewhat muted. In the case of a hyperempiric induction, the suggestor can allow himself to share imaginatively in the rising excitement and exhilaration brought about by the suggestion of expanded awareness. Such empathic responses often expedite the induction by adding implicit vocal and nonverbal cues that enhance the effect of the explicit suggestions contained in the induction. Indeed, some suggestors report empathically experiencing the effects of an induction themselves to a certain extent whenever they administer an induction to another; and it is asserted that this shared experience serves to facilitate rapport greatly, or the process of communication between suggestor and subject.

If the suggestor himself is a good trance subject, this enhanced rapport may be further augmented by allowing the subject to induce a trance in the suggestor, as soon as the initial induction has been completed, in a manner which is analogous to the procedure first described by Tart (1969). As is the case with self-induced trance experiences, either hypnotic or hyperempiric inductions may be employed, as long as both parties are sufficiently familiar with the procedure. After the induction has been administered to the first subject, he may be told, "Now you will be able to place me in a trance also, by administering an induction to me just as I have done to you." When this latter induction has been completed, the parties may take turns, administering at appropriate intervals, additional suggestions for deepening or heightening an increased rapport to each other until the desired degree of mutual imaginative involvement and shared credibility has been achieved.

A variation of this technique involves one of the parties inducing a trance in the other while simultaneously or shortly thereafter inducing a trance in himself by means of autosuggestion.

Mutual trance induction is particularly appropriate for use with various techniques involving fantasy and guided imagery.

At the conclusion of the proceedings, one party may terminate the experience for both by speaking the necessary suggestions aloud.

CHAPTER 5

Postinduction Tests of Responsiveness

At the conclusion of an induction, many suggestors may wish to test the subject's responsiveness before proceeding further. The first test administered for this purpose usually involves suggestions of eyelid catalepsy, or inability to open one's eyes when challenged, which is at the low or easy end of most suggestibility scales (Hilgard, 1965). These suggestions may be administered in the following manner:

> I'm going to count from one to five; and by the time I get to five, you will find that your eyelids have become stuck together so tightly that you will not be able to open them, no matter how hard you try; and the harder you try, the harder to open them it will actually be. But just relax and don't try it yet. Just listen to my voice now, as I begin the count from one to five.
>
> One. As I begin the count, you can feel your eyelids becoming stuck together, tighter and tighter. Two. Your eyelids are becoming stuck together more and more now, tighter and tighter all the time. Three. Your eyelids are becoming stuck together so very tightly, just like two sheets of lead. By the time I get to the count of five, they will be stuck together so tightly that it will be absolutely impossible to open them; and the harder you try, the harder to open them it will be. Four. It's becoming impossible to open your eyes now—a complete and total impossibility; and the harder you try to open them, the harder it will be. Five. It's completely impossible now. Try as you might, *you cannot open your eyes*. Go ahead and try, but the harder you try, the harder it becomes.

If the subject's eyes remain closed after a few seconds have elapsed, he is told that he can stop trying to open them (regardless of whether or not he actually appears to be trying), and suggestions may be given for further imaginative involvement (deepening or heightening the trance, as the case may be). On the other hand, if the subject does open his eyes, the suggestor should smoothly shift to another induction procedure without conveying the notion that anything is amiss. For example, if the "rubber raft" hypnotic induction was used initially, the suggestor may continue as follows: "All right, close your eyes once more, and I will show you how to go much deeper. With your eyes closed, please hold your right (or left) hand out in the air in front of you, with the palm up," thus making the transition to an alternate hypnotic induction using kinesthetic imagery.

After the second induction has been completed (or after the suggestions for further imaginative involvement have been given if the subject did not open his eyes), suggestions may be given for arm catalepsy as an additional test of the subject's responsiveness. Such suggestions may be administered as follows:

Please extend your right (or left) arm out in the air in front of you, and make a fist. That's right: arm straight out in front of you, with your hand clenched into a tight fist. Now, as I count from one to three, you are going to find that your arm will become more and more rigid, until at the count of three, your arm is going to be just as stiff and rigid as a bar of iron. And you won't be able to bend your arm at the elbow until I touch it, no matter how hard you try. In fact, the harder you try to bend your arm, the harder it will actually be to bend it.

One. As I begin the count now, you can feel your arm becoming stiff and rigid. You can feel your arm tensing up, more and more. Two. Your arm is becoming very stiff, as you feel the muscles beginning to tighten and lock it into place. By the time I get to the count of three, you won't be able to bend your arm at the elbow no matter how hard you try. Your arm is becoming as stiff as a bar of iron now, so rigid that you cannot bend it at all. It's totally impossible to bend it now. Three. Try as you might, you cannot bend your arm until I touch it.

At this point, the majority of subjects will sit with their arm outstretched, waiting for the suggestor to touch it so as to cancel the suggestions of stiffness. However, some subjects will cock their arm ever so slightly, as if to test the effects of the previous suggestions, before making a serious attempt to bend their arms. Thus, if a subject appears to be ready to reject these suggestions, the suggestor should have his own hand outstretched, ready to touch the subject's arm before he actually does bend it; for the essence of *trance*, from induction to termination, lies in establishing and maintaining the credibility of the experience for the subject (Kidder, 1972).

After a few seconds have elapsed—or sooner, if necessary—the following suggestions may be given: "Now, as I touch your arm, it is becoming completely normal again, and you can put it down. Now your arm is completely back to normal, and you can just let it rest comfortably as before."

The foregoing tests of eye and arm catalepsy tend to present the subject with a paradox. After assuring him that he will be able to resist any suggestion which he does not wish to accept, *challenge* items such as these appear to demonstrate to the subject that he is indeed in the *power* of the suggestor: that he cannot even open his eyes or bend his outstretched arm when challenged.

Of course, the subject is not really as helpless as these suggestions might imply. So-called challenge suggestions are effective because the subject wishes the trance itself to be effective, so as to enable him to achieve the goals which led him to undergo an induction in the first place; and for the sake of these ultimate goals (even if they comprise no more than the satisfaction of his own curiosity), a subject might allow himself momentarily to feel as if he had surrendered the ability to open his eyes or to bend his outstretched arm, as long as the suggestions that he will do this are presented in a sufficiently plausible manner and an appropriate degree of imaginative involvement has been attained. But as the culture continues to progress in a less authoritarian direction, many people who are capable of profound imaginative involvement with suggestions related to the satisfaction of their own personal goals are nevertheless disposed to resist any suggestion which appears to be aimed primarily at restricting their independence or demonstrating that they have surrendered a portion of themselves to the control of another. Thus, in purely applied contexts, I am inclined to agree with Hartland (1971), who finds little need for tests of responsiveness, and with Evans's (1978) observation that tests of this sort may actually be counterproductive, since failure to perform satisfactorily on any of the test items may adversely affect the credibility of subsequent suggestions.

As an alternative to the use of more formal procedures derived from various suggestibility, susceptibility, or "depth" scales, the degree of a subject's imaginative involvement with trance suggestions can often be assessed fairly well by asking him, "If you were to place yourself on a scale from one to ten, with ten representing the greatest degree of trance which you are able to experience and one representing the lightest degree, where are you on such a scale right now?'' If the subject responds with a low or intermediate number, additional suggestions may be provided for heightening rapport or imaginative involvement as are appropriate. But even this method may sometimes cause a less responsive subject to think to himself, "It isn't working very well," thereby lessening the credibility of suggestions which may be given later.

The subject's readiness to comply with a simple posttrance suggestion may most safely be assessed by wording the suggestion in such a manner as to allow him to exercise a choice between several different modes of compliance, in accordance with the characteristics of the subject's own personality (Erickson, Rossi, & Rossi, 1976). For example, he might be told:

After the trance has ended, you are going to experience a motive, an impulse, or a desire to reach over and touch the wall. But you won't experience it in terms of a conflict of wills, for it will be coming from inside of you, and you will just flow along with it, like you might flow with a piece of music. In fact, it might even tend to sneak up on you, and catch you unawares. Or you might find a plausible reason for touching the wall, regardless of the fact that I have told you that you would do so. But in any event, the longer you wait, the stronger the impulse is going to be. So within just a moment or two after the trance is ended, you will reach over and touch the wall.

If the subject has made no move to comply with this suggestion within a moment or two after the trance session has been concluded, additional facilitative suggestions may be worked into the ensuing conversation. For example, if the subject happens to glance in the direction of the wall, the suggestor may say, "Well, I see you looking over in that direction, so I know you must be thinking about what I told you." If the subject should happen to deny this, and he remembers the suggestion being given, he may be asked, "You're thinking about it now, though, aren't you,?" to which he must invariably reply in the affirmative, since this is now the topic of conversation. With the timely inclusion of an expectant pause or two, and additional comments such as, "It won't be long now," most subjects will eventually comply with such a suggestion. The degree of their responsiveness may then be inferred from the rapidity and the manner in which compliance took place, rather than from the fact that such compliance actually occurred. The subject may then be readministered an induction, and further tests or additional suggestions may be provided.

One of the more difficult tests, to which only about 5% of all subjects are capable of responding successfully, is a visual hallucination. It should be reiterated, however, that suggestions are only difficult in the sense that fewer people are likely to comply with them. It takes no more skill or ability on the part of a suggestor to administer a difficult or bizarre suggestion than it takes to administer an easy one, regardless of how impressive such a suggestion may appear to an untrained observer. One example of the manner in which a posttrance visual hallucination may be suggested, in combination with a suggestion for temporary amnesia for the test item, is as follows: After an induction has been given, the subject may be told:

> When the trance is over, as soon as you open your eyes, you are going to see me dressed differently. You will see me wearing a Santa Claus suit and hat, with whiskers, boots, and all. It's going to look completely real to you until I say the word "poof," at which time the suggestion will be canceled and you will see me dressed normally again, just as I am now. You will find the situation quite amusing, and you'll laugh about it and comment on it, but you won't remember that I have told you this until I say the word "poof." So even though you see me wearing the costume, you won't know why I look that way until the suggestion has been canceled.

After the subject has opened his eyes, if he appears to be responding satisfactorily, it is often desirable to allow him an opportunity to "feel" the whiskers before saying the key word which will cancel the suggestion. Some subjects, while asserting that they can "feel" the beard, will place their hands at the proper distance from the suggestor's chin, whereas others, still asserting that they can feel the whiskers, will place their hands either too close or too far away.

I am occasionally asked by students whether or not it is possible to tell if a subject is genuinely responding to the suggestions he has been given, or merely faking. Although a few highly responsive subjects are able to accomplish such feats as inhaling ammonia fumes with apparent relish after being told that they are smelling perfume, the majority do not; but it is possible for relatively unresponsive subjects to pass virtually any test of suggestibility if they are sufficiently motivated—even tests involving exposure to pain or other noxious stimuli. In applied settings, however, since the suggestor's sole purpose is to assist the subject in the attainment of the latter's chosen goals, the possibility of any form of deception—except perhaps momentarily in the name of politeness—is virtually nonexistent.

CHAPTER 6

The Less Responsive Subject

Since the base line of suggestibility has been found to be higher in the general population than was formerly supposed (Barber & Calverley, 1963), some subjects who are not sufficiently suggestible to experience a change in the perception of their own awareness as a consequence of undergoing an induction procedure will nevertheless be able to respond to suggestions of low or moderate difficulty, even though they may later assert that they "didn't feel any different," or that the experience was "not like I thought it was going to be," or they may even flatly state, "I don't think it worked on me."

For those who at best seem to be able to undergo only the most general or rudimentary forms of trance experience even though they respond appropriately to certain suggestions, it may be helpful to define the experience in more general terms, in accordance with their more limited capacities. If a subject appears to be in doubt as to whether or not an induction has actually worked, and his other responses to suggestion appear sufficiently adequate to make it worthwhile to continue to utilize a trance format, the suggestor may point out that the experience of trance is not fundamentally different from the kind of narrowing and focusing of attention which occurs when one is absorbed in reading a novel, watching a motion picture, or listening to music; and thus, it is potentially within the reach of anyone who is willing to cooperate with the instructions and suggestions he is given.

Strictly speaking, of course, the mere act of focusing one's attention does not automatically result in a trance experience unless one chooses to define it in such a manner, or unless such a definition is either directly or indirectly suggested. But, although many less suggestible subjects may still "feel the same" after an induction, such a definition will provide them with the necessary conceptual framework and ideological rationale to legitimize the acceptance of whatever additional suggestions they are able and willing to comply with, as is the case with others who are more responsive.

A broad definition of the nature of trance experience, such as the one just described, is also helpful in working with groups, in which individual levels of responsiveness may vary considerably but progress toward common or individual goals may be maintained even among the less suggestible members by a number of additional factors, such as the bond of trust and encouragement which develops between the group and the leader, the mutual support and encouragement which exists among the members, and the opportunity to model one's own behavior after the examples provided by certain members whose initial progress may have been more rapid or more dramatic than that of the others.

Traditional hypnosis has an "image problem" which may sometimes render induction difficult, even after reasonable efforts have been made to correct any misconceptions concerning what the subject is about to experience. Many people first encounter the concept of hypnosis, as I did, by watching a "monster" movie as a child. Indeed, ever since hypnosis first came into prominence in the nineteenth century, it has been associated in the popular media with unsavory personages both real and fictional: Trilby, Svengali, Cagliostro, Rasputin, and the Maddhi, to name but a few. Such misconceptions are probably due to the outward appearance of a traditional sleeping induction procedure, together with the use of challenge items as subsequent tests of responsiveness, which often may counteract previous assurances that a hypnotized subject does not surrender his will, even though these assurances are, of course, correct.

Because of the prevailing stereotypes attendant upon the concept of hypnosis, some individuals are still somewhat repelled by the notion of undergoing a hypnotic induction, even after an appropriate prehypnotic talk which is designed to allay such misconceptions. Since hyperempiric or alertness inductions have been found to be as effective as sleeping inductions in facilitating subsequent responsiveness to suggestion (Gibbons, 1976; Gibbons & Glenn, 1978; Katz, 1975; Severson & Hurlbut, 1977), I usually prefer to capitalize on the *positive* stereotypes currently associated with various forms of meditation and other mind expanding techniques by initially employing a hyperempiric induction unless the subject specifically requests hypnosis. Since alertness inductions necessarily imply that the subject will be even more in possession of his faculties at the conclusion of the induction than he was before, outmoded nineteenth-century Svengali-like stereotypes of an all-powerful hypnotist dominating a passive, weak-willed subject may thus be completely avoided.

It is also possible to merely omit the words *sleep* or *hypnosis* from a traditional induction procedure, perhaps substituting the word *relaxation* (Donk, Vingoe, Hall, & Doty, 1970; Swiercinsky & Coe, 1971; Vingoe, 1973). The suggestions that the subject is being hypnotized are then either implicit in the situation or they are communicated indirectly by means of gestures or tone of voice. However, some subjects are still likely to think to themselves, "This is something like hypnosis," or, "This is just another way to hypnotize me," particularly if the suggestor has a reputation as a hypnotist (Gibbons, 1974). Thus, although some otherwise refractory subjects may respond to such a "disguised" approach, it is usually simpler to employ a hyperempiric induction.

And what of the occasional subject who appears to be totally unresponsive? If, after a few repeated attempts, with perhaps different induction procedures, a subject still does not respond satisfactorily, then there is little to be gained in assuring him that he is responding well and that his performance will continue to improve each time he undergoes an induction procedure. But for every subject one encounters who responds poorly, one is statistically certain to encounter another who responds so well that perseverance in the use of induction techniques with those who are willing to try them will be amply rewarded.

CHAPTER 7

Administering Trance Suggestions

Suggestions should always be communicated with sufficient clarity that there is no possibility for the subject to mistake their meaning in his current uncritical frame of mind. For example, one woman who underwent trance induction to alleviate her insomnia was told that in the future she would "sleep like a baby." In response to this suggestion, she began to develop a pattern of going promptly to sleep and then waking up every four hours, just as a young infant is prone to do. Another subject, who was told that he would "feel tremendous" at the conclusion of a trance experience, reported sensations of extreme body distortion instead of the pleasant mood which had been intended. Equating "tremendous" with "gross," because of his German language background, the subject experienced a considerable amount of discomfort until corrective suggestions were administered.

The likelihood of such failures in effective communication can be considerably reduced if suggestions are always spoken slowly and carefully, with a considerable amount of repetition and deliberate redundancy—which also tends to heighten their effectiveness, in much the same manner that repetition and redundancy enhance the effectiveness of an advertisement.

Suggestions should also be worded in such a manner as to stress the positive consequences of an intended change rather than the negative consequences which may ensue if such a change should fail to come about. For instance, it is appropriate to suggest that as soon as a smoker who desires to quit has done so, he will begin to notice how much better his food tastes and how much he is starting to enjoy breathing fresh, clean air again. But one should *not* suggest that the smell and taste of tobacco will be highly unpleasant or revolting; for if the cessation of smoking should not happen to be permanent for one reason or another, self-punishing tendencies within the subject's own personality may cause the resumption of smoking to be accompanied by a great deal of unpleasantness. In fact, some subjects have even been known to vomit when they begin to smoke their next cigarette after receiving the apparently innocuous suggestion that the taste of tobacco will be very unpleasant to them in the future.

Of course, one should always remember to cancel specifically any suggestion which is not intended to persist. Although most such suggestions would probably not last long in any event (Perry, 1977), it would be rather embarrassing for all concerned if, for example, a subject were unable to open the door to leave at the conclusion of a trance session because his arm catalepsy had not been terminated.

Occasionally, a subject may not comply with a suggestion, or spontaneously come out of the trance, because he may find the suggestion to be objectionable for reasons of his own. One subject, for example, upon being told that he would have to leave the room and get a drink of water as soon as the trance session was concluded, remained steadfastly in his seat when the time came, even though he appeared to be thirsty and had been highly responsive to suggestion during the session itself. When questioned, it was learned that the subject originally came from a section of Europe where drinking plain water was considered appropriate only for the lowest class of peasants. Another subject, who behaved in an almost identical manner in response to a similar suggestion, subsequently indicated that she had always attended private schools in which the discipline was extremely strict; and thus, she did not wish to walk out on a teacher (which the suggestor in fact was) before she had been dismissed.

If a subject should open his eyes spontaneously during or after an induction, it does not necessarily mean that he has come out of the trance. Many excellent subjects are able to do this; and occasionally such a subject will open his eyes of his own volition. In such a contingency, if the suggestor should happen to inquire, "Oh, did you come out of it?" with the obvious implication that the subject *has*, the trance experience is virtually certain to be interrupted; but if he merely says, "Just close your eyes again—that's all right—and I'll keep talking to you," it is often possible to continue as before, perhaps with the aid of additional procedures designed to increase the degree of the subject's imaginative involvement.

Many subjects tend to find plausible reasons for carrying out a suggestion, rather than admit to themselves that they are merely complying with the wishes of the suggestor, or perhaps being unable to explain their actions because the suggestion itself is not recalled. For example, one subject was told that at the conclusion of a trance session she would touch a ceramic owl on my desk. As she was about to leave, she turned and said, "I know you told me that I would touch this owl before I left, but just to show you that I don't have to, I'm going to reach out and touch it now of my own free will!"

The length of time a suggestion will be effective depends on several factors. Suggestions which are strongly at variance with normal sensory input, such as suggested visual hallucinations, may generally be expected to wear off more quickly than suggestions which are not in direct conflict with subsequent sensory data. Moreover, the less responsive to suggestion an individual happens to be, the narrower is the range of suggestion-related techniques which may be utilized in order to assist him, and the more one is obliged to rely on indirect suggestions, double binds ("the harder you try to open your eyes, the harder it will be"), and disguised approaches, which are more difficult for the subject to counteract or deny (Erickson & Rossi, 1975; Erickson, Rossi, & Rossi, 1976; Haley, 1973), but are also more imprecise. Generally speaking, suggestions based on the use of fantasy and guided imagery may be used with all but the most refractory subjects; for virtually everyone is able to engage in fantasy. This type of suggestion is particularly useful in group settings, in which individual responsiveness may vary greatly. On the other hand, specific alterations in overt behavior usually require at least a moderate degree of suggestibility to be effective; for a major determinant of such changes is the subject's own conviction that they are actually going to work—and the more a suggested behavioral change deviates from one's everyday experience or customary patterns of conduct, the more responsive to suggestion one is likely to have to be in order to comply.

To some extent, specific behavioral changes induced by direct suggestion—such as the suggestions that a smoker will abstain from the use of tobacco, or that a dieter will not deviate from his diet—may be regarded as similar to a conviction or resolution that the subject has arrived at on his own. Regardless of whether one decides for himself that he is going to stop smoking, or whether a direct suggestion to that effect is administered, the ultimate outcome often tends to be the same: the subject will stop for a while, and then resume the habit as he discovers by experience how much more satisfying it is for him to smoke than not to smoke.

But the situation is not as hopeless as it might appear. First of all, the effects of suggestion may be prolonged by several methods. The means most commonly employed is simply to schedule the subject for a series of inductions, repeating the initial suggestions at each subsequent session before their effects have extinguished, and perhaps incorporating additional suggestions or new variations in wording. The subject may also be taught to use autosuggestion and self-induced trance experiences; and with appropriate instruction, he may be encouraged to employ cassette recordings of previous sessions to repeat the trance experience at a later date. Suggested amnesia may also facilitate the persistence of certain suggestions by making them unavailable for subsequent conscious recomputation.

However, such methods in themselves only tend to postpone the inevitable readjustment unless they help the subject to bridge the gap between his present circumstances and a new set of environmental conditions which act to maintain the desired improvements, as in the case of a girl who may easily be able to persevere on her diet as soon as she begins to experience the looks of admiration and approval which her increased attractiveness will evoke from those around her, together with the enhanced social and romantic life which is frequently a consequence of such attention.

Of course, human beings are capable of *learning* to be reinforced by a wide variety of situations; and regardless of the manner in which a suggestion is worded or the number of times it is presented, its greatest potential for relatively permanent behavioral change is generally to be found in the degree to which it facilitates the *learning of more adaptive patterns of behavior*. For example, a talented musician who is unable to perform adequately because of stage fright may not be able to experience the applause which would be his if his fear were not present; but with properly worded suggestions that he will experience most of his anxiety a few moments *before* going before an audience, rather than *during* the performance, he may be able to break the vicious circle of undue anxiety leading to poor performance, which, in turn, creates more anxiety that acts as a barrier to future accomplishments.

It should be emphasized, however, that suggestion is not a panacea for every type of situation, even though it is a tool of great versatility which may be usefully employed in a wide variety of settings. As is the case with other approaches (Schofield, 1964), the effectiveness of suggestion is greatly facilitated when it is administered in an atmosphere of competence and caring, in which the positive relationship between suggestor and subject is itself a major incentive for change; and when the suggestor himself is fully convinced that the procedure will be effective, and communicates this conviction to the subject both in and out of a formal trance setting. The possibilities of an approach using an induction format in combination with other approaches, such as behavior modification (Spanos & Barber, 1976), should also be considered.

It is generally desirable to limit oneself to one or two specific goals at one time. Occasionally, a subject will present a "shopping list" of several suggestions which he would like to receive simultaneously: to lose weight, stop smoking, study more effectively, and perhaps even to repair the leaky kitchen faucet which he has been ignoring for the past six months. Because the effectiveness of suggestion lies primarily in its potential as a tool to modify subsequent experience, however, and because the human capacity for experiential learning is less than the capacity to comprehend a new concept or an idea, it is generally desirable to deal with the most pressing matters first and to leave the less important ones for subsequent sessions.

Much has been written concerning the idiographic versus the nomothetic approach to the understanding of behavior (Allport, 1961), or the study of individual uniqueness versus the study of general psychological principles which apply in varying degrees to all. Although there may be individual exceptions (Erickson, Rossi, & Rossi, 1976; Haley, 1973), it is simply not possible for most of us to employ consistently an idiographic, or Sherlock Holmes approach, carefully scrutinizing the behavior of each individual subject for some clue which will enable us to formulate a sudden, dramatic, and unique solution for each individual problem. Such an ability, when it does exist, comes about as a result of many years of experience and is largely unteachable by present methods.

On the other hand, it is unwise to follow a purely nomothetic approach, presenting each set of suggestions in unvarying fashion as if it were an item on a standardized suggestibility scale. Obviously, such items induce changes in behavior; but there are always some who do not respond who would have done so if the item had been worded or presented differently. Thus, the verbalizations presented in this volume are intended to serve primarily as a starting point, as examples of the way in which one might go about dealing with certain types of situations; but as the reader becomes familiar with their content, he should immediately begin to modify and to adapt each set of suggestions to suit the unique individual requirements of the particular person or group he happens to be working with.

Many people who are familiar with the use of induction techniques are of the opinion that a subject cannot be made to do anything which is contrary to his ethics, morals, or religion by means of trance suggestion—or, more generally, that he cannot be made to do anything in a trance setting that he would not be willing to do otherwise. But it is also sometimes asserted that a sufficiently responsive subject could be made to violate his own customary standards of conduct—to participate in a robbery, for instance—if, after being administered a trance induction, he were provided with an appropriate rationale to legitimize such behavior. For instance, suggestions might be given to the effect that the subject is a member of the armed services, that the nation is in a state of war, and that he is acting under the orders of a superior officer to participate in a commando raid which is, in reality, the robbery itself.

Although this issue has been the subject of considerable discussion and debate (Conn, 1972; Kline, 1972; Orne, 1972; Watkins, 1972), properly controlled experiments designed to investigate such possibilities are difficult to carry out for a number of reasons, some of which are obvious and some of which are not so obvious (Levitt, 1977). For instance, if I were to administer a trance induction to a hundred subjects, hand them each a loaded gun, and then order them all to shoot themselves as a test of the coercive power of the trance state being suggested, what conclusions could be drawn if some of the subjects should happen to comply? Would not some of them, at least, have been inclined to suspect that the guns were loaded only with dummy bullets, or that some hidden safety device would be brought into play at the last moment to prevent such an experiment from reaching its grisly conclusion? And even if I were to find no compliance, or a lesser incidence of compliance, with such a suggestion in a control group, perhaps defining the situation for the first group of subjects as a trance induction might lead some of them to expect that they were supposed to comply with the instructions and suggestions which would be subsequently given, regardless of how dangerous such suggestions might outwardly appear. On the other hand, perceiving the situation as research, or as a psychological experiment which was sanctioned by a reputable institution and conducted by persons perceived as professionals, might tend to alter the expectations of both groups in such a manner that generalizing the findings to real-life situations might be difficult—assuming, of course, that an experimental test were selected which would be sufficiently convincing, but which would have less permanently damaging effects.

The issue becomes easier to resolve, however, when it is recognized that trance induction procedures have been in existence for a considerable length of time, and that these techniques are easily accessible to unscrupulous persons. It is generally agreed that an intelligent person can be taught the basic procedures involved in administering an induction in an hour or less; and many books, including this one, contain the necessary information to enable the reader to proceed without a teacher. Yet, in spite of these facts, no systematic, organized attempt to use such procedures by groups of criminals has ever been brought to light.

The reason for the absence of such "natural experiments" becomes clear when it is recognized that induction procedures themselves are primarily based on the use of fantasy. Thus, if a suggestion is fairly innocuous, or if a subject is willing to comply with it because he desires the other suggestions he receives to be effective also, he may be able to momentarily act and feel as if he could not resist a particular suggestion—for example, in responding to a challenge item on a suggestibility scale which involves an inability to shake one's head to indicate no. Indeed, the ability to experience such responses as involuntary may have a great deal to do with what has been commonly referred to as "suggestibility" (Spanos, Rivers, & Ross, 1977). But if the suggestor should attempt to guide the subject's behavior in a manner which the latter finds unacceptable, then he will either refuse to comply or he will awaken—that is, he will drop the trance fantasy altogether. In the unlikely event that a subject with poor reality controls, low self-esteem, and powerful hostile and/or masochistic tendencies should accept a suggested rationale for carrying out an act which the subject believes to be illegal, self-injurious, or immoral, it would be because he *wanted* to, rather than because he had been *programmed* to do so by the coercive influence of suggestion or of the suggestor (Kline, 1972).

With regard to the possibility of sexual encounters in the trance setting (which is often the first thing that comes to mind when the layman thinks of hypnosis), it would be naive to assume that fantasies of seduction occur only to male suggestors and never to their female subjects, particularly if the session is conducted in relative privacy and the subject should happen to find the suggestor physically attractive. Since an induction procedure does tend to enable the subject to feel less self-conscious, as evidenced by the antics so willingly engaged in by the subjects of stage hypnotists, it is possible that an occasional female subject may even take the initiative by signaling a willingness to accept sexual advances—although such behavior is usually quite rare, since sexual selection, at least in women, tends to be highly discriminating (Kroger, 1977).

If such a contingency should occur, the ethical responsibility for what may subsequently transpire rests solely with the suggestor, whereas the actual power in such a situation is primarily in the hands of the subject, in the form of potential legal, professional, and social sanctions which may subsequently be invoked. Indeed, to forestall even the *possibility* of such allegations being made by unscrupulous or unbalanced subjects who may wish to do so—which can often be as damaging to the professional reputation of the suggestor as though the alleged misconduct had actually occurred—it is generally desirable to have a third person present or nearby whenever trance suggestions are administered, or else to make a tape recording of the entire proceedings.

Some people occasionally point to the success of cults or totalitarian mass movements as evidence of the coercive power of mass hypnosis. However, such use of the term is far from accurate. When a person uses a political or a religious ideology to establish a cult or a mass movement, he may make considerable use of suggestion in the form of propaganda to achieve his ends; and such suggestions may have been carefully chosen with regard to the needs and desires of the intended recipients. In addition, the suggestions may have been administered when the recipients were deliberately placed in a receptive and uncritical frame of mind, as when their emotions were whipped into a frenzy in the course of a political harangue. But if a trance is neither directly suggested nor implied in the suggestions which are given, it is inappropriate to attribute the subsequent influence of such a demagogue to any form of suggestion-induced trance experience. Such effects may be explained much more accurately as an outcome of the demagogue's ability to influence the belief systems of his followers in other ways, and to his ability to control the material and psychological rewards and punishments to which he may have access.

CHAPTER 8

Terminating the Trance

Since most people find a trance experience quite pleasant, an occasional subject may take an extra moment or two to open his eyes at the conclusion of a trance session, much in the manner of a sleeper who does not immediately wish to interrupt his pleasant reverie. Since these subjects will usually show some outward signs of responding to the suggestions to terminate the session, such as a twitching of their eyelids, specific suggestions to accelerate these tendencies may be given as a means of facilitating the return to an everyday mental set: "Your eyelids are beginning to twitch now, as you continue to return from the trance, and soon your eyes will be completely open." This is usually sufficient to bring about eye opening within a matter of a few seconds. If the subject still does not open his eyes, the suggestor may continue: "All right, you can take a little bit longer if you wish, and soon your eyes will be ready to open. Now your eyes are just about ready to open, and any second now they will be open, almost ready, any second now."

It should be emphasized, however, that instances of a subject being reluctant to comply with suggestions for the termination of a trance are extremely rare and are almost invariably due to the pleasant nature of the trance experience. Thus, there is no reason for the suggestor to be nervous or alarmed if such a situation should occur; and, in particular, he should avoid communicating such feelings to the subject.

If a subject should still not open his eyes after a reasonable interval has elasped, it may be owing to the fact that he has been given a posttrance suggestion which, for some reason, he does not wish to carry out, or because he is aware that some previous suggestion ought to have been canceled and was not, or because he wishes to receive additional attention and/or suggestions before the session is finally ended. The reason for such a delay can often be ascertained by simply *asking* the subject why he does not wish to open his eyes, perhaps with the aid of ideomotor questioning or automatic writing, and wording subsequent suggestions accordingly.

If a subject's refusal to abandon the trance format constitutes an attempt to cling to his neurotic adjustments and defeat the efforts of the suggestor to assist him, it may be necessary to cancel some of the previous suggestions which have been administered and proceed in a more leisurely and indirect manner. On the other hand, if the subject is merely trying to assert his superiority or independence, suggestions of time condensation may be administered to enable him to make his point in a matter of minutes rather than hours, or to suggest that natural sleep will ensue, from which the subject may then awaken at a time when he is ready to do so (Kroger, 1977). Few individuals will continue for long to remain in trance if such behavior is not reinforced by the presence and attention of others. If the previously mentioned approaches have not been fruitful, and if one is dealing with a subject who is determined to demonstrate his superiority in a *passive-aggressive* manner by defeating every effort of the suggestor, the best thing to do is probably to leave the subject completely alone until a call of nature intervenes.

Most people in this culture are familiar with the stereotype of the hypnotized subject as a glassy-eyed zombie; and as long as the subject himself is aware of this stereotype, he is likely to start behaving in such a manner as he begins to respond to a hypnotic or sleeping induction. His breathing may become slow and regular, his head may begin to droop, his body may slump down in the chair, and so on, regardless of whether or not these responses have been directly suggested. Indeed, as long as the suggestor and the subject are both operating from the same frame of reference—that this is how a hypnotized subject is *supposed* to act—the presence of such responses may be taken as an indication that the subject is proceeding well. But the suggestor may define the situation differently if he so chooses: he may suggest that a highly responsive subject will be able to open his eyes and move around the room normally while continuing in trance, and even an experienced professional may not be able to identify the subject who is supposedly "hypnotized" if the latter is then allowed to mingle with a group of people who are not.

Because of this arbitrariness of the supposed "properties" of a suggestion-induced trance experience, I have chosen to eliminate posttrance amnesia (which is frequently used as an indication of *trance depth*) from both hypnosis and hyperempiria by including in the termination procedure suggestions to the effect that the subject will remember clearly everything that has occurred. Of course, these suggestions may be modified or eliminated in situations in which there may be something which the subject may prefer not to recall, or when the suggestor may specifically desire amnesia to be present. In general, however, I consider the trance relationship to be an active collaboration between suggestor and subject; and except where the elicitation of repressed or traumatic material is concerned, the communication inhibition brought about by the spontaneous amnesia—which may occur when a highly responsive subject associates being in trance with loss of consciousness—or by amnesia which is directly suggested, is generally much more of a hindrance than a positive contribution to the success of the endeavor.

The following suggestions may be employed to terminate a hyperempiric induction, a hyperempiric induction for children, and a traditional hypnotic or sleeping induction, respectively:

RETURN FROM HYPEREMPIRIA

In just a moment I'm going to count backward from ten to one, and by the count of one you will be back in the usual, everyday state of consciousness in which we spend most of our waking lives. Your mind will be clear and alert, and you will be feeling absolutely wonderful. You will remember clearly everything that has happened; for you are going to be thrilled and delighted by all your experiences in hyperempiria. But equally important will be your desire to communicate and to share these experiences with others.

Ten. Beginning to return now, as I start to count back to one. Nine. Coming down more and more now, and feeling perfectly marvelous as you continue to return. Eight. Seven. Six. Soon you will be all the way down, feeling calm and refreshed, and able to remember everything that has happened while you were in hyperempiria. Five. Four. Almost back now. Three. Two. One. You can open your eyes now, feeling wonderful. You can open your eyes, feeling *wonderful!*

RETURN FROM CHILDREN'S HYPEREMPIRIA

In just a moment, we are going to leave the enchanted cottage, and go back through the woods to the world outside. But you will remember everything that has happened here, and everything I have told you. And the things I have told you while we were here in the magic cottage will continue to be true, even after we return. But best of all, we will be able to come back to this special place whenever I tell you the magic story that takes us there.

Now we are going out of the door and starting back along the path. We are entering the woods now, and hurrying back along the way we came. Now we are beside the enchanted stream from which we drank. And soon we will be back in the world outside, feeling thrilled and happy because of all the wonderful things that have happened to us.

We're almost back now. Soon you will be able to open your eyes, feeling wonderful. Almost ready to open your eyes. Ready. Now we are back, and you can open your eyes, feeling *wonderful!*

AWAKENING FROM TRADITIONAL HYPNOSIS

In just a moment I'm going to count from one to five, and by the time I get to five, you will be wide awake and fully alert once more and able to recall everything that happened while you were in hypnosis. By the time I get to the count of five, you will be wide awake, and feeling absolutely wonderful.

One. Beginning to wake up now. Two. Waking up more and more now, and feeling perfectly marvelous as you do. Three. Soon you will be completely awake, feeling alert and refreshed, and able to recall everything that has happened. Four. Almost back now. Five. You can open your eyes now, feeling wonderful. You can open your eyes now, feeling *wonderful!*

CHAPTER 9

Sequelae to Trance Experience

Occasionally, some people may report feelings of dizziness, drowsiness, fatigue, a slight headache, or other sensations of distress after a trance session has been concluded. These occasional aftereffects tend to be of brief duration and of mild or moderate intensity (Hilgard, 1974; Hilgard, Hilgard & Newman, 1961), although there is one account of the persistence of a posthypnotic dissociative reaction because of important secondary gains and the opportunities afforded by this response for the expression of strong passive-aggressive tendencies within the subject's own personality (Starker, 1974). In the vast majority of instances, however, occasional aftereffects can best be understood and dealt with as the result of implicit expectations arising out of the induction format. That is, if a person has been inclined to assume that a trance experience is tiresome or stressful to some degree, his responding successfully to a trance induction will tend to *cause* him to experience feelings of stress or fatigue, just as if these feelings had been directly suggested. Usually, the effect of these implicit expectations can be countered by direct suggestions of well-being in the procedure for terminating the trance; but occasionally the earlier impressions are sufficiently strong that additional suggestions may be necessary to cancel their effects.

Often, when a subject merely reports a slight feeling of dizziness or fatigue, it is sufficient merely to remark, "That will go away in a minute or two—it won't last," and then to inquire after a few moments have elapsed whether or not the subject's distress is actually gone. If the subject still reports such feelings, he may be requested to close his eyes and a more elaborate set of suggestions may be employed *without* prefacing them by an induction. For example, if the subject reports that he has a headache which he did not have before the trance session, he may be asked to close his eyes, and the suggestor may say in a credible manner, "Now, as I count from one to five, your headache is going to go away, and by the time I get to the count of five, it will be gone completely. One. Your headache is beginning to go away now. Two. It's leaving, going away more and more. Three. It's leaving, leaving. Four. Now it's almost gone. Five. Now your headache is gone completely, and you can open your eyes, feeling fine."

Having just been exposed to a trance induction format, most subjects find it quite easy to return to a mental set in which suggestions such as the foregoing are accepted readily and easily. If, however, the subject should report that some aftereffects still persist, then it may be necessary to readminister briefly an induction that will enhance the credibility of the contravening suggestions. However, such instances are comparatively rare.

PART TWO

THERAPEUTIC SUGGESTIONS

"Now I'll give *you* something to believe. I'm just one hundred and one, five months, and a day."

"I can't believe *that!*," said Alice.

"*Can't* you?," said the Queen in a pitying tone. "Try again: draw a long breath, and shut your eyes."

Alice laughed. "There's no use trying," she said, "One *can't* believe impossible things."

"I daresay you haven't had much practice," said the Queen. "When I was your age, I always did it for half an hour a day. Why, sometimes I've believed as many as six impossible things before breakfast. . . ."

—Lewis Carroll, *Through the Looking Glass*

Retrieving Repressed or Forgotten Material

What is commonly referred to as "forgetting" seems to be due mainly to older memories becoming unavailable as new material blocks their recall (Miller, Galanter, & Pribram, 1960). That is, difficulty in remembering is primarily the result of difficulty in *retrieval* rather than to simply "having a poor memory," or the decay of memory traces over time. The ability of some people to recall more details of a previous event in response to the suggestion that they are actually reexperiencing that event is probably because such suggestions encourage subjects to portray the scene more vividly in their imagination (Barber, 1975). Thus, more stimulus elements are present in consciousness, and more associations to these elements are available for recall.

When memories have been denied access to consciousness because they are too upsetting to face directly, it is necessary to use an indirect approach to avoid premature confrontation with material which the subject may not yet be prepared to handle. Many of the following techniques make use of such indirect methods. As an added precaution, however, it is desirable always to include the suggestion, "You can forget any of this information, if you want to or need to, as soon as the trance session is over."

The procedures set forth in this chapter and in the next should by no means be considered a complete rendition of all possible therapeutic applications of trance suggestion; for when one is dealing with the potential uses of the human imagination, the total number of such possible therapeutic applications is limited only by the ability of the imagination itself to conceive of new ones. The interested professional reader seeking further information on the clinical uses of suggestion is referred to the works of Crasilneck and Hall (1975), Hartland (1971 a,b), Kroger (1977), and Kroger and Fexler (1976), as well as the *International Journal of Clinical and Experimental Hypnosis* and the *American Journal of Clinical Hypnosis,* both of which are published quarterly.

As is the case with other verbalizations presented in this volume, the following suggestions should only be administered by those who are properly qualified to do so by virtue of their professional training and experience.

ABREACTION AND CATHARSIS

During World War I, it was found that patients who were suffering from what was then termed *shell shock,* and which later came to be known as *combat fatigue,* would often manifest a dramatic improvement if they could be induced by means of suggested trance to relive their traumatic combat experience in all its emotional intensity (Ulett & Peterson, 1965). Although many soldiers were able to recall the events leading up to their difficulty, it was the emotional component of these events which had been repressed, and which thus needed to be reexperienced so as to become integrated into the patient's total personality.

As it is in combat, so it may occasionally be in life. Many people in contemporary society are unable to allow themselves to experience the feelings of pain and anger which constitute the natural somatic reactions to many of life's major and minor traumas. In the name of "dignity" and "self-control," or because other family members are trying so hard to restrain their own emotional reactions that they cannot permit the open expression of emotionality in others, strong feelings often tend to be denied expression in much the same manner as was seen in the shell-shock cases of World War I and subsequent conflicts.

Many humanistic psychologists have recently come to stress the importance to good adjustment of being able to "let go" on occasion (Greenberg, 1968; Perls, 1972; Schutz, 1967; Stevens, 1971). Of course, one cannot live one's entire life as though it were an encounter group;

and abreaction and catharsis should never be regarded merely as ends in themselves. But one reason why so many "release-oriented" therapeutic and "growth" techniques are currently in vogue is that many people in this culture were initially brought up never to show deep emotion—and perhaps never to allow themselves even to feel it—and, therefore, they are in need of finding some way to discharge this excess affect before they, too, become psychiatric casualties.

The trance format provides an excellent opportunity for such emotional ventilation in civilian as well as in combat settings. Occasionally a subject will spontaneously begin to show signs of emotionality soon after induction has been completed, or even before; and it may be clear from the context in which the emotional response occurs (or easily ascertained in response to questioning) that the reaction is not brought about by the situation itself, but rather that it is an outward expression of a need to release excess emotion. For example, one female student, who was pursuing a demanding schedule of musical and theatrical rehearsals during her undergraduate career, would appear regularly in my office once or twice each quarter saying, "I need to be hypnotized." After a few such appearances, our routine was quickly established. As soon as the induction had been completed, a tear would begin to roll slowly down her cheek. In response to my question as to whether or not there was anything about the induction procedure that was bothering her, she would invariably shake her head no. I would then proceed in approximately the following manner:

> Would you just like to go ahead and have a good cry, then, so that you will be able to feel better? All right. Just let the tears begin to flow. Let all that emotion you have been bottling up inside of you begin to come out now. And in a few minutes you will begin to relax, and you will be feeling *so* much better.

Occasionally, it was necessary to diminish the intensity of the release by adding such admonitions as, "Not so fast, now—take it easy," and to guide the termination of the catharsis with appropriate comments as the crying began to subside: "Now you are beginning to relax," etc.

With this particular subject, the need for such a cathartic release of emotion was invariably triggered by some environmental frustration, such as a quarrel with her boyfriend or failure to receive a coveted part in a play. She would talk freely about the situation after the emotional

release, but she would invariably find it uncomfortable to do so beforehand.

The induction procedure, plus the reassurances of the suggestor,
apparently were all that was needed to provide the necessary permission for the subject to abandon momentarily her tight self-discipline.
Because this permission was relatively weak in other contexts, suggestions to the effect that the subject would be able to have a good cry on
her own were largely ineffective. However, her need for such an
artificially contrived release pattern was terminated with the end of her
college studies and her simultaneous marriage to a fellow classmate
who provided, as she put it, "a better shoulder to cry on."

Suggested catharses are likely to be of particular benefit in
situations involving separation or bereavement if a similar blocking
should occur, in assisting crime victims to work through the emotional
trauma of their experience, or in helping a person to handle the
emotional stresses involved in dealing with chronic or terminal illness—whether it be the subject's own or that of one who is close to
him.

Pent-up emotion can often be most easily discharged by means of
abreaction. Suggestions for such revivification may be given in the
following manner:

I'm going to count backwards from five to one, and by the time I get to
one, you will be mentally back in the past, reliving and reexperiencing the
particular events which have been at the root of your difficulty. You will always
be able to hear my voice and to respond to questions, and I will return you to
the present time in a while; but until I do so, these events are going to be
completely real to you as you experience them once more.

Going back now: Five. Four. Going all the way back to the former experience we have chosen. Three. Two. Almost there. One. Now you have returned, and you are feeling and experiencing the event just as you did the first
time. Flow with it, and live it again, describing it to me just as it is happening.

As the subject begins to describe the event unfolding in his mind,
suggestions similar to those employed for catharsis may be given to
facilitate the accompanying emotional discharge—or to lessen its intensity if need be; for at times the degree of affect accompanying such
revivification may be considerable. As with induced catharses, relaxation suggestions may be administered as the intensity of the emotional
release begins to subside, and the abreaction may then be terminated
in the following manner:

Now I am going to return you to the present time, the time from which you left. I'll count from one to five, and by the time I get to the count of five, you will be all the way back in the present, but still very much in trance for a while. One. Coming back now. Two. Coming all the way back. Three. Four. Almost back. Five. Now you are all the way back in the present time, feeling much relieved as a result of your experience, but still very much in trance for a while, until we are ready to conclude it.

AGE REGRESSION

The following technique is a particularly useful means of allowing sufficiently suggestible subjects an opportunity to explore previously held attitudes and feelings which have a bearing on their present difficulties. Depending on the degree of their imaginative involvement, subjects may spontaneously come to manifest a childlike voice and vocabulary when they regress to a very young age, or they may simply describe the experience as if they were picturing it in their imagination. Since age regression may occasionally lead to spontaneous abreaction of repressed or traumatic material, even by subjects who may outwardly manifest no need of therapy, this technique should only be employed in settings in which the suggestor is prepared to deal with such material if it emerges. Needless to say, age regression should never be employed merely for purposes of demonstration or entertainment. At the completion of an induction, the following suggestions may be administered:

Now I am going to help you to return mentally to an earlier age, to enable you to recall what life was like at that time, and to help you to reexperience some of the events that were occuring then so that we can better understand them. You will always be able to hear what I am saying and to respond to my voice, as I guide and direct the experience. But until I return you to the present time, everything will be just as it was then, and you will feel just as if you were that age once more, seeing and experiencing everything just as you did at that time.

In a moment I am going to ask you to start counting slowly backward from your present age, counting slowly, out loud, all the way back to the age of three. And as you do, you will feel the years flying by one by one until by the time you get to the number three, you will be that age once more, and everything will be just the same as it was then. You will always be able to respond to my voice, and to answer any questions I may ask you. But in all other respects, everything will be just as it was then, and you will be able to experience everything I describe to you just as if you were really there.

Now you can begin to count, counting slowly out loud, backward from your present age to the age of three.

When the subject reaches the designated age, a great deal of information may be elicited by direct questioning, such as attitudes toward parents and siblings, or he may be asked to reexperience particular situations or events as if they were actually occurring, perhaps with the suggestor assuming the role of someone in the subject's past (see the discussion in the section on Induced Conflicts, page 96). As with the other techniques contained in this chapter, amnesia may be suggested for material which the subject may not yet be prepared to integrate into his everyday awareness.

The foregoing suggestions for age regression may be terminated before the conclusion of the trance by asking the subject to count forward, beginning with the age to which he has been regressed and ending with the number at which the subject initially began. If a subject is to be regressed to an age at which he did not yet know how to count, it may be necessary for the suggestor to count the subject into and out of the regression.

These suggestions may be presented in slightly modified form to enable subjects to recapture details of a previous experience which have supposedly been forgotten, or as an aid in locating lost objects. If the regression is to be measured in days rather than years—for instance, if the subject is to be assisted in reliving the events of the previous Thursday in order to help him recall where he might have misplaced his wallet—he may simply be asked to recite backward the days of the week, beginning with the present day, until he arrives at the day he is seeking.

When suggestions for temporal or age regression are employed, it is necessary to recognize that, because the subject usually wishes to comply with the suggested recall, regardless of whether or not he is actually able to do so, there will occasionally be a tendency to fill in the missing gaps with fantasy and to visualize or reexperience obligingly the fantasy as if it had actually taken place. This is the basis for such cultic practices as supposedly regressing a person to a time when, in fact, his nervous system had not become sufficiently mature to be able to store information in the form of comprehensive memories. Indeed, certain misguided individuals have elicited fantasy material by means of suggested regression as though it were actual recollections from early infancy, from the time of birth, from the moment of conception, and even supposedly from a previous lifetime.

In terms of its psychological consequences, it may not always be of great importance whether a person is actually recalling such information or whether he is merely fantasizing it; and the success of such cultists is primarily because they are sometimes able to induce valid changes in a subject's personality by bringing about a change in his belief system, regardless of whether or not these new beliefs are based on fact. For example, it may be a tremendous boon to a woman's self-confidence suddenly to "discover," through suggested regression to a previous lifetime, that she is the reincarnation of Marie Antoinette! However, the difference between believing that one is the reincarnation of Marie Antoinette and believing that one actually *is* Marie Antoinette is largely a matter of degree; for the underlying personality needs which are being met by such delusions often tend to be quite similar. Obviously, then, it is desirable to subject information obtained by suggestion-induced regression or revivification to the same objective validation as hearsay evidence which is obtained without an induction.

When such techniques are used as an aid in interrogation or in locating lost objects, it is not always necessary that the subject be sufficiently suggestible actually to relive the experience he is describing or attempting to recall. Quite often the relaxed atmosphere that is immediately provided by the induction format will be sufficient in itself to facilitate recollection, even though the subject may feel that he is merely imagining himself going through the experience instead of actually reliving it.

If the subject still appears to be "blocking" after suggestions for regression have been administered, or if it seems desirable to protect him from undue emotional stress which might be attendant upon actual revivification, as may be the case when one is interrogating crime victims, the free-association method or other subsequently described indirect techniques may be employed, either in lieu of suggested regression or in conjunction with it, as a means of getting the subject over the rough spots. For example, a campus rape victim was able to describe her assailant's automobile with much greater clarity after an induction procedure and subsequent suggestions to the effect that she was merely watching the event on television.

ARTIFICIAL MULTIPLE PERSONALITY

Each of us tends to be a somewhat different person in different situations, and in some people this tendency may be more pronounced than in others. A college student may appear to be one type of individual while having Sunday dinner at home with his family, and quite a different sort of person at a fraternity initiation party. When the stress engendered by conflicting environmental demands and pressures becomes sufficiently intense, particularly when the situation is further exacerbated by a need to shut out childhood trauma, the result may be a so-called multiple personality (Thigpen & Cleckley, 1957). Such a phenomenon, of course, is not due to the presence of two or more "souls in one body" (Goddard, 1927); but rather, each separate "self" may be seen as meeting a different segment of the patient's needs, thereby making its own contribution to the overall economy of the total personality (Murphy, 1947). The task of the therapist thus becomes one of helping the patient to "put Humpty Dumpty together again," by developing a life style in which the patient's needs can be met more parsimoniously.

In everyday life, many patterns of thought and behavior tend to be rejected because they are not perceived as being consistent with the concept of self (Lecky, 1945; Rogers, 1961). The following suggestions are designed to assist the subject to evoke such unaccustomed modes by temporarily inducing an artificial multiple personality, in a manner analogous to the procedure demonstrated experimentally by Kampman (1976), with a view to facilitating the subsequent selective incorporation of the material thus elicited into the subject's existing personality structure. At the conclusion of an appropriate induction procedure with a highly responsive subject, one may proceed as follows:

Now I would like you to be somebody else for a while. You are going to take on the identity of another person, with a new name and a different personality. It might be an imaginary playmate that you had in childhood, or someone you used to dream of being when you grew up, or perhaps somebody you would like to be now. You might even be some famous person or historical figure.

You will always be able to hear and to respond to my voice, and I will return you to your original identity in a while. But until I do, it is going to be exactly as if you were this person; and when we talk, you will be thinking his or her thoughts and feeling his or her feelings.

Now, as I count from one to five, you are going to experience this change of identity taking place. One. Your identity is beginning to fade away now, as you start to become aware of yourself as this other person. Two. Fading away more and more, as the new identity becomes clearer. Three. Soon the change will be complete. Four. Merging completely into your new identity now. Five. Now the transition is complete.

As the suggestor begins to converse and to interact with the new identity, the person to whom the suggestions are being given may be discussed in the third person, as though he were not physically present.

With appropriate changes in wording, the foregoing suggestions may be employed in a more directive manner, to elicit various specific aspects of the subject's personality: "I'm going to be talking to your best self, to the best person you are capable of becoming," or the subject may be given suggestions to the effect that the suggestor will be talking to the former's "worst self," with a view to abreacting and desensitizing dissociated material.

At the conclusion of the session, the following suggestions may be administered:

Now I am going to return you to your original identity by counting backwards from five to one; and by the time I get to the count of one, you will have completely returned to your original identity once again. But you will still be in trance for a while, until I bring you out. Five. Your new identity is beginning to fade now, as you start to return to your original self once again. Four. It's fading more and more, and you are beginning to be aware of yourself as the person you were before. Three. Soon the transition will be complete, and you will have returned to your original self once more. But you will still remain in trance for a while, until I bring you out. Two. Almost back. One. Now you have returned to your original self once again.

AUTOMATIC WRITING

In using the technique of automatic writing, it is desirable to provide the subject with ample writing space and an abundant supply of paper, as the customary rules of penmanship are not likely to be observed. After the induction has been completed, suggestions may be provided as follows:

Now I would like you to raise the index finger of the hand with which you write. That's fine. Now I am going to place a pencil in your hand, and some paper underneath it, and soon your hand will begin to write. It will write automatically, independent of your conscious awareness or control, as though it were writing all by itself. It will write freely and easily, but clearly enough that I will be able to read what is written. And your hand will be able to respond automatically to my questions, and to write about whatever topic I may suggest.

Now your hand is completely free of conscious control, and ready to begin to write, automatically and without your conscious awareness.

If no movement of the hand is observed, the suggestor may provide additional prompting: "Soon your fingers will begin to twitch, and then to write." If the subject's fingers merely manifest a slight twitch, but no further move toward compliance is observed, the suggestor may continue, "Now your fingers are twitching, twitching, and soon they will begin to write, clearly and easily, in response to what I have asked. Any second now, your hand will begin to write." If the subject still does not respond, the finger method of ideomotor questioning may then be employed as a somewhat slower substitute.

The technique of automatic writing is often rich in the production of condensations and neologisms similar to those encountered in dreams. These condensations may be explored for further meaning either by additional questioning using automatic writing or by subsequent free association to the material which is elicited by this method. Automatic writing may also be used in conjunction with age regression to elicit and explore previous traumatic incidents. Some subjects (though not all) may manifest a marked handwriting change, in response to such suggestions, which roughly corresponds to that of the age to which they have regressed.

Like ideomotor questioning, responses elicited by automatic writing will often be at variance with those that are elicited by direct questioning. Of course, information obtained by this method should not be regarded as more valid than information which is brought forth by any other means, but rather, as a manifestation of the subject's tendency to express conflicting attitudes and opinions in a dissociated manner. Indeed, some suggestors are inclined to facilitate such dissociative tendencies by addressing the hand directly and referring to the subject in the third person, as though he were not physically present.

Of course, the suggestions for manual dissociation should be canceled before the termination of the induction, as well as any additional suggestions, such as for age regression, which are not intended to continue beyond the time the trance suggestions are in effect. The automatic writing suggestions may be terminated in the following manner:

Now I'm going to count from one to three, and by the time I get to the count of three your hand will be completely normal again, no longer separated from your awareness or from your voluntary control. One. Now your hand is becoming completely normal once more, and by the time I get to the count of three it will be completely normal. But you will still stay in trance for a little while longer, until I bring you out. Two. Your hand is becoming completely normal once again, and completely returned to your customary awareness and voluntary control. Three. Now your hand is completely normal once again. But you will remain in trance just a while longer, until I bring you out.

CRYSTAL AND MIRROR GAZING

In this technique, the subject is asked to visualize an imaginary mirror or crystal ball and to describe what he sees as he gazes into it, perhaps free associating at appropriate intervals to the contents of his description. At the conclusion of a hypnotic or hyperempiric induction, suggestions may be administered as follows:

Now I would like you to imagine yourself seated comfortably in front of a large crystal ball, gazing into its depths. Continue to visualize the crystal ball and to focus on it, and soon you will begin to see the images appear within. You will be able to describe everything you see, just as it occurs; and I will be able to guide and direct the images as they appear, or to suggest new images from time to time.
Now you can picture the crystal ball very clearly in your mind, and as soon as you are ready, you can begin to describe the images as they appear.

Such a procedure is especially useful in enabling the subject to visualize the successful resolution of a problem at some point in the future, particularly when combined with suggestions of amnesia to instill confidence (Erickson, 1954). The image of a mirror instead of a crystal ball may be employed to elicit information about various aspects of the subject's perception of himself as he is now, as he was at various times in the past, and as he would like to be at various times in the future. Alternatively, the subject may be asked to visualize a stage in a theater, or a motion picture or a television screen, and be asked to describe the action he sees taking place, with the suggestor functioning as a "director." This approach is often helpful in assisting the subject to recall the details of a traumatic event, such as a crime he may have witnessed, while retaining a sufficient amount of detachment to enable him to remain insulated from the emotional charge which may accompany such memories.

DREAM INDUCTION

Suggestion-induced dreams are probably the richest and most versatile of all projective techniques; for the subject is free to supply everything that is not directly suggested to him, in accordance with his own needs and desires (C. Moss, 1967; Tart, 1965a, b). If left to his own devices, the subject will frequently bring forth dream imagery which is centered around new and hitherto-unsuspected themes. Suggestions may be given as follows:

Now you are going to have a dream. You will soon begin to see the dream images forming in your mind, and you will be able to describe to me everything that is happening in your dream, exactly as it occurs. Now the dream is beginning, and as the images become clearer and clearer in your mind, you can start to tell me what you see.

If the suggestor so desires, he may select a particular topic or situation to serve as the subject of the dream: "Now you are going to have a dream about flying." The suggestor may also wish to take a more active part in the dream itself, either to guide the situations which are depicted to a more satisfactory resolution, or to facilitate the examination of a symbolic material as it emerges. The subject may be told, "I will be able to direct the course of your dream by suggesting changes from time to time. And as I do, these changes will appear in your dream, exactly as I describe them."

FREE ASSOCIATION

Sigmund Freud, early in his career, studied hypnosis for a year at Charcot's clinic in Nancy, France. Freud soon abandoned the use of hypnosis, however; for he came to believe that no lasting cure was possible unless the patient developed insight into the underlying causes of his behavior—and for this to occur, it was necessary that he be fully conscious (Kline, 1950). It was not until several decades later that the versatility of a suggested trance experience was sufficiently developed to enable it to be employed as a means of facilitating the orthodox psychoanalytic procedures which Freud subsequently initiated (Arluck, 1964; Wolberg, 1945).

Free association, which eventually became the basic tool of psychoanalysis, is customarily conducted with the analysand reclining on a couch, and the therapist seated far enough away to be out of view. The analysand is then instructed to say whatever comes to mind, letting his thoughts run on in apparently aimless fashion, with absolutely no attempt on his part to control, direct, or censor them (Fromm-Reichmann, 1950). The assumption underlying this technique is that the apparently "random" thoughts generated by such a procedure are not really random at all; but that they are generated by problems with which the patient is futilely attempting to grapple, in spite of the fact that they are currently beyond the reach of consciousness.

The function of the analyst is to listen with trained perceptiveness—or "with the third ear," as it has been called (Reik, 1948) —guiding the analysand by means of an occasional question or judicious comment to a gradual lifting of the barrier of repression so that adequate insight may be attained and the patient's problems appropriately dealt with. As might be expected, however, such a process can be extremely time consuming—especially since the patient often manifests resistances to having his most intimate problems exposed in such a manner. These resistances may appear in the guise of many types of evasions and circumlocutions, such as talking about the weather or about one's tennis game instead of getting on with the business at hand, forgetting or coming late for appointments, personal attacks on the analyst, etc. Indeed, the process of attempting to recover a repressed complex of memories by means of free association as it is traditionally practiced may be likened to reaching for the brass ring on a merry-go-round: if one fails to grasp it on the first attempt, one merely goes around again and again until success is finally achieved. It should not be surprising, therefore, that progress in orthodox psychoanalysis is usually measured in terms of months and years.

Many analysands, however, lack both the willingness and the

financial resources to undergo seemingly interminable hours of free association, interrupted only occasionally by a question or a comment from the therapist. For this reason, many who were originally trained in the methods of orthodox psychoanalysis have come to make use of a number of additional techniques and to adopt a more eclectic orientation.

Often an induction procedure in itself is sufficient to relax the subject and heighten rapport in such a manner as to facilitate the process of free association (Hartland, 1971b). Specific suggestions for relaxation and for heightening rapport may also be added at the completion of the induction, together with the suggestion that, when the session is concluded, the subject will remember what he wants to remember and forget what he wants to forget concerning the information which has been brought forth, thus helping to prevent the material elicited by this method from being confronted at a faster pace than the patient is constructively able to accept (Ulett & Peterson, 1965).

When blocking, or the apparent inability to recall a bit of information occurs, one may follow the standard Freudian technique of placing one's hand on the subject's forehead and assuring him that a thought or an idea which seems to be momentarily lost to him will promptly come to mind (Hartland, 1971b). Other techniques presented in this section, such as automatic writing, ideomotor questioning, or dream induction, may also be employed.

IDEOMOTOR QUESTIONING WITH THE CHEVREUL PENDULUM

The Chevreul pendulum, which was described on page 45, may also be employed, after an induction has been completed, as a means of indirect questioning. Since the subject is generally unable to tell in which direction the pendulum is moving when he has his eyes closed, information may sometimes be elicited in this manner which the subject is consciously unaware of, but which may be of assistance to the suggestor in guiding the subject toward an eventual resolution of his difficulty.

After suspending the pendulum from the subject's fingers and instructing him to hold onto it while resting his elbow on a flat surface so that the pendulum may swing freely, the following suggestions may be given:

Now I am going to ask your unconscious to tell me some things about your situation that you may not be consciously aware of. Your unconscious will be able to answer my questions automatically, by letting the pendulum swing back and forth for yes, and from left to right for no.

The questioning is then begun, with sufficient time between questions for the subject to be able to respond and for the pendulum to change direction, and with prompting suggestions interspersed when necessary:

Soon the pendulum will begin to move, probably without your being aware of it. Back and forth in front of you for yes, and from side to side for no.

IDEOMOTOR QUESTIONING: FINGER METHOD

The following suggestions are particularly useful for subjects whose imaginative involvement with a suggested trance induction may be relatively slight and who might be disturbed by having to answer questions orally. This procedure may also be used with more highly suggestible subjects to elicit repressed or dissociated material which has been denied access to consciousness:

Now I am going to ask you some questions, and you will be able to answer merely by raising the index finger of your right hand to indicate yes, and the index finger of your left hand to indicate no. And if I should happen to ask you any question you do not know the answer to, or any question which you do not want to answer, you can simply signal me by raising your right thumb. The right index finger for yes, and the left index finger for no, and the right thumb for "I don't know," or "I don't want to answer." Now you can signal me this way to answer my questions. Are you ready to begin?

As is the case with automatic writing, some suggestors, when working with highly responsive subjects, prefer to phrase their questions in such a manner that the dissociation is made explicit: "Now your hands will be able to answer by themselves, without your being aware of what they are telling me." Subsequent questions may be worded as if one were addressing the hands directly and the subject were not physically present; for example: "Hand, will Laura be ready to talk about having sex with Daddy when the trance is over?" Such a dissociation may be terminated before the conclusion of the trance by the suggestor saying to the subject, "Now I'm going to count slowly to three, and by the time I get to the count of three, your hands will be perfectly normal once again, and completely under your own control once more; but you will remain in trance a little while longer, until I bring you out." The suggestor then counts slowly to three, interspersing assurances at appropriate intervals to the effect that the subject's hands are returning completely to his own control once more, and finally that they have done so.

INDUCED CONFLICTS

Much of what troubles people in the present is often unfinished business from the past (Perls, 1972; Stevens, 1971). A person who has been disappointed in love, for example, may constantly role-play in his imagination a host of conversations with the object of his affection, as if searching desperately for a clue which would have enabled him to cause the relationship to turn out differently. In much the same manner, one who feels that he has been insulted by an especially cutting remark of another may devote a considerable amount of time to a mental review of the offending conversation until he has come up with a sufficient number of cutting responses of his own to permit him to administer a verbal coup de grace to his opponent—at least in his own imagination.

The increased amount of imaginative involvement which often results from a trance induction may be used to facilitate the effectiveness of techniques which are aimed at reinvoking earlier conflicts so as to lead them to a more satisfactory resolution. For instance, at the conclusion of an induction, a sufficiently responsive subject may be asked to open his eyes and look at a pillow which has been placed in a chair in front of him. The subject may then be told:

As you continue looking at the pillow, you are gradually going to see your father sitting there. You will be able to talk to him, just as if he were really there. Now you are beginning to see him, more and more clearly, and now you can see him sitting right there. You can see your father very clearly now, and you can tell your father everything that you have always wanted to say to him;

everything that you have been storing up inside. You don't have to hold back any longer; just go ahead and tell him.

The result of such suggestions is sometimes a full-fledged catharsis, with the subject shouting, crying, and hitting the pillow—and experiencing a great deal of relief as a consequence. Alternatively, the suggestor may himself assume the role of the person with whom the subject has some "unfinished business" and guide the conflict to an appropriate conclusion, perhaps suggesting subsequent amnesia for the experience to prevent the possibility of conscious recomputation.

Such an approach may also be used to anticipate potential conflict or problem situations in the future, as a means of examining and strengthening the subject's coping strategies and skills—for example, in rehearsing an interview between the subject and a prospective employer who may be skeptical of the patient's personal history, with the suggestor playing the role of interviewer.

PARADOXICAL INSIGHT

The suggestions that follow are based on a technique reported by Hartland (1971b). By providing the subject with a sense of accomplishment and the assurance of further progress, the techniques facilitate the process of constructive change and, at the same time, shield him from a direct confrontation with material which he may not yet be ready to face. The specific content of the information elicited by this method may be subsequently investigated by means of automatic writing, dream analysis, or other indirect techniques:

Deep within your mind, at some level that is presently unconscious, you are aware of the real reasons for what has been causing your difficulties. I am going to count from one to five, and as I do, you are going to find these memories coming to the surface. At the count of five, and not sooner, you will fully and completely understand what it is that has been causing your problems.

But as soon as these memories have been recovered, you are immediately going to forget them once again, until we have time to bring them forth more gradually and deal with each of them in turn. And the realizations which you do gain from these memories, even though the memories themselves are going to be forgotten again for a while, will allow you to see how much progress you are already making and to know that you a re going to progress even faster, until you have become the person that you want to be.

Now I am going to begin the count, and by the time I get to five, but not sooner, you will remember and fully understand the reasons for everything that has been contributing to your difficulties; and then you will promptly forget them again, until we are ready to bring these reasons back.

One. Two. The memories are beginning to rise to the surface now, and by the time I get to the count of five, but not before, you will be able to recall and to understand them fully and completely. Three. Four. *Five!* Now you *know*.

But just as quickly as you have recalled them, you are starting to forget these memories once more, until we are ready to bring them back for a longer time. They are going away. They are going, going, almost gone. And now they are gone completely, until we are ready to bring them back.

This brief glimpse into the real reasons for your difficulties has enabled you to see how much progress you have made already and to realize how much more progress you are going to make in the near future, until you fully attain the goal of becoming the person you want to be. And that goal, as you now know, is not only within the range of your ability to achieve; it is absolutely inevitable, as long as you continue to desire and to strive for it.

CHAPTER 11

Behavioral Regulation and Self-Control

The kinds of questions we ask determine what sort of answers we will obtain; and often they may also determine whether those answers are useful or not. A child who is always getting into trouble, for example, may cause those around him to wonder from which side of the family he has "inherited his mean streak," or what sort of "mental disease" may be producing these troublesome symptoms—or even whether or not this may be a "rotten kid" who deliberately chooses evil whenever he is given an opportunity to do so. But a psychologist will usually ask a different sort of question, in the hope of obtaining a more useful answer; namely, *"What's the payoff?"* More specifically, what is the child getting out of his behavior which makes him continue to engage in it?

Because human needs are so varied, however, the same type of problem behavior can be engaged in by different people for vastly different reasons; and since multiple causation is the rule rather than the exception in human behavior, the solution to individual difficulties may at times be complex indeed. The potential dangers of failure to ascertain the cause-and-effect relationships which may underlie a subject's presenting problem may be illustrated by the predicament of a very obese student who was once referred to me for help in losing weight. After ascertaining that the student had recently been examined by a physician and that no underlying medical difficulty such as edema or hypothyroidism was involved, I casually mentioned

99

that sometimes people may have a tendency to overeat to divert their attention from other problems, and asked the student if he was aware of anything else which might be bothering him. It was then that he told me that he would frequently "stuff his face," as he put it, to divert his attention from recurring sadistic homosexual fantasies involving little boys.

I do not know whether or not the subject's overeating would have been replaced by even more maladaptive (and dangerous) behaviors if suggestions for dieting had been routinely or mechanically administered; but clearly, the lad was in need of prolonged psychotherapy.

The following verbalizations are not intended to imply, then, that there is only one cause for a particular difficulty, or only one way to proceed in attempting to resolve it. Neither are they intended to serve as a *substitute* for therapy. They may be useful, however, when administered by properly qualified professionals who have established that the task at hand is simply one of improving or changing habitual behavior patterns, or when the nature of the subject's problem is sufficiently understood to insure proper management within a therapeutic context.

ALCOHOLISM

It is generally agreed that the alcoholic must first admit that he has a problem and be willing to seek help before he can begin to make any real progress toward the goal of sobriety. Yet many alcoholics are not willing to take this essential first step until they have literally hit bottom—which for some people is the grave.

Although hereditary and constitutional factors may also play a part, one of the principal reasons why it is so difficult for the confirmed alcoholic to stop drinking is that he finds its immediate consequences to be highly reinforcing in spite of the additional problems which his drinking may cause him in the long run. For the timid, highly anxious, or overly dependent person who needs to use alcohol as a crutch to function, this immediate reinforcement can be great indeed. Eventually, however, a vicious circle is established, in which the alcoholic must drink to escape from the problems which his drinking has created; and finally, to forget the fact that he is an alcoholic, with all the attendant feelings of guilt and self-devaluation which invariably accompany such knowledge.

As his habit becomes more firmly entrenched, the alcoholic may also come to use his drinking bouts in a passive-aggressive manner, either to test the loyalty of those around him or to punish those whom he believes to be responsible for his predicament. This inclination to blame others for one's own conduct may often represent an attempt to cope with the intense feelings of guilt and self-devaluation mentioned previously; for to the extent that one is able to see oneself as a victim, whether it be of fate or of the machinations of others, one may feel free of the need to accept responsibility for one's own conduct.

Such freedom is illusory, of course. Since each person must experience the consequences of his own actions regardless of whether those consequences are desirable or undesirable, no one can ever truly escape responsibility for his own behavior, regardless of the circumstances. Although it is often true that many sources of frustration which may be viewed as contributing to the alcoholic's drinking pattern may be found in the environment—failure to receive a coveted promotion or an unsatisfactory marital relationship, for example—the essential underlying cause of the alcoholic's excessive drinking may frequently be traced to his tendency to "quarrel with fate" instead of learning to adjust and cope with it. For those who are able to recognize that they have a drinking problem, organizations such as Alcoholics Anonymous (AA), combined if need be with psychotherapy, may offer the best opportunities for developing the necessary attitudes and coping skills to bring about a remission.

Drugs such as Antabuse have been employed in alcoholic rehabilitation to induce severe nausea and vomiting as soon as a drink has been taken, thus causing the patient to associate the consumption of alcohol with immediately punishing rather than immediately rewarding consequences. If a subject is sufficiently responsive, however, such an outcome may also be directly suggested, in which case the connection between drinking and nausea may be established more easily—particularly when suggestions of amnesia are given to forestall the possibility of conscious recomputation, since the alcoholic is then unable to attribute his nausea to merely having taken a drug. Suggestions may be administered as follows:

> You will not remember my telling you this, but if you should ever take a drink containing alcohol from now on, you will immediately begin to experience feelings of queasiness and nausea; and these feelings will keep on getting stronger and stronger with every passing second, until they make you vomit

up the drink. You will, of course, be able to eat normally and to drink beverages that do not contain alcohol. And as soon as you have vomited up the drink, you will feel all right again, until the next time. But any time you take a drink with alcohol in it, you will immediately become so sick to your stomach that you will have to vomit. And because you will not remember that I have told you this, you will believe that it is your system that is rejecting the alcohol instead of attributing it to the suggestions.

Hartland (1971b) advocates the use of such habit-breaking suggestions in conjunction with other suggestions similar to the following, which are aimed at weakening the alcoholic's desire to drink and transferring the craving to something else:

With each passing day, your desire to drink is going to become less and less. You are going to feel stronger and stronger, and your need to drink will be correspondingly decreased. With each passing day, you are going to derive more and more pleasure out of life, and so you will have less and less need to dull your senses with alcohol.

And if you should ever still feel a need for alcohol, all you will have to do in order to make the need go away, or at least to cut it down so that it is easily manageable, is simply to take a piece of candy instead, and you will find that the candy is usually enough to satisfy your craving completely. For as soon as you have taken the candy, you will find your need to drink becoming weaker and weaker.

Of course, eliminating an addiction can never be made completely free of effort; but even this may be used therapeutically. Festinger (1957) has stated that in many situations which involve decision and personal commitment, if the value of the goal to be attained does not initially match the amount of work required in order to achieve it, the individual may come to increase the value of the goal to bring it more into balance with the effort he actually expends. This upward shift in value may be particularly helpful in the treatment of alcohol and other addictions, and may be facilitated by the following suggestions:

The harder you work to achieve your goal of total abstinence, and the more effort you put forth to attain it, the more highly you will come to value this goal, and the more you will become convinced of the certainty that you will succeed.

The use of suggestion need not be confined to drinking itself, however. During the period of withdrawal, the alcoholic may also be assisted by the use of suggestions for time condensation and for the relief of physical discomfort, to alleviate insomnia, and to aid in the reestablishment of normal patterns of sleeping. Directly suggested sleep may also be utilized when desirable. As rehabilitation proceeds, training in techniques of suggestion-induced relaxation and in autosuggestion and self-induced trance experiences may also be employed. The alcoholic's changing personality structure and perceptions of the world about him may be explored by such methods as free association, automatic writing, ideomotor questioning, and dream analysis. Suggestions for achievement motivation, ego strengthening, and emotional enrichment may also be used as part of long-term rehabilitation.

Of course, the true alcoholic will never be able to drink in moderation as other people may. Complete abstinence is his only hope of bringing about a permanent improvement; for there is no such thing as a "cure" for alcoholism. However, many people who are not alcoholics in the usual sense of the word may be termed *situational* drinkers. That is, they may tend to overindulge on specific occasions, such as when they are entertaining friends or when they are at a party, but they tend to drink moderately the rest of the time if indeed they drink at all.

Situational drinking may also be engaged in as a means of meeting other needs, as in the case of the unattached person who may not allow him- or herself to participate in a sexual encounter until first becoming intoxicated, as a means of escaping from a sense of responsibility for his or her own actions. Situational drinking may also be indicative of a prealcoholic personality pattern, especially when it seems to be directly related to environmental frustrations of an episodic nature.

ALLERGIC AND SKIN REACTIONS

Many allergic reactions are intensified by physical or psychological stress; and to the extent that stress is a contributing factor, such reactions may be lessened or avoided by the timely use of techniques such as relaxation training or suggestions for the relief of insomnia. Additional therapeutic approaches should also be considered if the contributing stress appears to be prolonged or intensive, or if its causes are not readily apparent.

Suggestions may also be administered to alleviate specific allergic response patterns. For instance, after a subject has mastered the technique of self-induced trance experience and has been taught how to administer autosuggestions for relaxation, suggestions for the relief of asthmatic symptoms may be administered as follows:

> If you ever feel any more attacks coming on, or even if one has already started, you will be able to place yourself in trance very rapidly, just by closing your eyes and silently repeating the necessary suggestions to yourself. Then you will be able to drive away the symptoms completely by slowly counting to fifty, with each count taking a deep breath and clenching your fists, and then unclenching your fists and letting your body relax as much as possible each time you let a breath out, silently repeating to yourself the word *calm* each time you exhale. And when the count is completed, you can terminate the trance in the usual way, feeling fine once more.

Suggestions for alleviating nasal allergies may be presented in similar fashion, with the subject visualizing himself standing atop a snowy mountain and breathing in cold dry air, silently repeating to himself the word *cool* as he clenches his fists and inhales in the previously described manner, and continuing to repeat the word *calm* as he exhales to the count of fifty.

Because the skin is such an active participant in emotional changes—reddening in anger or embarrassment, blanching and shivering with fear, perspiring with worry, and developing "goose bumps" with cold or excitement—many allergic reactions and infections of the skin have been associated with excessive stress. As in other forms of illness, the possibility of so-called secondary gain, or reinforcement in the form of extra attention and the opportunity to escape from unpleasant social and work obligations, must also be taken into account. It has long been accepted that any response of which an organism is capable can, through learning, be attached to any stimulus to which the organism is sensitive, regardless of whether or not the response in question is a "voluntary" one or merely a change in physiological functioning.

Barber (1978) has indicated that just as blood flow to the sexual organs may be influenced by the imaginary portrayal of various sexual stimuli, so may circulation in other parts of the body also respond to suggestions which make use of appropriate imagery. Suggestion may thus be of potential benefit in alleviating many skin conditions in which faulty circulation is either a causal or an exacerbating factor; and normal healing processes may be facilitated in certain other conditions by accelerating blood flow to the afflicted part. For example, warts appear to be particularly responsive to suggestion, and the folklore of many lands is rich in time-honored rituals to hasten their demise. With slight modification, the following suggestions for the alleviation of warts, modeled after a procedure described by Hartland (1971b), may be adapted to other types of skin conditions. At the conclusion of an appropriate induction procedure, one may proceed as follows:

Now I am going to stroke your hand, and as I do, you will gradually begin to be aware of feelings of warmth flowing from my hand into yours and flowing all through your hand, as these feelings of warmth continue to grow stronger and stronger with each passing moment. As I stroke your hand now, you will soon begin to notice these feelings of warmth flowing into your hand from mine, and as soon as you do, you can signal me by nodding your head.

After the subject has nodded his assent:

That's fine. Now, as the warmth continues to grow stronger, you are going to feel it becoming concentrated in the warts themselves. And soon the warts will begin to feel warmer than the rest of your hand. As I stroke the warts now, you can feel the warmth flowing into them from the rest of your hand. And as soon as you can feel the warmth in the warts themselves, you can signal me by nodding your head once more.

After the subject has nodded his head once more:

Very good. Now, as you continue to feel the warmth flowing out of my hand and concentrating itself in the warts while I continue to stroke them, the warts are going to start to heal. And this healing process is going to continue until the warts are gone completely.

Over the coming days, your warts are going to become flatter and smaller, and soon they are going to disappear completely. Before very long, they will be completely gone. Within a very short time, your warts will be gone completely.

DRUG ABUSE

Baumann (1970) has reported that adolescent drug users are frequently able to relive a previous drug experience after a hypnotic induction, and that they are even able to "make it better" in response to the suggestion that they can do so. Students have reported similar results with hyperempiric inductions. Responsive subjects, for example, seem able to reexperience quite easily the sensations of smoking marijuana if, after either type of induction, they are handed an ordinary cigarette and are told that it is a "joint"; and their enjoyment of such a "trip" may also be guided and enhanced by means of direct suggestion.

In the same article, Baumann also relates that he has obtained good results using such a technique as a temporary substitute for narcotics during the process of rehabilitation—with the exception of marijuana users, who tend to be poorly motivated because they are inclined to view marijuana smoking as a harmless custom akin to the adult cocktail hour. "You could give them something that would make them feel ten times better," a student once said to me in the same vein, "and they'd still smoke pot because there are so many social things attached to it." However, enough people apparently *are* able to be helped by such a procedure to make it a valuable addition to the therapist's armamentarium. At the conclusion of an induction, suggestions may be given as follows:

Now I would like you to think of one of the most enjoyable drug experiences you can possibly imagine. This should be an experience which is within the range of your own abilities, and one which you would like to undergo right now. As soon as you have an image of the experience firmly in mind, you can signal me by raising the index finger of your right (or left) hand.

After the subject has complied:

That's fine. Now I'm going to help you to experience the high that you have envisioned, just as you have imagined it to be, and perhaps even better.

As I continue speaking, you can already feel the high beginning, as you start to experience it yourself, just as you have imagined it would be. You will always be able to hear and to respond to my voice, and I will be able to guide and direct the experience as it progresses. You will be able to talk and to answer questions, and I will bring you back down when the experience is over. But for now, just let yourself go on getting higher and higher, until you are experiencing just the same high that you imagined, in just the way that you imagined it. And when you are there, you can signal me by raising the index finger of your right (or left) hand once more.

Because the subject may tend to become rather passive in response to the foregoing suggestions, he may need to be prompted: "Soon you will be experiencing the high you have envisioned, and your finger will rise to signal to me that you are there. Any second now, your finger is going to rise." When the subject has given the aforementioned signal, he may then be asked to describe his experience, with the suggestor guiding and directing it as appropriate. Suggestions for time expansion may also be employed if desired. During the course of the trip, the subject may be left on his own for a moment or two, to experience a period of free fantasy. After an appropriate interval—which usually need not be longer than a few minutes—or when the subject indicates in response to questioning that he is ready to come down, the following suggestions may be given:

Now I am going to count backwards from five to one; and by the time I get to the count of one, you will be all the way down and feeling just fine, but you will remain in trance for a while longer, until I bring you out. Five. You are beginning to come down now, and by the time I get to the count of one, you will be all the way down, feeling wonderful. Four. Coming down more and more now. Three. Halfway, and continuing to come down. Two. Almost down, but still in a trance for a little while longer. Almost down. One. Now you are all the way down, and feeling wonderful, but still in a trance for a while, until I bring you out.

The subject may then be given suggestions specifically intended to decrease drug usage: "As a result of this experience, your desire for narcotics will be considerably diminished, and in the future, you will continue to be able to satisfy your need mentally, in the way I have shown you."

Suggestions for time condensation and other techniques of pain control may be employed to assist the subject during the withdrawal phase. It may also be suggested that he will handle the most stressful portions of withdrawal through a form of dissociation which is sometimes referred to as an *out-of-the-body experience*:

During the times when you may be experiencing more stress, you will begin to feel as though these changes were not happening to *you*; but instead, you will feel as if they were happening to *a* body, which you temporarily happen to inhabit. You will realize that you are *not* this body, and it will be as if you were merely watching these changes occur. In fact, there may be times when you feel as if you were somewhere else, watching this body from another part of the room. But that will be all right, for you will always be aware that as soon as it is comfortable for you to do so, you will feel as if you are back in your own body once more. And when your body is feeling comfortable once again, all sense of separation between your body and your consciousness will vanish completely.

The subject may also be encouraged to make use of dissociative autosuggestions, repeating over and over again during stressful periods such affirmations as, "I am *not* this body"—which is apt to be particularly effective when used within a spiritual frame of reference.

Techniques such as dream induction and automatic writing may be used to establish or to corroborate the reasons for the subject's excessive use of drugs—to "get back at" one's parents, to seek "do-it-yourself" chemotherapy, etc.—and the motivation for change may be explored and strengthened by the use of fantasy and guided imagery techniques presented on pages 149–164.

ENURESIS

Nocturnal bladder control depends first on maturation and then on learning; for until a child has become sufficiently mature to control the sphincter muscles of the bladder, sleeping through the night without urinating is physiologically impossible. Relatively large individual differences may exist between children in the same family in the relative rate of maturation leading to the development of such control, although girls generally tend to be a few months ahead of boys; and occasionally lateness in the development of bladder control may appear to be a family trait. Although a very few children are able to remain dry throughout the night at the age of one year, with only an occasional "mistake" to remind the parents of earlier days, the majority of children acquire this ability between the ages of two and three, with only an occasional child still wetting the bed after age three. At times, however, the problem may even persist into adulthood.

The ability to sleep through the night without wetting is often attained before daytime toilet training has been completed, and sometimes before it is even begun, because of the normal tendency of the kidneys to produce a smaller amount of more concentrated urine during sleep. Such control may be more difficult to attain, however, owing to a wide variety of organically-based causes, such as hyperacidity of the urine, diabetes, or a reactive kidney condition which operates to reduce the level of blood sugar before it has actually become excessive. If a child has a tendency to sleep so deeply that he does not respond to the usual signals which indicate a state of bladder distension, medication may sometimes be prescribed to lighten the depth of sleep until the necessary stimulus–response connections have been established—that is, provided such deep sleep does not result from some pathological condition, or from mere exhaustion. In this connection, it should also be noted that unduly profound or excessive slumber may at times constitute a neurotic attempt to escape from an intolerable environment (Hartland, 1971b).

If failure to attain nocturnal control of the bladder is not merely the result of lack of maturity or some underlying pathological condition, the problem may be due to various problems within the family, such as the birth of another child or impending parental separation. Like many other problem behaviors of childhood, bed-wetting may serve as a means of getting extra attention, or as a way of expressing resentment or hostility toward the parents, as well as an expression of underlying insecurity; and at times it may serve all three of these functions simultaneously. In any event, the child should not be blamed for his inability to exercise proper nocturnal control of the bladder; for it is generally agreed that punishment in such instances is ineffective, and excessive punishment may only serve to make the situation worse. Instead, the parents should accentuate the *positive* aspects of the child's behavior whenever possible, congratulating him whenever he does awaken with a dry bed, and even praising him whenever he awakens with a bed which is even *half-dry* instead of scolding him for having a bed which is *half-wet* (Spock, 1957). Of course, the parents should also insure that the child is provided with sufficient affection and security, and that major sources of stress in the environment are either removed or dealt with in such a manner that their effect is minimized. Care should also be taken, however, that the child does not gain the upper hand by using his behavior as a form of blackmail to force the parents to comply with his wishes. In other words, he should not be allowed to play the role of "disturbed child," who must constantly be given attention or else his "trouble" will get worse. Indeed, the way in which the parents selectively encourage the child's behavior in the desired direction usually spells the difference between success and failure.

There are also a number of rather obvious but essential practical steps which should be taken if training in nocturnal control of the bladder is to succeed. The child should not be given anything to drink the last hour or so before going to bed, and he should be required to visit the bathroom before retiring. The parents may also awaken the child briefly to have him repeat the visit before they retire themselves if the child's bedtime is sufficiently ahead of that of the parents and if he has relatively little difficulty in falling asleep again. An alarm clock may also be employed for this purpose.

The child should be encouraged to refrain from urination a bit longer during the day, particularly if he is in the habit of urinating more frequently than he actually needs to, as is often the case with enuretics. He should also be encouraged to interrupt the stream of urine several times as he is voiding; for both of these procedures may be useful ways of strengthening the sphincter muscles of the bladder and of increasing the child's control over them.

If functional enuresis should persist into adolescence or adulthood, or if it should return at such an age without having been brought about by disease or organic injury, it may be indicative of a poorly developed concept of self with strong accompanying feelings of personal inadequacy and a considerable degree of hostility directed against the self. Functional enuresis in adolescence or adulthood may also serve a defensive function, preventing the establishment of marital and family relationships or other close personal ties which the individual may find threatening. In addition to specific suggestions to eliminate bed wetting, suggestions for ego strengthening and relaxation training may be provided for the late enuretic in the context of therapy which is aimed at discovering and changing the symbolic or instrumental function of such behavior.

If the subject is a child, the following suggestions may be given at the conclusion of a hyperempiric induction for children:

As you look around the room we have entered, here in the enchanted cottage, you see a fireplace at the far end of the room, with a warm log fire burning brightly, and beside the fireplace is an easy chair, which looks so comfortable that you decide to go over and curl up in it for a while.

Our journey here has made you sleepy, and as soon as you curl up in the chair and begin to watch the fire, you find yourself starting to drift off to sleep. You are getting very, very sleepy there in the chair, in the enchanted cottage. You are so very sleepy. And now you have begun to sleep, soundly and comfortably, there in that soft easy chair.

Now you are sleeping very soundly. But in just a minute or two, you are going to have to go to the bathroom. And as soon as you begin to feel that you have to go to the bathroom, you are going to start to move around, and you will open your eyes and wake up before you have wet. Your eyes will open, and you will be completely awake before you actually start to do anything. And when you do open your eyes, you will be back here with me, and not in the cottage any more. We can go back to the cottage after you have gone to the bathroom. But first, you will open your eyes and wake up, ready to go to the bathroom before you have wet. And from now on, whenever you are asleep at night, you will wake up before you have wet, just as you are going to do now.

Any time now, you are going to feel that you have to go to the bathroom, and you will begin to move around, and your eyes will open before you have wet.

If the subject is an older child or an adult, a hypnotic induction may be employed, after which similar suggestions may be given: "Now you are sleeping very soundly, but in just a minute or two, you are going to have to go to the bathroom."

After the subject has awakened and complied with the suggestion that he will visit the bathroom and urinate, the initial induction may be repeated and additional suggestions given reiterating that in the future the subject will be sensitive to signals from his bladder indicating a need to urinate, and that these signals will be effective in awakening him.

Since most people are able to produce at least some urine even when the bladder is not fully distended, and since most individuals—especially children—occasionally fool themselves into thinking that they have to urinate when little urine is actually present, the foregoing suggestions are likely to be effective with most suggestible subjects.

HYPERTENSION

Recent advances in biofeedback techniques have enabled some patients to learn to monitor and control deviations in their own blood pressure within certain limits (Friedman & Taub, 1977). Biofeedback makes use of modern electronic instrumentation to provide the subject with a continuous flow of information concerning various physiological changes which are taking place within his own body at the moment they are occurring. By attending to these momentary changes, the biofeedback trainee is able to learn just what subjective feelings accompany such changes. Eventually, the subject may be able to bring about these changes himself, merely by generating the same subjective feelings. Biofeedback is often referred to as "the Yoga of the West," because the procedure enables on to obtain voluntary control over processes which are normally thought to be involuntary, in much the same fashion as Eastern yogis have occasionally been able to do. But since the use of electronic instrumentation makes the task of attending to one's own internal bodily processes a great deal easier, the time required to gain control over such processes by means of biofeedback is often measured in hours and days rather than months and years.

To the extent that stress is a factor in precipitating hypertension, its effects may also be mitigated by suggestions for relaxation, which serve to disrupt the stress pattern and countermand the excessive arousal and alarm signals which are being transmitted to the body (Deabler, Fidel, Dillenkoffer, & Elder, 1973). Instructions for relaxation training are presented on pages 128–129.

Changes in the subject's environment and in his customary routine which are aimed at removing him from unnecessary stress are also frequently desirable, as is counseling in order to modify needlessly high standards of performance or to reduce the tendency to worry excessively over life's frustrations and petty annoyances. Further therapeutic intervention may also be necessary to deal with other underlying problems which may be contributing to the disorder, and ancillary medication may also be required.

INSOMNIA

Many people may complain of insomnia when what they really need is a new job, or a new hobby, or to get the mother-in-law out of the guest room and into an apartment of her own. Being chronically in need of sleep can also be a means of "holding back," and not committing oneself fully to a round of daily activities that one dislikes. Prolonged sleeplessness, of course, may also be symptomatic of some underlying organic disease process, or it may be symptomatic of a deeply rooted personality disturbance. Some people may find it hard to go to sleep, for example, because of the nightmares which plague them when they do fall alseep. In many other instances, however, insomnia is primarily the result of faulty habit patterns which are readily modifiable by means of direct suggestion.

According to Hartland (1971b), some people have become chronically poor sleepers because they literally try too hard. They are so concerned about the possible effects of prolonged sleeplessness on their work or on their health that they may lie awake for hours worrying about their insomnia. However, most of those who claim that they "didn't sleep a wink all night," or that they "haven't slept for days," are probably exaggerating the situation; for under such circumstances it is easy to drift in and out of sleep for brief periods without realizing that one has been asleep at all. Moreover, as any parent who has ever tended a baby afflicted with colic will confirm, it is possible to adapt to drastically reduced amounts of sleep for relatively prolonged periods with few side effects save an increased sense of fatigue.

Once it has been established that a subject's pattern of sleeplessness is primarily owing to habit, it is first desirable to assure him tactfully that he is probably getting a great deal more sleep than he actually thinks he is; and that he is in absolutely no danger of ruining his health or "overtaxing his brain" simply because he is not getting enough sleep.

When the vicious circle of losing sleep because of worrying about one's insomnia has been broken, or at least weakened, the subject should be encouraged to examine his nightly routine with a view to modifying it in ways that are conducive to slumber. One should take care to retire at the same hour each night if this is at all possible. Emotionally stressful activities late in the evening should obviously be avoided; and it is often helpful to follow the same ritual pattern of "unwinding" the last hour before going to bed, such as taking a relaxing shower or tub bath followed by a warm beverage which does not contain stimulants. If it is acceptable to the subject, a small amount of alcoholic beverage, such as brandy or cognac, may be consumed shortly before retiring. For many people, sexual intercourse at bedtime is also conducive to sleep.

The following suggestions may be used at the conclusion of an induction to assist the subject to be able to drop off to sleep whenever he wishes. Thus, they may be helpful not only to people who suffer from insomnia, but also to those with a demanding schedule of evening activities who would like to learn to cap nap during the day. If the subject has previously come to rely on chemical soporifics, the dosages may gradually be reduced as the new procedures become effective. Because most people who suffer from insomnia tend to resist direct suggestions of sleep, it is generally preferable to precede the following suggestions with a hyperempiric induction rather than a hypnotic one.

For the occasional subject who may feel so keyed up that any further increase in alertness may be discomforting, a modifed hypnotic induction may be employed in which the words *drowsiness* and *relaxation* are used:

Picture yourself standing all alone on a tropical island, beside a jungle pool which is fed by a waterfall. Just hold the scene in your mind and continue to focus on it, and soon you will be able to experience everything I describe to you as if it were really happening. The water looks so clear and inviting that you decide you would like to go for a swim. Since you happen to be wearing a bathing suit beneath your other clothing, you quickly remove your outer garments and prepare to enter the pool.

The water is slightly heated by underground volcanic rocks, and tiny clouds of steam are rising from the surface in the cool morning air; but the water is still so crystal clear that you can see all the way to the bottom. It's just the right temperature for bathing, and you wade into the pool slowly, savoring every second of the experience. Feel the soothing warmth moving up from your feet to the calves of your legs, and then on up to your knees and thighs. Feel this gentle warmth spreading throughout your entire body now, as you immerse yourself completely and begin to swim over to the waterfall.

Directly underneath the waterfall is a large flat rock which is just big enough to stand on. You climb out underneath the falls and feel the warm water cascading over your body and gently massaging you all over. And it's as if all the worry, and all the tension, and all the care that you have ever felt are being washed away by these endless streams of infinite, boundless peace, tranquility, and calm.

Just savor the experience for a few moments, and continue to feel these beautiful sensations of infinite peace and relaxation, tranquility and calm, flowing through every muscle, and every fiber, and every nerve in your body.

Now you step out from under the waterfall and stretch out on a smooth, sunny rock to take a nap. The fresh air and the sunshine, the warm rock beneath you, and the soft jungle sounds in the distance, all combine into such a pleasant, soothing sensation, making you feel so very drowsy, so peaceful, and so calm.

And whenever you wish, you will be able to recapture these feelings of peacefulness and drowsiness by going over this experience again in your mind. This will enable you to drift off to sleep promptly and easily, and to sleep soundly all through the night, waking up the next morning completely rested and thoroughly refreshed. And the more often and the more carefully you practice this technique for putting yourself to sleep, the better you are going to be at it, and the more easily you will be able to doze off whenever you wish.

It is sometimes desirable to suggest that a trance experience will change directly into natural sleep without an intervening period of activity. This approach is particularly useful during and after periods of prolonged or intense stress, as in situations involving chronic pain or during the period of withdrawal from addictive drugs. The subject should be reclining comfortably in a setting which is free of distractions, so that he can sleep for a fairly long period without being disturbed. After an initial induction, which can be either hyperempiric or hynotic, depending upon the situation and the needs and preferences of the individual subject, as previously discussed, the suggestor may proceed with the material just presented, omitting the last paragraph and substituting those that follow:

Now just let yourself continue to relax, deeper and deeper. Feel yourself continuing to soak up this peace, tranquility, and calm as you relax more and more. Soaking up peace, soaking up calm, just like a piece of blotting paper, as you continue to relax deeper and deeper.

As you continue soaking up these feelings of peace and calm and relaxation, soon your trance is going to change into natural sleep; and you will sleep deeply and peacefully, continuing to be completely relaxed, tranquil, and calm. You will sleep as long as you need to, and you will be able to get all the rest you need. You will awaken rested and refreshed, feeling very much better, after one of the most restful, most refreshing sleeps that you have had in a long, long time. So just let yourself drift now, as you relax more and more, and soon you will be asleep.

The suggestor should be cautioned to avoid the use of suggestions of time expansion in conjunction with this approach. Some lay hypnotists, for example, are occasionally inclined to tell a subject that five minutes of sleeping trance experience will be as beneficial as five hours of natural sleep. Although the subject may *feel* rested for a time, in response to explicit or implicit suggestions to that effect, there is nothing to be gained in the long run by fooling the subject into thinking that he has received more rest than is actually the case. The proper function of suggestion in these circumstances is to create the appropriate attitudinal conditions to maximize the opportunity for the body to get the natural rest and sleep it requires.

If the subject should happen to be a nonswimmer, trance logic will usually make this fact irrelevant as far as the foregoing imagery is concerned. However, since some subjects do possess an actual fear of water, it may be well to mention briefly to the subject ahead of time the general nature of the imagery that is to be employed.

NAIL BITING

In addition to the immediate oral gratification which nail biting may provide, the habit may also serve to divert attention from troublesome thoughts and situations, thereby perhaps giving evidence of underlying feelings of insecurity or other problems which may be more in need of attention than is the actual nail biting (Hartland, 1971b). Nail biting may also serve a passive-aggressive function, in that it may provide a child with an opportunity to annoy his parents as a means of "getting back" at them for real or imagined offenses, or for failure to give him as much attention as he desires. A child may come to use nail biting as a form of self-punishment (Crasilneck & Hall, 1977), particularly if it leads to punishment from the parents. The habit may intensify with the advent of stress situations, such as parental separation or the birth of a sibling (Hartland, 1971b); and it is possible that the response may tend to become fixated, or unusually resistant to change, if excessive punishment has been employed in attempts to correct it (Maier, Glaser, & Klee, 1941).

It is generally to be expected that as long as the child is made to feel emotionally secure and the environment is kept relatively free of emotional stress, the less attention that is paid to his nail biting the more readily the habit will tend to disappear. However, when nail biting becomes deeply rooted through long practice or early fixation, it may occasionally tend to persist into adulthood.

Although the habit is essentially harmless, occasionally there may be sufficient concern over the possibility of minor dental malocclusion to justify attempts to correct the behavior. Older children and adults may also express concern about the appearance of their nails, or the fact that nail biting makes them feel excessively self-conscious. When there is little in the present environment which appears to reinforce such behavior, the following postinduction suggestions may be helpful. It may be necessary to modify the wording slightly when one is dealing with children who are very young:

Every time you bite your nails from now on, you will have to bite them with your hand turned *completely upside down* from the way you usually hold it. You are going to be absolutely unable to bite your nails in the way you have been doing it, because every time you start to bite your nails in the usual way, you are going to *have to turn your hand completely over* before you do.

Every time you feel like biting your nails, your desire to *stop* biting them is going to be felt too. And this is what is going to make you do it in such an awkward and uncomfortable way. You won't be able to express one desire without expressing the other one at the same time, so if you do let yourself bite your nails, you won't let yourself enjoy it.

And when you do turn your hand upside down to bite your nails, you will soon find that this position is *so* awkward, and *so* uncomfortable, that your desire to bite your nails is going to get weaker and weaker, until your desire to bite your nails is *so* weak, and it is just *so* much trouble, that you will just give it up completely.

PAIN CONTROL

In a Hollywood motion picture of the 1940s, a girl who has never been in love asks her roommate to describe the experience. "When you fall in love, you'll know it," the friend replies, "because, when your boyfriend kisses you good-night, it will seem as if the whole sky is filled with bombers overhead." The plot then proceeds, in typical Hollywood fashion, with the girl becoming acquainted with a boy to whom she is very much attracted, who eventually asks her for a date. At the conclusion of a delightful evening, with a strong relationship already beginning to develop, the boy starts to kiss the girl good-night—when suddenly, the audience is treated to the sight of dozens of bombers roaring across the screen.

As in most forms of humor, there is a grain of truth behind the exaggeration. People tend to experience events—including the act of falling in love—in ways that are in accordance with their expectations. It is rare to be able to tune up and down the radio dial without interrupting a song in progress which describes the glories of being in love; and because one's expectations have been so structured from childhood on, when the experience does occur, it is apt to possess an intensity bordering on psychosis, in spite of the fact that in many other cultures romantic love as we conceive of it is indeed virtually unknown.

Of course, the ability to develop a high degree of organismic involvement in a given experience in accordance with one's previous expectations is not confined solely to the experience of falling in love. In Victorian times, women were expected to faint at the slightest provocation—particularly if the air in a room happened to be rather stale, or if someone swore in their presence—as *prima facie* evidence of their femininity; and apparently enough of them did to maintain this stereotype for a time as a form of self-fulfilling prophecy.

By the same token, the experience of pain can either be brought about or considerably intensified by catastrophic expectations concerning the nature of the experience which one is about to undergo (Chaves & Brown, 1978). Physicians and dentists have long been aware of the need to avoid such catastrophizing tendencies on the part of their patients by guiding the patients' thoughts in other directions. For example, a dentist may say, "You may feel a little pressure in a moment," instead of telling a patient, "We are very close to the nerve now, so please try not to move."

Previous catastrophic expectations may occasionally result in a generalized dental phobia which prevents the patient from seeking dental assistance, or which virtually guarantees that the experience will be painful. Occasionally this is even the case when the work to be performed involves nothing more than routine inspection and cleaning. When such a phobic reaction is merely the result of patient catastrophizing, relaxation training may be employed, as well as a desensitization procedure analogous to the one described in the section on phobic reactions (see page 124). Direct suggestions may also be administered after an appropriate induction, to the effect that any strong sensations which may still be present in the situation will be reinterpreted and experienced as pressure (A. Moss, 1977; Tinkler, 1971).

Menstrual cramps also provide an illustration of the manner in which expectations of pain can frequently be a major source of its occurrence. Provided that such discomfort is not owing to any underlying organic condition; and provided it is not merely an outward somatic expression of marital disharmony or other emotional conflicts, dysmenorrhea may often result from erroneous impressions gleaned from one's mother or other relatives and friends, who in turn acquired the mistaken notion in their own formative years that menstruation is inevitably accompanied by pain. Such misconceptions may frequently be alleviated by means of appropriate discussion and reassurance, bolstered by direct suggestions at the conclusion of an induction to the effect that menstrual discomfort will no longer occur, since the subject now realizes that it is unnecessary (Hartland, 1971b).

Most pain tends to serve an adaptive function, as a signal that something is wrong and as a warning to the person to decrease his activity until the healing processes have run their course. For this reason, it is generally not desirable to remove *all* perception of pain from an injury, such as a sprained ankle, or from any other bodily condition for which pain is serving a valid purpose. However, when pain is present in excessive amounts, it may be dealt with by means of the suggestions contained in the following paragraph. If necessary, the subject may be instructed in ways of maintaining their effectiveness through auto suggestion and self-induced trances, after being cautioned to observe the proper limitations so that only the excess pain is removed. Such a procedure may often be more effective than chemical analgesics in taking away just the right amount of pain without impairing the subject's general efficiency or his overall ability to function:

After the trance has been concluded, you will find that your pain is almost completely gone. There will still be a little discomfort remaining, just to serve as a reminder for you to take it easy; and you will still continue to let up as much as you need to for the healing to proceed properly. But the extra pain, which serves no useful purpose, is going to be completely taken away. And you are going to be greatly relieved at how much better you will feel.

Occasionally, of course, it may be desirable to induce complete local anesthesia as a temporary first-aid measure and to help forestall the onset of shock. This can be accomplished by suggesting glove anesthesia for one hand, and then transferring the anesthesia to the portion of the body where it is needed. Suggestions may be given as follows:

Now I would like you to concentrate on your right (or left) hand, and upon the sensations you experience there as you continue listening to my voice. I am going to show you how to take away the feeling in that hand, and then we are going to transfer this lack of feeling to where it is needed most. Just continue listening to my voice, as I begin to count from one to five, and by the time I get to the count of five, your hand is going to be completely numb. One. As I begin the count now, you can feel your hand beginning to tingle a bit, almost as if you had been given a shot of Novocain at the dentist's office. Two. Your hand is beginning to feel more and more numb, as the sensation continues to leave. Three. The feeling is going away, going away, going away more and more, as I continue the count, and by the time I get to five, your hand will be just as numb as a piece of stone. Four. The sensation in your hand is almost gone now, and your hand is almost completely numb. Five. Now you have lost the ability to feel anything in your hand, and your hand is just as numb and just as insensitive as a piece of stone.

The subject may then be instructed to place his hand gently upon the afflicted part. It may then be suggested that the subject can feel the anesthesia flowing into the afflicted part as normal feeling gradually returns to his anesthetized hand. Rubbing or stroking may also be employed to heighten the effectiveness of the suggestions for transferring anesthesia from one bodily part to another. For example, when this approach is employed for the alleviation of the pain of a toothache or in preparation for dental treatment, it is usually helpful to instruct the subject to rub the gum with the anesthetized hand instead of merely placing it over the desired spot while suggestions for transferring the anesthesia are administered. In another variation of this technique, the suggestor himself may rub or stroke the afflicted area, suggesting as he does so that the subject will gradually begin to feel the area growing warm (or cold); and that as this change continues, the pain will begin to leave, until finally it is completely gone (A. Moss, 1977; Tinkler, 1971).

If complete anesthesia is not produced by these methods, it may at least be possible to reduce the amount of chemical analgesic which is required. When some pain does remain, it may be possible to suggest that the pain is going to be felt in a smaller area, or that the location of the pain is going to shift to a more comfortable spot. With less responsive subjects, goal-directed imagery may also be employed as a means of minimizing catastrophic expectations and encouraging the subject to use his thought processes in a more adaptive fashion (Chaves & Brown, 1978). For example, a subject with a painfully injured arm who is awaiting medical treatment may be instructed to visualize the arm as a wooden log or a roll of tightly packed cloth. Even in the absence of a formal induction procedure to heighten the credibility of such imagining, a subject may often be able to achieve a sufficient amount of dissociation to lessen his distress considerably.

The pain problem most frequently encountered in everyday life is most likely to be that which results from migraine and vascular headaches (Andreychuk & Skriver, 1965; Graham, 1975). Most people who suffer from migraine and other forms of stress-induced headache tend to be "over-doers" with a strong sense of duty, for whom being tired is simply not enough justification to stop whatever they are doing and take a rest. Life for such people often becomes little more than an endless list of things that simply have to be done—that is, until their headaches enter the picture. Brought on initially by the accumulating anger and frustration which result from the pattern just described, such headaches tend to recur with increasing frequency because they provide what is often the only acceptable means of escape from such a pattern—even if the price of such a temporary respite is pain so severe that it *forces* one to stop.

Hereditary predispositions, of course, also play an important part in determining whether the eventual outcome of such a stress pattern happens to be chronic headache or some other ailment, such as high blood pressure or a peptic ulcer. The immediate physiological cause of migraine headaches is to be found in excessive dilation of the arterial walls within the brain itself, while so-called vascular headaches are caused by constriction induced by the contraction of muscles surrounding the skull. Whereas vascular headaches typically involve constriction of the blood flow in both hemispheres, migraines are generally experienced on one side of the brain only, although they may occasionally become more diffuse or shift from side to side. A variation of the usual migraine pattern is the so-called cluster headache, which occurs in rapidly repeating sequences of pain rather than a single sustained onslaught.

I have had excellent results with the following suggestions, which use vestigial remnants of the diving reflex to alleviate the discomfort of migraine and other stress-induced headaches. By slowing the heartbeat and decreasing blood pressure by means of this technique, circulatory congestion in the head may be alleviated and the headache symptons gradually cease. (Of course, *suggestion* also plays an important—and perhaps the *most* important—part in enhancing the effectiveness of this underlying physiological rationale.)

The effect of the following suggestions may be enhanced by requesting the subject to assume a sitting position prior to the induction, and, as the "diving" suggestions are given, handing him a cloth moistened in cool water to hold against his face as he bends forward slightly and puts his head down:

Picture yourself now as a dolphin, swimming lazily along just below the surface of the sea. Feel the water above you gently warming your back; and feel the cooler water beneath you, as you swim lazily along. Just let yourself continue to swim slowly along, concentrating on the images and the sensations which you feel as you continue to listen to my voice, and soon you will be able to experience everything I describe to you just as if it were actually happening.

You think how refreshing it would be to dive down, all the way to the bottom. Let yourself begin to dive now, diving easily and gently, all the way down to the bottom. Feel the cooler currents against your face as you angle your body toward the bottom, and feel yourself beginning to adjust to the increasing depth and the pressure of the water around you as you continue to descend.

Any previous discomfort you may have felt is fading away now, as you feel the cool, soothing currents rushing by as you sink deeper and deeper, and your system continues to slow down in response to the increasing pressure and cold. The water continues to grow even colder now, as you continue to sink, but your body adapts to it easily and comfortably. You continue to drift down and down, sinking past seaweed forests and deep coral canyons, sinking all the way down to the bottom, almost there.

Now you find yourself drifting slowly along, exploring the bottom of the sea. Just savor the experience for a few moments and enjoy the cool freshness as you swim along.

In just a short while, I'm going to return you to your normal sense of time and place; but after you return, this feeling of peace and well-being will remain with you, and all traces of your previous headache will have vanished. Even after you have returned to your normal sense of time and place, you will continue to feel just as good as you do right now. So just continue to let yourself explore this undersea world for a moment or two, experiencing all the enjoyment and pleasure that goes with it; and soon it will be time to return you to the environment from which you left.

After a moment or two has elasped, suggestions may be given to the effect that the subject is slowly rising back to the surface, followed by suggestions that the scene is fading and that the subject is becoming fully aware of himself as a person once more, still in trance and still retaining the feelings of relaxation, peacefulness, and well-being which were part of his undersea experience. The trance may then be terminated in the usual manner, together with suggestions that the subject will continue to feel peaceful and relaxed, with no further trace of discomfort.

At the conclusion of the trance session, the subject may be instructed to repeat the foregoing imagery at appropriate intervals by means of autosuggestion, either to ward off an oncoming headache or to alleviate one which has already begun. More responsive subjects should eventually be able to experience similar sensations merely by closing their eyes and silently repeating to themselves the word *dive*.

It may not always be necessary, of course, to employ such an elaborate procedure if the headache happens to be a mild one, or if one is working with a particularly good subject. (An example of the use of direct suggestion to alleviate a tension-induced vascular headache with a highly responsive subject is presented on page 48.) By the same token, adjunctive medication may still be necessary, at least on occasion, for certain subjects who are less responsive to suggestion, although in many instances the dosage may be reduced.

Relaxation training is also helpful in assisting the subject to alter the basic stress pattern which may be contributing to the onset of his headaches, and in combating any tendencies to unduly catastrophize over life's problems and annoyances.

Sometimes it is not possible to eliminate completely the experience of pain by these or any other methods, in which case the goal must be to help the subject learn to live with his discomfort (Crawford, 1978). In this connection, it is necessary to consider what benefits, if any, the patient may be receiving from continuing to experience his pain instead of giving it up. People can learn to be reinforced by almost anything; and for some individuals, the rewards of not having to get up and go to work each day, or not having to look after a busy household, may be considerable indeed—especially when they are combined with the extra care and attention which a person's illness may elicit from those around him. Conversely, it may be possible to put up with even a considerable amount of pain now and then if a person happens to be engaged in pursuits that are sufficiently gratifying in themselves.

The following suggestions may be helpful in assisting a subject to get through a particularly stressful period, such as a painful convalescence, which is not unduly exacerbated by underlying personality conflicts or by various "secondary gain" factors such as those mentioned in the previous paragraph. These suggestions may also be employed, together with directly suggested sleep as discussed in the section on insomnia, to assist a seriously or terminally ill patient in coping with intervals of unusually severe discomfort. In the case of terminal illness, however, such suggestions should usually not be relied on to the extent that they may deny the patient sufficient time to accept and to come to terms with the fact of his own impending death; and other patients who may learn to use such techniques by means of autosuggestion should be cautioned not to employ them to avoid having to cope with problems which ought to be dealt with instead of merely being endured, such as the periodic drinking bouts of an alcoholic spouse.

After a hypnotic or a hyerempiric induction has been administered, one may proceed as follows:

As a result of what I am telling you now, your awareness of the passage of time is going to be changed, so that the days (or hours) will just seem to be flying past, and you are going to be pleasantly surprised at how swiftly they have gone. You will be able to carry out all of your routine activities in the usual manner, for this will have no effect on the speed with which you do things; but just as a few minutes can seem like an hour at times, and an hour seem like only a few minutes, your perception of the passage of time is being changed now, so that every minute that passes is going to seem much, much shorter than it actually is.

As with other techniques, it may be necessary to repeat the foregoing suggestions at appropriate intervals (or to teach the subject to do so by means of autosuggestion) for them to remain effective for the desired length of time. But it should also be made clear to the subject that these suggestions are only intended to be effective for a limited period of time. This can most easily be accomplished by adding the following sentence each time the suggestions are administered, whether by the subject himself or by another:

These suggestions will be effective only until————, at which time your normal sense of the passage of time will be fully restored.

Suggestions for time condensation may also be used in conjunction with suggestions for emotional enrichment as a means of counteracting unpleasant or negative affect by directly suggesting the opposite sensations (Sacerdote, 1977).

PHOBIC REACTIONS

A student once requested that I hypnotize her to alleviate her recurring nightmares about snakes, which would inevitably awaken her, leaving her terrified after each occurrence. Although the possible sexual symbolism was immediately obvious, I replied, in a more general fashion, that since she was not merely afraid when she *saw* a snake, it seemed as if the fear were somehow pursuing her.

"Yes," she replied, "and lately I've become afraid to use a public rest room for fear of being bitten by a snake." To see what else she might initially have to say, I confined my response to a restatement of my previous comment. Nodding in agreement, she added without prompting, "And now it's turning into a fear of sex."

At this point, I told her gently that I would like to suggest the possibility that she had been afraid of sex all along, and that she had previously displaced it to snakes as a means of symbolically disguising it to avoid having to confront her fear directly. I then suggested that she would probably wish to seek therapy to get the matter resolved. The probable reason for her emerging awareness of the true nature of her fear, and perhaps the reason why her nightmares had been bothering her so much of late, was evident in her reply, "Well, I'll have to—I'm engaged!"

Phobic reactions may serve an instrumental as well as a symbolic function. Dollard and Miller (1950) report a case in which a woman patient was unable to venture downtown in the city in which she lived without being overcome by sudden feelings of anxiety. She was physically very attractive, and before her marriage she had developed a pattern of frequent and casual sexual encounters which she was strongly tempted to resume. To protect herself from the realization of just how intensely she desired to return to her former life-style, in spite of the fact that she deeply loved her husband, she did not admit to herself that the problem even existed; but whenever she found herself downtown, her anxiety began to surface, for it was here that the chances of such an encounter were the greatest. Her anxiety was further reinforced since it caused her to withdraw from the situation, thereby escaping temptation without even having to think about what was really bothering her.

Most phobic reactions, of course, are the result of direct experience with the object or situation concerned. A high school student of my acquaintance who was involved in a serious automobile accident developed such a strong fear of automobiles that he was no longer able to drive. The therapeutic approach which was chosen to alleviate his anxiety was systematic desensitization, based on the principles of classical conditioning (Wolpe, 1961). The patient was first requested to construct a list of several situations related to automobile driving which he feared, and to rank them in order, from the one which was least disturbing to the one which caused him the greatest amount of discomfort. He was then taught deep muscle relaxation and asked to visualize each of these scenes, in turn, while remaining deeply relaxed, beginning with the situation which was the least stressful and gradually working his way up the list. When this is done with sufficient care and patience, the strong feelings of relaxation can be expected to overcome gradually the weak feelings of anxiety brought about by merely imagining oneself to be in the situation at the bottom of the list; and with practice, this result can be expected to generalize to the actual situation, as well as to similar situations further up in the hierarchy. Thus, by starting at the bottom of the list and gradually working one's way to the top, the entire problem should eventually be eliminated. In the present instance, the student had resumed his normal driving routine at the end of one week of such training, and reported no further discomfort.

Systematic desensitization may easily be adapted for use within a trance induction format (Gibbons, Kilbourne, Saunders, & Castles, 1970; Gibbons, 1971), as a means of alleviating phobic responses which are not due to unconscious symbolic substitutions or emotional displacements, and which are not primarily instrumental in the satisfaction of other needs. As an illustration of the manner in which this may be accomplished, the following suggestions are designed to alleviate a fear of flying which is simply the result of inappropriate past experience, or lack of appropriate experience, with flying itself:

First of all, I want you to make yourself quite comfortable and relaxed; and when you are feeling thoroughly peaceful, and completely comfortable in every way, you can signal me by raising the index finger of your right (or left) hand. So just let yourself relax completely now, and soon your finger will rise.

After the subject has responded:

That's fine. Just continue to relax even deeper now; and with every word that I utter, you will find yourself able to follow my suggestions more easily. Just let your imagination drift along with my words, and let yourself flow with the experience I describe, and soon you will be able to feel everything I suggest to you, just as if it were really happening.

Now, as you continue to relax more and more, I want you to picture yourself at home, getting ready to go to the airport. But the relaxation you are feeling now will remain with you, and if you should happen to feel any tension later on, you can just raise your index finger again, and I will take you back to an earlier part of the trip and we can proceed more slowly. So just picture yourself here at home, feeling very relaxed as you begin to pack and to make all the other preparations for your trip. And as you do, just notice how relaxed you are, and how calm you have become.

Now you are taking your luggage out to the car and putting it into the trunk. And now you are getting into the car, ready to go to the airport, and still feeling perfectly calm. All the details of the trip have been taken care of up to this point, and you can just relax and enjoy the drive.

You will be able to answer yes or no to my questions by shaking your head in the appropriate manner. You are still feeling very calm and relaxed now, aren't you?

Pause. If answer is yes:

That's fine. Now we can proceed. And if you should happen to feel any anxiety at any time, you can just signal me by raising your index finger, and we can go back to an earlier stage in your journey and let you relax a little more deeply before going on. But I doubt that you will need to do this, because you are still feeling so very deeply relaxed and calm.

Now you are pulling up to the airport and getting out of your car in order to give your luggage to an attendant who will see that it is checked onto your flight. You get back into your car and proceed to the parking area. You park your car and calmly stroll into the waiting room, feeling perfectly calm every step of the way. Now you are waiting in line at the ticket counter, picking up your ticket, looking at it, and now you are walking to the gate where you are to board your flight.

On the way to the gate, you pass a newsstand, where you notice a paperback book which looks extremely interesting. You stop a moment to purchase the book to take along with you on your flight. Now, still deeply relaxed, you are going through the security check on the way to the gate. You remain deeply relaxed as you think about the book you have just purchased, and about how interesting it appears to be.

Now you have completed the security check and you are approaching the gate. You give your ticket to the attendant, who stamps it and gives you your seat number. You take a seat in the waiting area and begin to thumb through the book, becoming more and more interested in it with each passing second. It looks like it is going to be one of the most interesting books you have ever read.

As your flight is called, you rise from your chair and prepare to board the plane along with the other passengers, still feeling very deeply relaxed and thinking about the fascinating book you have just started to read.

Now you enter the plane and make your way to your seat, still feeling perfectly calm and relaxed. You sit down and fasten your seat belt and open the book once more, quickly becoming so absorbed in your reading that you scarecely notice the takeoff.

You interrupt your reading long enough to enjoy the meal which is brought to you, and you are pleased to discover how good everything tastes. You are still deeply relaxed and you enjoy your meal thoroughly before returning to your book.

So absorbed in your book have you become once again that you are surprised to discover that the plane has landed and is taxiing up to the ramp.

You leave the plane, feeling relaxed and happy. You have had a very enjoyable flight, and you have remained perfectly calm during the entire trip. And now that you have seen how pleasant flying can actually be, you know that whenever you fly again in the future, you will have a similar relaxing and enjoyable experience in store for you.

RELAXATION TRAINING

In response to a physical emergency, the human organism will respond almost instantly with a number of changes which are often collectively referred to as *fight-or-flight* reaction, preparing an individual either to fight for his life or to run away (Cannon, 1929). But a perceived threat to one's cherished values and goals may be just as much of a threat to his "existence," as he has come to define it, as is a threat to his physical survival (Lecky, 1945; Rogers, 1961). Under the countless day-to-day pressures of modern life, the body is often flooded with messages of alarm which would be entirely appropriate in dealing with a physical emergency such as an encounter with a bear in the woods, but are of little value in coping with "psychological" emergencies such as an impending loss of status related to the loss of one's job.

When such stress situations are frequent or prolonged, the body eventually begins to lose its adaptive capacity and a host of functional ailments may develop (Selye, 1956). Because psychological stress patterns occur so frequently in this culture, it is often useful to learn ways of consciously countermanding the virtually constant pattern of alarm signals which are thereby transmitted to the body. The following suggestions may be employed after an appropriate induction, either by themselves or in conjunction with suggestions for specific stress-related difficulties such as migraine or insomnia:

Now I would like you to visualize yourself seated before a control panel which has one large dial. Continue to hold the image in your mind as I describe it, and soon you will be able to experience the scene just as if you were really there. The dial can be turned to any setting from zero to ten, representing all the various levels of tension and relaxation which your body is able to experience, with the number zero standing for all the relaxation it is possible for you to feel and the number ten representing as much tension as your body is able to experience at one time.

Now you can begin to look closely at this dial which monitors and controls the level of tension in your body. See what the dial reading is now on the scale from zero to ten, and see yourself reaching over to turn it down. See yourself turning the dial down ever so slowly, down and down, just a little bit at a time, and feel your body relaxing more and more as you do.

Feel the tension in your body lessening more and more as you turn the dial all the way down. Turning the dial all the way down to zero, as all the tension in your body ebbs away. Soon the dial will be turned all the way down to zero, and your entire body will be just as relaxed as it can possibly be. And all your previous tension will be replaced by peaceful feelings of total relaxation, tranquility, and calm.

Now the dial is all the way down to zero. Now your entire body is completely relaxed and free of tension. It's as if all the tension and all the worry and all the care that you have ever felt have been driven out by soothing currents of peace and tranquility and relaxation. And you can feel these currents gently coursing through every muscle and every nerve and every fiber of your being.

And from now on, you will be able to relax just like this whenever you wish, merely by sitting or lying down and closing your eyes for a few moments while you visualize yourself turning down the dial on this control panel, just as I have shown you.

And as a result of this new ability to relax whenever you wish, you will be able to rest better at night and to sleep more soundly, awakening each morning completely refreshed and ready for each new day. You will be able to work more efficiently, without being bothered by people or situations which might otherwise tend to upset or annoy you. And you will be able to derive a great deal more enjoyment out of leisure time activities, because you will be so much more able to relax and just let go.

Rest, work, and leisure, every aspect of your life will be considerably improved and enriched by your new ability to relax whenever you wish, and you are going to be absolutely delighted at the results.

And the more you practice this new ability, the more deeply and the more easily you will be able to relax, and the longer these feelings of relaxation will remain with you.

The following palliative suggestions may be included to provide relief from minor situational tensions and anxieties which are not the result of some underlying neurotic conflict and which do not require additional therapeutic measures:

Whenever you should find yourself in need of an additional measure of reassurance, you will only have to close your eyes for an instant and silently think to yourself the word *calm*; and this action will serve as a stimulus which will release from the depths of your being a great wave of steadiness, confidence, peace, and relaxation which will be more than adequate for all your momentary needs.

Often an inability to relax is the result of a lifelong tendency to reproach oneself for real or imagined previous failures—a tendency which must also be corrected if the relaxation training is to be effective. From both the learning theory and the psychoanalytic points of view, children learn to reward and punish themselves as a means of keeping their own behavior on an even keel and thereby getting more of the "good" things of life—such as a little extra dessert at dinnertime, or a visit from Santa Claus at Christmas—and also as a way of avoiding the undesirable consequences of their misbehavior, such as a spanking or a scolding from parents. Indeed, such training in self-control is at the very core of the socialization process; and those who fail to receive an adequate amount of such training are often labeled as *sociopaths* or *psychopathic deviates*. If this training is too prolonged or too severe, on the other hand, a person may develop an intropunitive life style, in which he habitually tends to blame himself for everything that goes wrong, regardless of whether or not he is at fault. Such an individual often spends a great deal of time feeling guilty, depressed, and anxious over his inability to live up to standards and ideals that are probably much too high to begin with (Coleman, 1976).

The basis of such an intropunitive orientation is often rooted in the tendency of many middle-class parents to rely on the withdrawal of love as a means of hastening the socializaton process. If a young child spills his oatmeal, for example, his mother's angry words and stern expression assail his ears until the child begins to cry and sincerely promises never to make that mistake again. Whatever the mother herself may believe, the emotional import of such a procedure tends to communicate to the child that his mother no longer loves him, and that sincere repentance on his part constitutes his only hope for regaining her lost affection. Parents who rely too heavily on such methods may become very adept at instilling excessive amounts of guilt and anxiety in their offspring—eventually, with as little as a glance or a sudden silence.

A large proportion of the problems with which many counselors, ministers, and physicians are routinely confronted may thus involve an excess amount of intropunitive fear and guilt. When these responses have become habitual, direct suggestion may be of considerable help in bringing about the necessary readjustments, particularly when it is combined with counseling aimed at helping the subject to develop more realistic goal expectations and more positive feelings of self-worth. Of course, one should not attempt to remove *all* potential for experiencing guilt; for it is only the excess which may cause a person to encounter difficulties; and some capacity for self-reproach is probably essential if he is to retain sufficient concern for behaving ethically in regard to others. There is certainly nothing to be gained in terms of net adjustment from turning a neurotic into a sociopath.

The following postinduction suggestions are based on a similar technique which involves the imagery of releasing a red balloon to carry one's excess feelings of guilt away, as first related by Walch (1976):

The guilt which you have been carrying around with you for whatever you may have done, or neglected to do, in the past, is like borrowing from a miser—you pay and pay, and because the rate of interest is too high to start with, you never seem to be able to get out of debt. You just go on paying and paying, long after the actual debt has been paid off.

I'm going to help you get rid of this extra burden of guilt now; for the real debt of guilt that you may have incurred in the past—if you ever had any real debt to begin with—has already been paid off long ago.

Just picture yourself standing before an open fireplace, where a cheerful log fire is burning brightly, as you continue listening to my voice. Continue to picture the scene in your mind, exactly as I describe it, and continue to listen to my words, and soon you will be able to experience the situation just as if you were really there.

Over to one side, lying in a pile on a small table, are all of the extra payments of remorse, grief, self-doubt and depression which you have felt required to make because the interest on your debt of guilt has been so excessive, and because you have tended to demand more of yourself than is really necessary to meet life's obligations. You know that these extra payments have all been unnecessary; for anything you might ever have owed on these debts of guilt has been paid off long ago.

See yourself picking up these unnecessary charges now and dropping them into the flames one by one. See them slowly being turned to ashes; and feel how great a relief it is as you watch them being consumed in the flames, until all that remains of these false and unnecessary burdens are the ashes themselves, as the final, smoldering evidence that they are gone, and that they will never bother you again.

SELF-REINFORCEMENT

In the taking up of a new bahavior or the leaving off of an old one, the most important thing to remember is to *be kind to oneself*. If the change is sufficiently satisfying to begin with, very little in the way of deliberate effort or resolution is necessary to bring it about. But in many instances in which the benefits of altering one's customary pattern of conduct lie in the future rather than in the immediate present, any change in one's current habits is experienced as entailing extra work. The more distant the rewards, and the more one has to sacrifice in the present to attain them, the more it seems necessary to push oneself to do the work instead of being free to push the work alone. In such a situation, unless one is both willing and able to teach oneself to *like* the new pattern, the chances are that one is sooner or later going to give it up (Deibert & Harmon, 1977; Schmidt, 1976).

There are, of course, many ways to learn to like a new habit, or at least to make it less unpleasant. An acquaintance of mine who achieved top honors in graduate school bought an elaborately de-signed adjustable easy chair several months before he was scheduled to take his comprehensive doctoral examinations. He would study for several hours each night, deeply relaxed in his *comps chair*, as he called it; and to strengthen further the association between relaxation and studying, he was careful *not* to study in any other place, and not to do anything else but study while he was actually sitting in the chair. In similar fashion, many people have found that dieting is no longer much of a problem if they are able to afford an evening menu which is frequently centered around a well-trimmed broiled steak; and those for whom balancing a checkbook was once a virtual impossibility have frequently been surprised at how easy this has become after purchas-ing a small electronic calculator which has allowed them to convert this task from an onerous chore into a game.

In addition to altering the environment as a method of altering one's behavior, much of the incentive for change can come from what one *tells* oneself about the new course of action. If a person believes that the change is really worthwhile, he may allow himself to "feel good" about it, even in the absence of external rewards. On the other hand, if a person is merely in the habit of telling himself that he *ought* to do something, but figuratively "beats himself over the head" with the task as he goes about it and then neglects to enjoy having finished, he may soon be disappointed at his apparent "lack of resolution" as he finds himself drifting back into the old ways (Lee, 1978).

The following suggestions are designed to assist an individual in developing a greater capacity for self-reinforcement so that he will be less dependent on external sources of reward—and hence, better able to determine the course of his own conduct. Of course, numerous concrete applications are possible:

Now I would like to help you to experience the feelings of satisfaction and achievement which come with the attainment of an important goal, so that you can learn to practice and strengthen these feelings and apply them to the attainment of other goals in your life. First of all, I would like you to think of a time in the past when you had just achieved something that was very important to you—something that gave you a strong sense of pride and accomplishment, and meant a great deal to you at the time. It may have been graduation from high school, or the day you got your first driver's license, or almost anything else you can think of, as long as it was something you really felt good about when it happened. Take your time, and as soon as you have thought of a situation which fits this description, you can signal me by raising the index finger of your right (or left) hand.

After the subject has responded:

All right. Now let yourself get in touch with the feelings of achievement and satisfaction which you were feeling when you were actually in that situation. Let yourself go back and experience those feelings once more, and feel them growing even stronger as I speak. Growing and growing, and becoming clearer and stronger and more intense with every passing second. And all the time I am speaking to you, until the trance is over, these feelings are going to continue growing stronger by themselves.

And when the trance is ended, your normal, everyday mood will return. And of course, you will have no need to balance things out by feeling bad, just because you have been allowing yourself to feel so good. But because you have been able to recapture and to strengthen these feelings of pride and accomplishment, and the sense of deep personal satisfaction that goes with them, it will be much easier for you to feel good in the future over all the things you do that you ought to feel good about, and to give yourself a pat on the back whenever you have it coming.

SEXUAL DYSFUNCTION

A student once requested that I hypnotize him because he could not remember anything that had happened during his sixteenth year. He was becoming more and more preoccupied over this inability to recall, and he wished to use hypnosis as an aid in overcoming this amnesia. I pointed out to him that his difficulty in remembering might be because of unpleasant events which could have occurred during the period in question, and which he was not ready to deal with at the time. I then mentioned that his increased concern over his inability to remember might be taken as a possible indication that he was ready to come to grips with whatever had transpired, and I asked him if he was willing to try. He readily agreed.

To shield the subject from the possible deleterious effects of too sudden and too direct a confrontation with whatever information might emerge, when the induction was completed I first attempted to use the television screen technique as described on page 91. Although the subject reported that he was able to visualize the screen quite clearly, it remained blank.

I then suggested that the subject would continue to feel stronger and better able to cope with both the present and the past; and that as he did so he would begin to have a series of nocturnal dreams pertaining to the memories he was trying to recall. I suggested that these dreams would gradually provide him with the information he sought, but only as fast as he was ready to deal with it effectively. The dreams were never to reveal so much information that they would constitute a source of increased anxiety; but rather, they would provide him with reassurance and relief as the memories returned at a rate which matched his increasing capacity to deal with them. I asked the subject to remain in close contact with me for a while and to let me know as soon as the dreams had begun.

Three days later, the subject returned and recounted the following dream from the previous night: "I was driving a Jaguar XK-7 along a dirt road which kept getting narrower and narrower, until finally it became stuck in a big mudhole and I could not pull it out. The next thing I knew, I was back in my father's garage, working on the car in order to get it back in shape. There were some tools and parts lying on a workbench behind me, and when I turned around to get them they were gone. I knew that my father had taken them, and I was very mad about it. I went out and found my brother, and grabbed him by the sleeve, saying, 'We've got to do something about this!' "

The subject also said that he could now remember two especially trying events which had occurred during his sixteenth year; and with the recall of these two events, his memories of the remainder of the year had apparently been restored also. It was during this period, he now recalled, that he had been molested by a priest; and it was also during this interval that he had had his first heterosexual experiences, which had caused him a great deal of guilt because he was not emotionally attached to the girl and had been dating her primarily because of her physical attractiveness.

The phallic symbolism in the first part of the dream, and the "father who had been taking his parts" described in the second portion, were likely symbolic expressions of the subject's concern over the two events just described, and the ambivalence in his own sexual orientation which they may have exacerbated. Although the subject denied experiencing any sexual difficulties at the time he came to see me, he admitted some two years later that he had been unable to maintain an erection long enough to experience a climax or to satisfy his partner; but after his recalling the two experiences from his sixteenth year, this difficulty was eliminated. In retrospect, it is likely that his impotence constituted a defense against (and possibly also a simultaneous expression of) latent homosexual tendencies which had been intensified by the advances of the priest and the subject's own guilt over his first heterosexual experience. With the emergence of later heterosexual emotional ties, the earlier events had become less threatening; and the subject himself had initiated attempts to recover and to deal with the "forgotten" information.

Of course, not every sexual problem necessarily requires an approach based on the recovery of repressed memories of traumatic events, accompanied if necessary by abreaction and catharsis and followed by the development of realistic insights into the underlying causes of one's difficulty. Previous failures to satisfy one's partner, or less than fully satisfying experiences on one's own part, though less than traumatic in themselves, may generate expectations of poor performance in the future, which operate in much the same manner as negative suggestions to bring about just such a result.

Negative expectations of this type can often be reversed by means of direct suggestion. One particularly effective method for administering such suggestions, first originated by Erickson (1954), is as follows. At the conclusion of an induction, a crystal gazing technique is employed as described on pages 91–92. When the subject indicates that he can clearly visualize the crystal ball, he is told:

Now, as you continue to watch the crystal ball, you are gradually going to be able to see an image appear within it of yourself at some time in the near future, making love extremely well. I will not ask you to describe the scene;

but as you continue to gaze into the crystal ball, you can see that both you and your partner are going to be fully and completely satisfied. And now, as this is occurring, the scene is beginning to fade, and the crystal ball is fading away too. And even though you will not be able to recall the memory of the crystal ball when the trance is over, you will still be aware that you are irresistably headed for certain success; and that your future sexual experiences will be just as pleasurable, and just as enjoyable, as you have already seen that they will be in the crystal ball.

Amnesia for the specific details of the experience is suggested so that factual discrepancies between the details of the visualized scene and the actual experience, when it does take place, will not negate the validity of the positive expectations engendered by this procedure.

Since women are generally slower than men to achieve their initial climax, and since more women than men are capable of routinely experiencing multiple orgasms, the ability of the male to delay his own climax and maintain an erection until his partner has been fully satisfied often requires a great deal of restraint on his part. Many men, especially those with relatively less experience, find it virtually impossible to delay a climax when exposed to intense sexual stimulation for more than a few moments, particularly under conditions of relative deprivation (Richardson, 1978).

As Richardson also points out, the prospect of being unable to fully satisfy one's partner may constitute such a threat to some males they they may occasionally find it difficult to develop an erection sufficient to begin or maintain coitus. The following suggestions are aimed at reestablishing the subject's confidence when the problem is essentially one of developing the necessary control:

Please extend the index finger of your right (or left) hand straight out in the air in front of you. That's fine. Now, as I continue to speak, you will soon notice that your index finger is becoming very stiff and very rigid. And as it does, you will also find that you are completely losing all feeling in it. Soon your index finger will be just as stiff and just as numb as a bar of iron. It's becoming just as rigid and just as numb as an iron bar now. Your index finger is just as rigid as a bar of iron, and just as insensitive.

Now please clench your jaw firmly, three times in a row. And as you do, you notice that feeling is returning to your finger, even though it continues to be stiff and rigid. The feeling is returning completely now; and even though your finger remains as rigid as before, the feeling in it is entirely normal once again.

And now, in order to make the stiffness go away, all you have to do is to decide that you are ready for it to do so. And notice as you do that your finger has become completely flexible once again. Just bend it a couple of times to assure yourself of this fact, and then go ahead and put it down.

From now on, each time you are ready to have intercourse, you will find that at the proper time your penis has become just as stiff and just as rigid as your index finger was a moment ago. And it will also be just as numb, as stiff and as numb as a bar of iron.

You will be able to maintain your erection and prolong intercourse for as long as necessary to fully satisfy your partner. And when you are ready for normal feeling to return, you will only need to clench your jaw firmly three quick times in a row for this to happen. But even after your sensitivity does come back, you will still be able to maintain your erection as long as necessary so as to achieve your own orgasm.

Additional sessions may be necessary until the subject has achieved the necessary control. When this has been accomplished, subsequent suggestions should emphasize retaining progressively more feeling in the penis until the subject has clenched his jaw three times, allowing more and more restraint to be developed, until finally such suggestions are no longer necessary.

When one has remained with the same partner for an extended period, normal cues for arousal may also tend to extinguish, in spite of the fact that affectional ties remain strong. Such a predicament may at times be corrected fairly easily by means of suggestions such as the following:

Sometime during the next few nights, when you are asleep in bed with your partner, you are going to have a pleasant dream which you will find sexually very stimulating. The dream will be formed out of images and sensations which you find especially pleasant and arousing at the time, and you will be so excited by them that you will awaken even before the dream is completely over, fully aroused and ready to make love.

The arousing effects of the dream will persist for some time after you wake up. They will add new dimensions of richness and pleasure to your lovemaking, and they will enable you and your partner to discover new avenues of pleasure, and new channels of communication, which will deepen your relationship considerably.

You will be particularly pleased to find that your orgasm will be unusually profound and satisfying, and it will seem to last much longer than it usually does.

And you will continue to have dreams of this sort at appropriate intervals in the future, which will continue to enrich and deepen your relationship in just the same manner.

Inability to initiate and maintain coitus may also be symptomatic of a more general feeling of helplessness and impotence with regard to life, in general, as part of an overall pattern involving a poor self-image and an inability to achieve. This is particularly apt to be the case when the patient is an alcoholic or shows other evidence of general maladjustment (Richardson, 1978).

The various projective techniques described in Chapter 4 may be especially useful in identifying the underlying causes of a sexual difficulty, whether they may result from an unconscious identification of the partner with one's mother, a desire to punish the partner (or perhaps oneself) for previous infidelities (Araoz, 1978), early lectures on the evils of masturbation, latent homosexual tendencies, or a host of other possibilities. Specific suggestions for relaxation training, alleviating phobic reactions, ego strengthening, and emotional enrichment may also be employed as part of an overall corrective approach.

Finally, it is also necessary to point out what is sometimes perceived as a sexual problem may not be a sexual problem at all, but merely the result of lack of appropriate information. Sexual desire is probably normally distributed in the general population, after taking age into account; yet the media-fed emphasis on sexuality may frequently lead one to feel that he or she is both personally and sexually inadequate unless a high level of sexual activity is maintained throughout one's adult life. As is frequently the case in other situations in which individual behavior may be at variance with the prevailing cultural ideal, what may actually be needed is not professional assistance, but merely for the therapist or some other authority figure to provide the necessary reassurance to the subject that "It's all right to go on being *you*" (Levitt, 1978).

SMOKING

As with other forms of drug addiction, the temptation to resume smoking is the greatest during the period of withdrawal, immediately after the habit has been discontinued. Specific suggestions to the effect that the smoker's craving will diminish are particularly helpful during this period of initial abstinence, as is the timely use of such dissociative autosuggestions as, "I am *not* this body," or, "Don't feel sorry for yourself." But long after the last traces of nicotine have vanished from the bloodstream and all the necessary physiological readjustments have been completed, the smoker may still find himself tempted to return to his former habit if abstinence is experienced as less satisfying than smoking was—which is often the case, at least intermittently. Thus, the inclusion of self-reinforcement techniques is particularly useful as a means of assuring that the suggested abstinence is more likely to remain.

After a hypnotic or a hyperempiric induction has been administered and the previously presented suggestions for self-reinforcement have been given, one may proceed as follows:

And when the trance is over, you are going to continue to feel just as good as you do now, over the fact that you have stopped smoking. Your normal, everyday mood will return, but it will be a source of deep personal satisfaction to you that you have been able to stop smoking. You are beginning to realize that the reason you feel so good right now is because you have decided to quit, and in the future, you are going to continue to feel just this good, whenever you think about the fact that you *have* quit.

Your desire to smoke will vanish completely, for it will be driven out by the strong feelings of pride and accomplishment which you are experiencing now, and which you will continue to feel whenever you think about the fact that you have quit. The smell and taste of tobacco will no longer be appealing to you, and the situations which used to tempt you to smoke will no longer awaken an urge to smoke within you. It will be a special source of deep personal satisfaction to you whenever you refuse an opportunity to smoke. And because you feel so good about the fact that you have stopped smoking, you will not experience any sense of frustration or deprivation over having done so, and you will have no need to turn to any substitute activity.

As time continues to pass, your feelings of satisfaction over the fact that you have quit will continue to grow even stronger, for you will continue to find new reasons to be glad that you have stopped, and you will continue to find new reasons for not wanting to start again.

THUMB SUCKING

Thumb sucking may generally be considered as a habit which is similar to nail biting, in that it is an essentially minor annoyance which is reinforced by immediate sensory gratification—perhaps providing an outlet for insufficiently satisfied sucking needs—and which tends to disappear in time if little attention is paid to it and the child is provided with a sufficient amount of emotional security and freedom from stress

(Hartland, 1971b). Like nail biting, thumb sucking may be learned as a means of gaining extra attention, or it may serve a passive-aggressive function which provides the child with an opportunity to annoy his parents in return for real or imagined offenses on their part. It may begin or intensify during periods of heightened emotional tension, such as after parental separation or the birth of a sibling; and thus, it may betray the existence of other difficulties which may be more in need of attention than is the thumb sucking itself. Regardless of its etiology, punishment for thumb sucking is generally considered to be counterproductive (Cheek & LeCron, 1968); and in extreme cases, punishment may even serve to fixate the response so that it becomes even more resistant to change. In fact, thumb sucking which persists well beyond the age at which such behavior is normally discontinued may occasionally be rooted in childhood trauma (Morban-Lancer, 1961).

When thumb sucking is primarily because of habit, and there is no evidence of underlying emotional difficulties, the parents may be asked simply to ignore the behavior when it occurs, taking care to provide the child with sufficient attention and affection at other times. Abandonment of the habit is likely to be facilitated by postinduction suggestions such as the following, which are similar to the approach recommended by Crasilneck and Hall (1975):

> You are going to suck your thumb less and less from now on, because you just won't feel like it as much as you used to. And if you do suck your thumb at all, you are going to suddenly start to notice how *bad* it tastes.
> If you do suck your thumb any more, this bad taste is going to get worse and worse as time goes on. And soon it is going to taste *so* bad that, if you still feel like sucking a finger, you are going to have to stop sucking your thumb and start sucking one of your other fingers instead.
> But when you do, you are going to find that the other finger soon begins to taste bad, too. And all the time your desire to suck any of your fingers is going to keep on getting weaker and weaker. And soon you are going to have to give up sucking any of your fingers because they will all start to taste bad, and the bad taste is going to be so awful that you just won't want to put any of your fingers in your mouth anymore.

WEIGHT CONTROL

When a person who is overweight decides to go on a diet, whether or not a satisfactory outcome will be achieved depends not only on his ability to follow through with his reducing plan, but also on the reasons for his being overweight in the first place. Among the possible physiological causes of obesity are edema, or the tendency to retain an excess amount of body fluids, deficiency in thyroid functioning, heredity tendencies toward a stocky physique, and weight gain which is associated with the onset of certain diseases such as diabetes. Overfeeding during specific periods in infancy and childhood may also be a contributing factor, as such a practice may lead to the production of an excess number of fat cells in the body, thereby resulting in a lifelong tendency to lose weight only with difficulty and to gain it back again with relative ease (Nisbett, 1972).

Of course, the most common cause of a person's being overweight is poor eating habits which result in the intake of more calories than he expends in activity. People who were physically active in adolescence, and people whose parents may have constantly urged them to "clean their plate" at every meal when they were children, may be especially prone to develop "middle-aged spread" as they become more sedentary in later life (Kroger, 1977). In some instances, however, the whole matter can be entirely illusory, as in the commonly encountered example of the well-endowed girl who may feel that she is "overweight" because she is not as slender as most of the models whose photographs appear in fashion advertisements. "You can never be too rich or too thin," the saying goes—and some of us are inclined to believe it.

A person may also tend to overeat as a reaction to stress. The practice may serve as a means of diverting one's attention from other problems, or as a source of consolation when one is lonely, bored, or tired. In some families, food may be customarily employed as a means of expressing affection; and thus, the person who is in need of solace, if he was raised in such a family, may be inclined to turn again to food in order to find it as an adult. Overeating may also serve as an outlet for frustrated sexual tensions, or as a means of protecting oneself from the possibility of romantic or emotional involvements which one has unconsciously come to fear. Some husbands may subtly encourage their spouses to overeat because they are afraid of losing them to other men if they should remain slender and attractive. It is even possible that being overweight may possess some bizarre symbolic significance for the individual concerned, as in the case reported by Lindner (1976) of a psychotic, middle-aged spinster for whom being overweight symbolized being pregnant.

Finally, it should also be pointed out that any behavior which is immediately enjoyable is difficult to abandon once it has become a firmly entrenched habit, regardless of the fact that it may be unpleasant or even damaging in its long-term consequences. Some modification of the concept of self may also be necessary for a person who has long been overweight to accept the possibility that he, too, can be thin and attractive to others.

The following suggestions are intended for use in the large number of instances wherein it has been determined that the primary cause of a person's being overweight is simply a habitual preference for too many high-calorie foods. However, a word of caution is in order. Many people tend to be either diabetic or hypoglycemic, or to have various vitamin and mineral deficiencies, without being aware of the fact. Before this or any other approach to weight control is employed, the subject should have a complete physical checkup, with an adequate diet prescribed by a physician. Because of the high caloric content of most alcoholic drinks, the person's drinking habits should also be examined.

After a hypnotic or a hyperempiric induction procedure has been administered and the previously presented suggestions for self-reinforcement have been given, the following suggestions may be administered:

When the trance is over, you are going to continue to feel just as good as you are feeling now over the fact that you are following your diet. Your normal, everyday mood will return, but when you think about the fact that you are following your diet, just as you want to, you will feel very, very good about it, just as good as you are feeling now. And it will be a source of deep personal satisfaction to you that you are continuing on your diet.

As you do continue, you will also be happy to find that you are eating a bit more slowly than you normally have in the past. And because this enables you to enjoy eating smaller amounts of food just as much as if you were eating more, and to begin to feel full before you have eaten as much as you are accustomed to eating, you will find yourself taking smaller helpings and fewer second helpings than you normally would.

Even though you still eat as much as you are supposed to, you will not want to eat any more than that. You may even find yourself leaving a little food on your plate at the end of a meal, without feeling at all guilty about doing so, because you will only be eating as much as your diet prescribes. And the only time you will want to eat anything between meals is about half an hour before a regularly scheduled mealtime, when you might occasionally want to take *just a bite* of something sweet to take the edge off your appetite when the meal is served.

Your taste preferences are going to change a great deal also, for even though you continue to eat the balanced selections called for in your diet, you are going to find that you are no longer even attracted to the high-calorie foods which you have previously liked. And if you ever should be tempted to eat something now and then that you know you are not supposed to have, all you will need to do is to picture it in your mind, covered with the most awful thing you can think of, and the craving will immediately disappear.

Low-calorie foods, on the other hand, are going to become a lot tastier to you than they have ever been, and you are going to be pleasantly surprised at how much more you are going to enjoy them.

And as time goes on, you are going to continue to find other reasons of your own to be glad that you are staying on your diet, as you follow these suggestions and observe the results. You will not be discouraged by any temporary setbacks which may occur; for you will continue to look forward eagerly and confidently to all the satisfactions which will be yours when your ideal weight is attained, and you will spend a great deal of time thinking and daydreaming about how much fun it is going to be. For the contnuing loss of weight which all these changes produce will be a source of great and continuing fulfillment to you as you gradually approach, and finally attain, the weight which you have selected as your goal.

Many dieters have tried several approaches before, but to no avail; and they may turn to trance induction as a last resort, perhaps unconsciously hoping for some sort of "magic spell" which will do for them what they have been unable to do for themselves. Thus, it is usually important to stress the fact that a great deal of effort and cooperation will be required which only the subject can provide: that while you may be able to draw them a road map which shows them how to get to their eventual destination, it is they who must make the journey.

Repeated inductions, at the rate of one or two a week, may be useful in helping the subject to bridge the gap between his present and his desired weight. During this period, it is not only the suggestions themselves, but also the personal relationship and encouragement provided by the suggestor, which may contribute a great deal toward bringing about the desired improvement. Such social facilitation may be further augmented by working simultaneously with several individuals in a group setting if the subject appears to respond appropriately to the initial induction.

Specific habit patterns which provide unusually strong temptations to deviate from the requirements of the subject's diet may also have to be modified or abandoned. Some people have developed such a strong association between snacking and watching television, for example, that it may be necessary to reduce the time spent in front of the television set as the easiest way of eliminating this snacking behavior until the new dietary pattern has been firmly established. If necessary, this may be accomplished by posttrance suggestions that television will begin to lose much of its customary interest and appeal for a while. By the same token, since food consumption is so frequently the center of informal social activity in this culture, it may be necessary to discuss with the subject the possibility of a need to modify such customary patterns of social interaction. One student who recently came to me with a request that she be hyptonized because she was unable to lose weight in spite of the fact that she had "tried everything," was in the habit of holding nightly sessions with her friends in her dormitory room, during which time she would invariably consume vast quantities of popcorn drenched with butter.

Whether or not the desired weight loss will be maintained once it has been achieved depends primarily on the availability of appropriate environmental incentives after the use of trance suggestion has been discontinued; and some time should be devoted to identifying these incentives in advance and utilizing them in an appropriate manner to facilitate and maintain the desired improvement. For instance, a woman who has begun to make satisfactory progress on her diet, but who seems to be in some danger of backsliding, may be encouraged to purchase an especially attractive article of clothing which is slightly smaller than she can comfortably wear at present. Whenever she is tempted to abandon her diet, she may be encouraged to look at the coveted apparel, and to imagine herself wearing it, as an incentive to continue (Kroger, 1977). The subject herself should be able to tell with a good deal of accuracy whether or not such an incentive will be effective in enabling her to continue dieting to the point where the new apparel can actually be worn, rather than being simply a waste of money.

It may also be helpful to encourage a change in the subject's social or recreation habits, such as joining a sports group or a dancing class, to provide an outlet for any feelings of increased loneliness or isolation which may be attendant on no longer indulging oneself with food, while at the same time providing enhanced opportunities for the development of new friendships and/or romantic attachments which may strengthen the subject's desire to adhere to a proper diet.

It should be noted, however, that because of the large number of factors which may result in a person perceiving himself as overweight, some of which may be completely beyond his control—as is the case when one simply happens to have inherited a stocky physique—sometimes it may be more appropriate to encourage the subject to select a smaller weight loss as his ultimate goal, or even to come to like and accept himself as he is.

PART THREE

SUGGESTION AS AN INSTRUMENT OF PERSONAL GROWTH

Your old men shall dream dreams
Your young men shall see visions
—Joel 2:28

CHAPTER 12

Guided Fantasy Techniques

When we are asleep and dreaming, there is a tendency to experience the events occurring in our dreams as if they were actually happening. Pleasant dreams may cause us to smile, and even to laugh aloud at times, while nightmares may cause us to awaken fearful and apprehensive. It is generally not until after we awaken that we realize that the "events" which we have just lived through have all been figments of our imagination. Similarly, *suggested* alterations in conscious awareness may also enhance the tendency to experience imagined events as if they were actually taking place. If a sufficiently suggestible subject is administered an induction and then told that he is Enrico Caruso, and that he is about to sing some lines from a famous opera, his subsequent efforts may sound to us like the baying of a lonely coyote; but to him, they are the work of the master artist he temporarily believes himself to be.

This readiness to confuse subjective and objective reality in response to suggestion has been the source of a great deal of mischief in the hands of ignorant and uninformed people; for if the suggested events happen to fit in reasonably well with the personality needs of the subject or with his preexisting belief patterns, he may continue to believe that the suggested events actually did take place, even *after* the trance experience has been concluded. For example, the rather plain girl with a "wallflower" personality who asked me to hypnotize her because she suspected that she was actually the reincarnation of Marie Antoinette, wished to use hypnosis to see whether or not this was actually the case. (Needless to say, she probably would have become convinced that indeed she was the reincarnation of Marie Antoinette; and needless to say, after tactfully explaining my reasons for doing so, I refused to oblige her.) Such situations are reminiscent of the practice in some so-called primitive societies of attempting to "even the score" with someone after dreaming that one has been in a fight with him and lost. After all, if another person's spirit picked a fight with your spirit in your dreams the previous night, this individual obviously needs to be taught a lesson in order that it will not happen again.

In our own culture, we are well aware of the differences between sleep-induced fantasies and actual events; but some people are not quite so sophisticated when it comes to fantasies induced by suggestion. There are still a number of old books gathering dust on library shelves which contain subjective accounts of people who have supposedly been led to "recall" the details of a previous existence on the planet Mars after undergoing a hypnotic induction, including vivid descriptions of vast cities connected to one another by an intricate network of canals. Nowadays, we know too much about the planet Mars for such fantasies to be mistaken for objective reality; for satellite exploration has revealed that the markings which were once thought to have possibly been canals are really rills, or temperature fault lines. Since the notion of Martian canals has been discredited, the current fashion among suggestion-cultists is to induce subjects to "recall" the details of a previous lifetime on the "lost continent" of Atlantis. Perhaps in a few more years, when the details of sonar mapping of the ocean floor are more widely known, we can expect to hear of suggestion-cults which center their practices around the purported recall of previous lifetimes somewhere in another galaxy—where they should be safe from exposure by the continuing advance of human knowledge, at least for a while.

In the late 1950s, a great deal of interest was aroused by the publication of an account of a young woman who was supposedly able to recall many details of a previous lifetime in Ireland before the turn of the century (Bernstein, 1956). She claimed that her name had been "Bridey Murphy"; and while responding to suggestions that she was in a hypnotic trance, she was able to produce a wealth of information about the region in which she supposedly lived, and about the daily habits of people living there at the time. When her "recollections" were compared with actual historical records, many of them were found to be substantially accurate. However, the resulting publicity soon attracted the attention of some investigative reporters who began making inquiries around the woman's childhood home in Chicago. Thus, it was discovered that when she had been a little girl, she had had a nursemaid who used to entertain the child with tales of her own girlhood in Ireland before the turn of the century; and that most of the details of the woman's purported previous existence as "Bridey Murphy" could be traced to this source (Gardner, 1957).

A more sinister use of suggestion which was recently brought to light in the popular press involved a fortune teller and hypnotist who, for a fee, would supposedly place his "hypnotized" clients in telepathic communication with an ancient Egyptian goddess, so that the clients might receive "advice" from the goddess about how to manage their personal affairs. Needless to say, it was the hypnotist who stood to gain more than anyone else from such advice.

The success of such individuals is not hard to fathom. Events rarely turn out exactly as one expects them to; and it is therefore hardly surprising that charlatans who claim to be able to provide a direct pipeline to truth may develop a large following, even, or perhaps especially, in the modern world, where people are beset with the necessity of making so many choices whose long-term consequences are difficult if not impossible to foresee.

The practices just described have led many responsible individuals to reject the use of suggested fantasy as too irrational and too akin to the occult to be of any practical use in fostering personal growth and in helping to solve life's problems. Yet, most of these same individuals will readily attend a motion picture or a theatrical performance, giving little thought to the fact that most of the events portrayed never really took place at all, and that they are merely the figments of someone's imagination. If these skeptics should be asked why they are willing to suspend momentarily their critical abilities and allow their imagination to enter freely into the mood of an entirely fictional event, they are likely to respond that such fictional portrayals can not only be an important source of entertainment and recreation, but can also provide many new and useful perspectives which may broaden one's understanding of oneself, of others, and of life in general.

As it is with standard fiction, so it is with suggested fantasy trips. As long as we recognize that we are *only* dealing with fantasy, suggestion can be employed to create a "theater of the mind," in which the scenes portrayed may be enjoyed more fully because of their enhanced reality, in a manner somewhat akin to the "feelies" described by Aldous Huxley in his book, *Brave New World* (1932). But to derive the full benefits of such an approach, there is certainly no need to continue to believe in the reality of such experiences after the fantasy has been concluded.

The several examples of fantasy experience that follow may be brought about with subjects who respond well to suggestion and who are free from any existing impediment to normal imaginative functioning. Although some suggestors are in the habit of employing fantasy trips without a formal trance induction, it is my own belief that fantasy experiences are considerably more vivid and more effective when they are presented after a hypnotic or a hyperempiric induction. Because of the enhanced subjective reality which an induction may produce, however, sufficient care should be taken to avoid exposing anyone to suggested fantasy material who is likely to be upset or frightened by the experience, as would probably be the case if a person with a fear of water were to experience the Undersea Fantasy, or if an individual who was afraid of heights were to participate in the Fantasy of Flight. Such contingencies are easily disposed of by appropriate preliminary discussion concerning the nature of the fantasy experience which is about to be presented.

Regardless of whether or not a preliminary induction has been employed, certain initial steps should always be taken to insure a sufficient degree of imaginative involvement with the material. These include providing a sufficient amount of initial information and discussion to insure that the participants know what to expect and that an appropriate degree of interest has been established, and selecting an environmental setting which is free of distracting noises and interruptions. A low level of illumination and appropriate background music or other sound effects are also generally helpful.

People who derive the greatest enjoyment from fantasy trips tend to be those who have the keenest imaginations; and subjective accounts of their experiences often reveal a tendency to change or to elaborate upon various aspects of the fantasy to suit their individual tastes. In fact, those fantasies which are reportedly the most effective often turn out to have been "joint productions," to which the participants have added numerous refinements and finishing touches of their own. Accordingly, it is often helpful to insert occasional pauses here and there, to encourage the participants to take a more active part in the direction of the fantasy themselves.

It is also useful to allow for an appropriate period of discussion at the conclusion of the fantasy experience, particularly when working with groups, to allow the more responsive subjects an opportunity to model the appropriate responses for those whose degree of imaginative involvement has been less, so that the latter individuals can have a better conception of what they are supposed to experience and what to look for in future sessions.

Additional material on the use of guided fantasy may be found in Anderson and Savary (1972) and Masters and Houston (1972).

THE CELEBRATION OF LIFE—
A GROWTH FANTASY

I would like you to visualize yourself now as a tiny songbird, about to burst out of its shell. Continue to hold the image in your mind and to focus on it, and the feeling of reality will grow stronger and stronger with each passing second, and soon you will be able to experience fully everything that I describe.

It's a beautiful spring day outside, and through the thin wall of the shell which surrounds you comes the sound of wind gently blowing in the trees around your nest, and the song of other birds chirping merrily, as if inviting you to come out and join them in their celebration of life.

You are a little baby songbird, encased in its shell and ready to peck its way out into the world. Let yourself experience the situation fully now, and everything that goes with it. Feel how cramped you are in the shell, and feel the urge to break out growing stronger with each passing second.

The surging life forces within you may no longer be denied. The shell which has been your home up to now is no longer able to contain you. You *must* break through into the world that lies waiting outside; for the forces of life and growth are becoming stronger and more insistent with every instant that passes.

You are beginning to peck away at the shell now, slowly at first, and then with ever more rapid movements. And the shell is beginning to crack, and now it is starting to give way before your insistent efforts. Now a tiny piece of the shell has fallen away, and you are able to catch a glimpse of the tantalizing world outside. It is a fascinating place of indescribable beauty; and you feel a renewed surge of strength and joy as you redouble your efforts in response to the promise of all that is to come.

More pieces of the shell are falling away, and now you are able to push your head completely through the opening you have created. With a great burst of strength, you cause a crack to appear along the entire length of the shell, and the crack becomes larger and larger with each repeated shove. Until at last your shell has broken apart, and with a great surge of triumph you stand blinking upon the threshold of a new life. You are completely free from all the constraints of the past. You are completely free from everything that has been holding you back.

You are ready to begin a new phase of your existence, and ready to unfold and to use the new talents and abilities which have been quietly developing there inside your shell. And as you stand there upon the threshold of a new existence, you can feel the stirrings of a song rising up within you. A song of victory, and a song of joy, a song of growth, and a celebration of life. And as you flex your wings fully for the very first time, you can feel the notes bursting forth clear and strong. Hear the song in your mind now, and listen to it mingling with the music of the birds around you.

(*Twenty-second pause:*)

Now the scene is fading, and you are becoming aware of yourself as a person once more. But the feelings of triumph and of joy will remain with you. You will continue to carry the lesson of this experience with you, and each time the experience is repeated, the feelings of strength, of triumph, and of joy will become even stronger, and their beneficial consequences in your everyday life will be correspondingly increased.

The following fantasy experience is best preceded by the hyperempiric induction "On the Beach at Night" (see p. 31). Suggestions may then be administered as follows:

FANTASY OF FLIGHT—
A FANTASY FOR ENTERTAINMENT

Now, as you stand there on that sandy beach, the early morning sun has broken through the fog and begun to flood you with its warmth. You decide that it would be fun to stretch out on the sand for a few moments and enjoy the sunshine. You lie down, feeling perfectly content as the combination of the cool sand beneath you and the warm sun above you begins to flood your entire being with a sensation of perfect balance, happiness, and contentment.

And now you are about to undergo a marvelous adventure; for as you continue to lie there upon the sand, enjoying the sunlight, you glance upward and notice the outline of a large, graceful bird soaring majestically above you in the heavens. You are thrilled and delighted by the grace and the beauty of this magnificent creature, and as you continue to watch, you realize that it has seen you and that it seems to be putting on a show just for your benefit as it soars and circles, soars and turns again, drawing ever nearer to the spot where you are lying.

As the bird draws nearer, you are able to see that it is an eagle, and it soon becomes apparent that it is going to land. And as it alights, you realize that it is larger than any bird you have ever read or heard about; for it is so big that it could easily carry a person on its back.

The bird turns slightly to one side, gesturing with its beak as if inviting you to climb on for a ride. Seizing a nearby strand of seaweed, you quickly fashion a harness for yourself and loop it around the bird's neck as you leap onto its back. And suddenly, you are on your way.

At this point, I usually like to introduce as background music Richard Wagner's "The Ride of the Valkyries," from *die Walküre,* beginning at low volume and then increasing it as appropriate.

Rising rapidly above the beach, you marvel at the breathtaking view before you; for you are able to see for miles in every direction. But the eagle is continuing its ascent, heading directly for a cloudbank high above. You are drawing closer and closer to the bank of clouds. And now you are completely enveloped by them; but the bird continues to climb.

Now you have broken through the other side of the cloudbank. Majestic cloudpeaks rise above you, and feathery cloud canyons stretch out beneath you: pink and white and occasionally a dusky gray. You are nearly overcome with awe at such a scene of indescribable beauty.

Now the eagle is taking you to explore these peaks and valleys, soaring and diving and turning as it was doing when it first appeared to view. Sometimes it swoops so close to the clouds that you can almost reach out and touch them; and sometimes it dives directly into one before turning and soaring back to even greater heights.

Enjoy your flight now, and in a few moments you will return to the beach. But in the meantime, you can just continue having the time of your life as you and this magnificent bird experience together all the beauty of free and unrestricted flight, as you soar high above the clouds.

(After a two-minute interval of free fantasy:)

Now it is time to return, and the eagle is beginning to descend back through the clouds. You are being taken back to the very same spot from which you departed. But you will always remember this wonderful adventure, and whenever you wish to do so, you will be able to experience the joys of free flight in fantasy once again.

Now the bird is landing, and you are ready to alight. You loosen the harness, and the bird immediately takes flight once more. You wave goodbye as it circles and swoops low one final time, and begins a rapid ascent into the heavens. And soon it is but a tiny speck in the sky, eventually becoming lost to view. But each time this experience is repeated, its vividness will increase; and your capacity for enjoying it will be correspondingly enhanced.

GANDOR'S GARDEN—
A PROJECTIVE FANTASY

Now, as you continue to listen to my voice, you find that the scene is changing. You are walking down a lonely forest path, early on a summer's afternoon. Suddenly, you come upon a large mount of earth, freshly dug, with a round wooden door to the side. Curious, you leave the path and walk up to the door, which is standing slightly ajar. As you peer inside, you find what appears to be a tunnel, with firm, dry walls which look almost as if they had been whitewashed. But the most intriguing thing of all is that there seems to be a glimmer of light coming from the other end, even though the tunnel slopes gradually downward.

Determined to investigate further, you enter the tunnel and begin to make your way along its length as it plunges downward ever deeper into the earth, and the light at the other end grows steadily brighter. Then, suddenly, just as you have almost reached the end, the ground beneath you gives way, and you tumble head-over-heels into a well-lit garden, coming to rest safely but in a heap at the foot of a grassy knoll, just a short distance from where the tunnel would have ended in the first place.

Glancing upward at the ingenious system of skylights which provides the illumination for this underground garden, you are startled by the sound of high-pitched laughter. Turning, you see before you a smiling elf, standing almost at your elbow, who takes the pipe out of his mouth and gestures grandly about him with his staff. "I am Gandor," he exclaims, "and this is my garden. I bid you welcome! You are free to walk around and explore to your heart's content; for you are to be my guest today." And with a final wave of his staff, the elf disappears before your eyes.

Now you begin to explore the magic garden. First you notice a tiny reflecting pool, nestled in the grass by the side of the knoll where you first entered. Gazing into its depths, you begin to see more of what makes this garden so very special; for there in the pool, gazing back at you, is the image of yourself not as you are, but as you would like to become—and suddenly, the image begins to speak, telling you something about yourself which you had not previously realized. So just listen a moment to what this reflection of your ideal self has to say about you, and then it will be time to move on and explore the rest of the magic garden.

(Twenty-second pause:)

As the reflection finishes speaking and begins to fade away, you continue along the pathway through the garden—and as you round a bend in the path, you suddenly come upon a little child, happily skipping rope. The child smiles and beckons to you, as if wanting to tell you a secret. You bend down and the child begins to whisper in your ear, telling you something about yourself which you have almost forgotten—something from your own early years, which needs to be remembered now to help you live more fully in the present. So listen now to the secret which the child is telling you, and then it will be time to continue on through the garden.

(Twenty-second pause:)

As the child skips happily away and you resume your walk, you come upon a small clearing in which there are three butterflies dancing joyfully in the air. As you come closer, you realize that they are humming a tune to accompany their dance; and gradually you can even begin to make out words to the tune. It is a song about happiness, and about what constitutes the true secret of being happy. Just listen a moment now to what the butterflies are singing.

(Twenty-second pause:)

Now their dance is ended and the butterflies glide away. You are almost at the end of the path which leads through the magic garden, but you still have one more surprise in store; for there beside the pathway sits an old man, cross-legged and with his eyes closed, as if to meditate. He opens his eyes and smiles as you approach, as if he has been expecting you. And now the old man begins to speak; and from his lips you gain some especially wise counsel regarding a matter which has been of concern to you. So just listen a moment to what the old man has to say, and then it will be time to move on.

(Twenty-second pause:)

Now you have come to the end of the pathway which leads through the magic garden, and there is Gandor waiting to greet you once again. "You will be returning in a moment to the world outside," says he, cheerfully puffing on his pipe, "and after you return, you will remember with a special fondness everything that has happened during your stay here; for you are going to be very pleased by the fascinating insights which will grow out of your experiences here in the magic garden. And each time you return, there will be still more surprises, and more insights, which will be waiting for you."

And even before the elf has quite finished speaking, the scene begins to fade.

A JUNGIAN FANTASY

Now, as you continue to listen to my voice, we are beginning to travel backward in time. We are traveling backward together in time, backward through the centuries, until we arrive at the destination which has been our goal.

Now we are in ancient Egypt, late at night, standing before the cavelike entrance to a large pyramid which towers above us, its top completely lost to view in the darkness, for the sky is completely obscured, and the night is totally black. The only light to be seen is a faint glow, proceeding from the entrance itself.

As we enter the pyramid, we discover that the passageway is brightly lit by torches which are fastened to the wall at regular intervals. The passage slopes suddenly downward as we continue along its length, but we follow it eagerly, for this pyramid presents the mind with an image which will enable us to explore together the deepest levels of your awareness.

Let yourself continue to be guided by my voice now, as we travel ever downward, plunging to greater and greater depths, until suddenly, at the very end of the passage, we come upon a vast storage chamber, filled with treasures of every description.

We have entered into the storehouse of all the vast untapped resources within you, wherein resides all the potential for good and for accomplishment which you have not yet turned to your advantage. All these treasures are rightfully yours, for they have been denied you through the force of circumstance, and unless you are able to carry them back into the world outside, to share and to enjoy with others, they will eventually be sealed up inside this chamber and lost forever.

Your gaze is suddenly drawn to one particular jewel which is infinitely more brilliant than all the rest, embedded in the forehead of a huge, forbidding statue in the center of the room. And as you continue to look at it, the jewel appears to glow with an eerie light of its own.

This statue, holding within its forehead this softly glowing stone, is the embodiment of all the negative and sinister forces of failure and defeat within the personality of each one who looks at it; and it has been placed in this room as a guardian of the treasure which is here, making all other guardians unnecessary.

In order to liberate this vast storehouse of your potential, you must first overcome the tendencies within you which are acting to prevent this, personified in the statue before you. Reaching out and grasping the stone firmly with both hands, you take it from the statue's forehead and turn it over, replacing it now with the obverse turned outward, so that the stone shines with a positive glow.

Stooping quickly to scoop up as many of the treasures as we can, we hurriedly retrace our steps to the entrance. And as we leave the pyramid, we discover that it is no longer night, for the sun has just appeared over the distant horizon. The way is clear before us, and now we can see for miles in every direction.

And as we stride purposefully away, you know that in your everyday life the treasures which we are bringing back will manifest themselves in the form of new habits, new ideas, and new directions. You are going to be absolutely thrilled and delighted by the improvements which the recovery of these potentials will bring about. And because your potential for growth is truly infinite, each time we return to this treasury of your unconcsious, the storehouse will never be empty.

A MINIVACATION

Now I would like you to think of a vacation trip you would like to take, and to picture in your mind some enjoyable experience which would constitute one of the best portions of the vacation. It might be racing down a ski slope in

Switzerland, or fishing in a small mountain stream, or perhaps standing at the rail of an ocean liner late at night and gazing out to sea with someone you are very close to. It could be almost anything, as long as it is a vacation experience which you would especially enjoy.

When you have chosen the particular situation which you would like to experience, continue to hold this image in your mind and to focus on it, and soon it will be just as if you were really there. You will always be able to hear and to respond to my voice, and I will bring you back to the present setting at the conclusion of the interlude: but until I do, every aspect of the situation you have chosen to experience will be completely real to you. And even though the experience may actually last for only a few moments, it will seem to have been going on for a much longer period, so your enjoyment of the experience will be correspondingly increased.

Now I'm going to count backwards from five to one, and as I do, you will mentally be transported to the scene which you have chosen, and by the time I get to the count of one, it will be just as if you were really there. Five. Your awareness of the present scene is growing dim now, and you can begin to be aware of yourself being mentally transported to the situation you have chosen. Four. The present situation is becoming dimmer and dimmer in your awareness, as you continue to be mentally projected to the scene you have selected. Three. You are beginning to be aware of yourself in the other situation now, and it is becoming clearer and clearer in your mind. Two. Almost there now. One. Now your awareness has been completely projected into the situation which you have chosen to experience. You will always be able to hear and to respond to my voice, but until I bring you back, every aspect of the situation you have selected will be completely real to you, and you will be able to experience it all, just as if you were really there.

Let yourself live the experience now and enjoy it to the fullest, and even though the experience may actually last only a few moments, it will seem to be going on much, much longer, and your enjoyment of the experience will be correspondingly increased. You will be able to return rested and refreshed, feeling absolutely wonderful as a result of the good time which you have had.

(A few moments later:)

Now I am going to bring you back by counting slowly from one to five. After you return, you will remain in trance for a while, until the trance itself is terminated. You will remember everything that has happened with a special clarity and vividness, for it will be just as if you have had a refreshing bit of vacation. And it will leave you feeling thoroughly rested, refreshed, and happy.

Five. Your awareness of the vacation scene is dimming now, as you begin to return. Four. You are beginning to be aware of yourself back here with me now, as your awareness of the vacation scene continues to fade. Three. Coming back more and more now. Two. Almost back. One. Now you are completely back and fully aware of yourself in the setting from which you left, feeling refreshed, rested, and happy, as a result of the wonderful time you have had.

Under the guidance of a suggestor, the act of listening to music may stimulate many highly imaginative subjects to produce vivid and elaborate fantasies of their own. Such procedures are often particularly effective in group settings, with an appropriate induction administered beforehand. At the conclusion of the induction, the suggestor may proceed as follows:

MUSICAL FANTASY

Now I am going to play some music which will direct your consciousness to a series of pleasant and meaningful images. As you listen, the images will flow naturally and effortlessly into your awareness. So just relax and listen to the music, as the images begin to flow, and savor their richness and their beauty.

At the conclusion of these suggestions, virtually any number of selections may be played. Many people report experiencing particularly vivid and meaningful imagery while listening to Ravel's *Daphnis and Chloe*, Musorgski's *A Night on Bald Mountain*, one movement of Brahms's Symphony No. 1 in C, Respighi's *The Pines of Rome*, Debussy's nocturne, "Les Sirènes," or his *Afternoon of a Faun*. If one is more inclined toward contemporary music, Pink Floyd's "Echoes," from his album entitled *Meddle*, is also particularly effective.

As is the case with the other fantasy experiences, a period of reflection and discussion should follow the conclusion of the fantasy and the cancellation of the induction to provide an opportunity for the subjects to integrate and to interpret the images that have been called forth.

Additional material on the use of musical fantasy is to be found in Bonny (1973).

The Shared Fantasy procedure is based on the technique of "mutual hypnosis" developed by Tart (1969). The present version involves the simultaneous administration of either a hypnotic or a hyperempiric induction to two or more persons, with the following suggestions provided after the induction has been completed.

SHARED FANTASY

In just a moment, you are going to have a pleasant dream about _____. The images may appear faintly at first; but gradually, you will be able to see them more and more clearly, and soon it will be just as if the dream were really happening.

You will be able to describe your dreams to each other while they are still going on. And as you do, the same features you are describing will appear in the dreams of the other(s), so that your separate fantasies will gradually merge into a single common dream which you will share with one another while it is occurring, guiding and directing each other, in turn, as the experience continues; one dream which you will all be sharing together.

You will always be able to hear and to respond to my voice, and I will be able to share in the direction of the dream, guiding it along with you to a satisfactory and a happy conclusion.

And now you will begin to see the dream images forming in your mind. Soon you will see them very clearly. And when you do, you can begin to describe what you see. Then the others will begin to see the images, too, exactly as they are described by the one who is dreaming them first.

Now you can see the images forming in your mind, and you can begin to describe them to one another.

Subjects may occasionally have to be called upon individually to initiate the descriptions or to maintain momentum if the participation should begin to lag. However, most individuals seem to enjoy the shared aspects of the fantasy experience, and show little inclination to retreat into a world of their own private imaginings.

The following fantasy experience is best preceded by the hyperempiric induction "On the Beach at Night" (see page 31).

UNDERSEA FANTASY—
A FANTASY FOR ENTERTAINMENT

You are standing alone now upon the shore of a small island surrounded by mist. Suddenly, as you peer into the mist, you notice the outline of a large yacht coming toward you, with light streaming through the portholes and gently illuminating the water around it, making the sea appear as if it were glowing. The yacht pulls up to the pier, and a gangplank mysteriously lowers for your ascent. You climb aboard without further hesitation.

As you stand upon the deck and begin to look around, you decide that you will explore the boat fully. It has several staterooms, a small galley, and a game room. No one else is on board, so just let yourself walk around and explore the boat for a while.

(After an appropriate interval of free fantasy:)

Now you are coming back on deck, and as you do, the first thing that you notice is that a small table has been set for you, with a mysteriously alluring beverage in a glass on top of it. You sit down and begin to sip, and as the beverage begins to take effect, you begin to be ever more aware of how delightfully different this magic potion is causing you to feel.

Suddenly, you notice that the gangplank has been raised and the yacht has pulled away from the pier. It's so quiet and peaceful drifting out to sea, all alone and completely secure in the knowledge that you will be well taken care of by this mysterious force that seems to sense your every need.

Now you have arrived at a place far out of sight of land, where the waters are completely quiet and crystal clear; and you notice that the boat is slowing down and getting ready to anchor.

The water looks so clear and inviting that you find yourself thinking how much fun it would be to go for a swim; and as soon as the thought enters your mind, you find yourself clad in a swim suit of your favorite style and color. You go to the railing and look down into the green-blue water. It looks so inviting that you just can't wait another moment, and so you leap in.

The water feels so warm and refreshing as you dive beneath the surface. And because it is so completely clear, you find that you are able to see almost as well under water as you can normally.

The undersea world is teeming with life; and you begin to notice details and creatures that you surely would have missed ordinarily, but the magic liquid which you drank has made everything you look at appear much more vivid. And to your own astonishment, you find that it is now possible for you to breathe underwater, so let yourself begin to explore this undersea world now, rejoicing in all its richness and beauty.

You travel downward through beautiful coral valleys which contain all the colors of the rainbow. And as you go, you can see little groups of multicolored fish scampering about between bunches of coral and lumps of seaweed. There are dozens of starfish about, and if you look carefully, you can see many other undersea creatures which blend in almost perfectly with their surroundings.

Suddenly, you see before you a mermaid. She is applauding your graceful movements as you swim rapidly along, and she seems to want to join you and be your guide. You motion to her to come ahead, and together you swim and dance and twirl, having a marvelous time as everything around you seems to come to life with a beauty and brilliance which is only to be found here in this magic world beneath the sea.

Dozens of tiny seahorses swim by, drawing a giant clam shell as a chariot behind them. The mermaid motions for you to climb aboard. You do so, and are off to even greater depths of the sea. You know somehow, without her telling you, that you are going to a vast undersea city.

Go freely now, into the depths, and drink in the beauty and the details of the city you are about to visit. Let yourself go and savor the experience. When it is time to return to the yacht, I will again call you. But for now, enjoy your journey and your visit to the undersea city.

(After a two-minute interval of free fantasy:)

It's almost time to return now. You have spent an entire day beneath the sea; for above the surface, the sun has already begun to set, and the undersea world around you is beginning to grow dim. You say goodbye to all your new friends and promise never to forget them.

The seahorse chariot arrives again, and you mount and begin your ascent to the surface. You are back at the yacht now and climbing up the side ladder. You turn for one last glimpse of the chariot, but it has already vanished.

Suddenly, you find yourself completely dry and back in your normal clothes. The yacht is heading back toward shore, and you know that your adventure is almost over. But you will never forget your day beneath the sea; for it will always be a source of wonder and delight to you that you have had such a fantastic journey. And each time that you return to this fantasy world beneath the sea, you will have new and exciting adventures in store for you.

The Visitor fantasy experience that follows is open-ended, so that the suggestor may direct the remainder of the fantasy himself. With this introduction, the possibilities for the development of subsequent themes are virtually unlimited.

THE VISITOR

Now you can begin to dream, as you find yourself guided by my voice to a new situation. Just allow the images to form in your mind, in response to my words, and soon it will be as if you are really there. It is late at night, and you are all alone in the woods, just nestling down in your sleeping bag to watch the dying embers of your campfire after a long day of hiking. As you are about to doze off, you notice a large, silvery object in the sky, which appears to descend from the clouds some distance away. "It's probably just a searchlight beam," you think to yourself; and you close your eyes, determined to get some sleep.

You are awakened some time later by the sound of footsteps. The night has grown very dark, and there is no sound at all except for the footsteps themselves—and now even these have stopped. Groping for your flashlight, you turn it on and quickly shine the beam up into the face of a stranger, who stands there looking down at you with a serious but friendly expression.

The thought gradually enters your mind that you have come face to face with a visitor to our world who is from another part of the galaxy, many light years away. The stranger nods and smiles, as if to confirm his thought projection, and asks in the same manner if you would like to accompany him on a journey from whence he came, promising to return you to the same point from which you left. You eagerly agree, and the stranger begins to project his thoughts into your mind once more.

He speaks slowly and distinctly:

"Let yourself relax, now, and I will tell you about the journey we are going to take. I have traveled the pathways of this journey many, many times before. We will travel—in spirit, in consciousness, beyond the barriers of space and time. Because I have made this journey so many times before, I am able to take you along with me, but to do this, our awareness must blend together completely for awhile.

"This will not be difficult as long as I have your full cooperation, for even as I continue to speak, you can feel your body and your mind relaxing even more. Your mind is becoming completely free of all other thoughts. We are drifting, drifting, floating through space and time as our minds touch, communicate, and become one. We are explorers, we are wanderers. Our minds are functioning in total harmony. And we are able to travel on together through space, time, and infinity to visit any part of your own planet, or of the universe."

CHAPTER 13

Improving Creativity and Performance

It is not enough for most of us merely to live out our lives free of ailments. To be truly healthy, in the fullest sense of the term, means to grow, to develop, and to strive to be the best person one is capable of becoming (Rogers, 1961). And herein lies the greatest potential of suggestion; for not everyone needs to be made well, but surely everyone is capable of growth.

The first popular use of suggestion as a means of actualizing human potential was initiated by the French pharmacist, Emile Coué. Coué (1932) held that the "unconscious mind" was most receptive to suggestion during the moments when a person was hovering between wakefulness and sleep; and if one were able and willing to take full advantage of the opportunity thus afforded for direct communication with the "unconscious," it would be possible to divest oneself completely of all the negative thoughts and feelings which had accumulated over the course of a lifetime and which were preventing a person from realizing his true potential. The way to accomplish this mental housecleaning, Coué believed, was to use these crucial moments between sleeping and wakefulness to repeat silently over and over to oneself the affirmation, "Every day, and in every way, I am getting better and better!"

Coué's teaching was initially received with a considerable amount of enthusiasm; and numerous individuals readily attested to dramatic improvements in their lives and fortunes, which changes they attributed to the faithful use of this technique. But as more and more people came to try it and found that it did not seem to work for them, Couéism soon fell into decline.

Every few years since the advent of Coué's technique, a new "positive thinking" movement has made its appearance (Bristol, 1957; Maltz, 1960; Silva & Miele, 1977). Such books generally tend to follow the same set formula. First, they make use of a new and appealing name which sets the current technique apart from those which have gone before. Then, like their forerunners, each new tome asserts that all human beings possess a vast reservoir of untapped abilities if only they were willing to make use of it. A ritual or a set of exercises is also included which, it is asserted, will enable the reader to actualize this potential if the procedures set forth are faithfully and diligently followed; and finally, some portion of the book is devoted to a collection of anecdotes and/or testimonials illustrating how the new technique has indeed changed people's lives for the better, bringing health and prosperity to those who were formerly devoid of hope.

Just as a properly timed and appropriately delivered pep talk can occasionally transform a losing athletic team into a winning one, so can a belief in positive thinking occasionally shift an individual from a losing to a winning pattern in the battle of life; and such persons can be expected to attempt eagerly to spread the word to others concerning the degree to which the new system has supposedly been of help to them. But as more and more people come to try the new technique and find that its effects are only temporary as far as they are concerned, if indeed the system seems to work at all, the method begins to lose popularity rapidly and the stage is set for the next positive-thinking movement to come along a few years later.

The principal reason why such approaches have only been effective with a minority of the general population is the inability of those using these systems to distinguish between situations for which the particular suggestions they contain may facilitate the learning of more adaptive ways to behave, and other situations for which it may be merely a form of wishful thinking. As a student once said to me, "Those positive-thinking books all seem to be saying, 'You're better if you think you are,' and I can't believe that!" She was right, of course, in pinpointing the central assumption underlying most such movements; but the fact remains that some people are actually "better" if they think they are.

The situations in which suggestion seems to operate most effectively are those in which it tends to function as a *self-fulfilling prophecy* (Jones, 1977). In other words, workable suggestions are those which tend to come true simply because they *have* been accepted and believed in—as illustrated by an account of a shy, retiring, and painfully self-conscious boy with a large birthmark on his cheek who was able to change his demeanor almost overnight because his grandmother had told him that this birthmark was a special sign from God that he had been singled out as a child destined for greatness. Needless to say, this once forlorn and unhappy lad grew up to lead an adult life full of accomplishment—an existence which he would probably *not* have led, were it not for his grandmother's prophecy, which, because it was accepted and believed in, acted to bring about the very conditions which it had predicted.

Hypnosis and hyperempiria, by making subsequent suggestions more plausible, and by providing a format which is particularly well suited to communicating messages of encouragement, reassurance, and inspiration, serve to increase greatly the number of situations in which self-fulfilling prophecies may occur; for to be effective, of course, such prophecies must first be accepted and believed in by those whom they are to benefit.

The following suggestions are designed to function as self-fulfilling prophecies when the subject has been made properly receptive by means of a hypnotic or a hyperempiric induction. However, it is also necessary to point out that such procedures should be used with caution. There will always be a number of aspiring athletes, musicians, and writers who would eventually be better off in some other field of endeavor. If the following techniques are employed as a means of fostering personal growth or improving performance for its own sake, well and good; but if one should attempt to employ such methods as a means of underpinning a new career or of rescuing one which is in trouble, the essence of wisdom will consist in knowing when to use them and when not to do so.

As is the case with the other examples presented throughout this volume, it will frequently be desirable to vary the wording of a particular suggestion to meet the needs of an individual subject and the requirements of a specific situation. Moreover, the examples provided tend to be interchangeable to some degree, or applicable to other situations in addition to the ones for which they have been presented;

for instance, the suggestions for writing ability may be used with slight changes in wording as a means of enhancing artistic expression, in addition to the suggestions which are specifically presented herein for this purpose; and the suggestions for public speaking may be employed as a guide in formulating suggestions designed to prepare subjects for a crucial interview or an oral examination which they may have come to fear. Thus, the examples which follow should never be regarded as ironclad prescriptions to be carried out to the letter, but merely as general guides upon which the reader should feel free to improvise for himself.

ACADEMIC PERFORMANCE

I was once seated in a college coffee shop next to a student who was futilely poring over a statistics text, attempting to study for an examination which was to be given the following hour. "I can't do 'stat,' " he kept repeating to himself as he turned the pages, "I just can't do 'stat.' "

Of course he couldn't. Telling himself over and over that he could *not* learn the material he was in the very act of attempting to study, and believing these statements implicitly as he made them, was in effect administering *autosuggestions* which acted to negate all the efforts he was putting forth. The following suggestions are designed to provide positive attitudes and expectations which will enable a student to perform more in accordance with his potential.

IMPROVING STUDY SKILLS

As a result of what I am about to tell you now, you will find many helpful improvements taking place in your study habits, and in the effectiveness with which you utilize your abilities in studying. Whenever you have any studying to do, you will find that you will be in just the right mood for it. You will *really feel like studying,* and as a result, you will be able to dig into the material with a lot more energy and a lot more enthusiasm than you usually have. You will be able to use your study time much more effectively; for you will be able to concentrate much more easily and to remember with much less effort what you have learned.

Each time you complete a period of study, you will find that you experience very strong feelings of pride, achievement, and accomplishment because you have been able to perform so effectively and so well. These feelings will reward you for the time you have spent in study, and you will come to look forward to your study periods in the same way that a trained athlete looks forward to a good workout. It will be a source of deep personal satisfaction to you that you are able to use your abilities so fully and so well, and you are going to be thrilled and delighted at the results.

TAKING EXAMINATIONS

From now on, you will be able to approach your examinations calmly and to feel calm and relaxed as you take them. When you enter the room in which the test is being given, the act of walking through the doorway will serve as a stimulus which will release within you a great wave of additional peace and tranquility, confidence and calm. And it will drive out completely any tension which might be reawakened by your starting to take the test, so that by the time the test begins, you will be in just the proper mood to function most effectively.

You will be able to recall a great deal of information which might otherwise be blocked because of tension. Your mental processes will be much more flexible, and you will be able to draw on vast reserves of potential which will enable you to concentrate much more easily on the questions asked and your answers to them.

You will be able to remain perfectly relaxed and calm throughout the entire test as the ideas, facts, and concepts continue to flow smoothly into your awareness and to organize themselves naturally and almost spontaneously, as if they were flowing onto the paper by themselves. You are going to be thrilled and delighted at how much easier the entire process of taking examinations is going to be, and at how much better you will be able to perform.

FACILITATING CLASS PARTICIPATION

From now on, you will find that the subject matter of all your classes has taken on a great deal more meaning. You will want to ask many more questions in class, and you will be very interested in the answers which are provided, both to your own questions and to the questions of others.

As you continue to participate more and more in the give-and-take of class discussion, you will become ever more interested in everything that is being presented. You will become more and more absorbed in the content of what is being taught, as each new fact and concept to emerge becomes more vivid and more interesting than those which have gone before.

As time continues to pass, your personal involvement will continue to grow, for you will constantly be discovering new ways to relate the material to your own life and experiences. And these applications will give rise to still more questions, resulting in an even greater desire to know.

As these new questions are satisfied in turn, the process will continue at an ever-increasing rate, for the more your aroused curiosity is fed, the stronger it is certain to become.

Additional information on the use of suggestion-related techniques for problems related to school and studying can be found in Lawlor (1976).

ACHIEVEMENT MOTIVATION

Many people ask to be given suggestions to improve their "will power," in the apparent assumption that the *will* is some general mental ability which, like physical strength, may be enhanced by appropriate stimulation and weakened through disuse. It is usually necessary to point out to such individuals that virtually everyone seems to possess a great deal of will power for some things in life (such as camping or trout fishing, perhaps), and that there are many other activities for which the necessary will power may be comparatively weak (such as mowing the lawn or washing the car). Rather than speaking of the will as a separate mental ability, then, it is more appropriate to speak of motivation with respect to a specific goal or class of activities.

Perhaps the closest thing to what the layman refers to as *will power* comes under the general heading of achievement motivation (Atkinson, 1957; Atkinson & Litwin, 1960). Laboratory research has tended to support the assumption that performance in an achievement-related situation is influenced by two basic motives: the motive to approach success and the motive to avoid failure. Since everyone has had numerous experiences involving both, everyone presumably possesses both of these motives in varying strengths, depending on how much of each type of experience one has encountered in the past. Contrary to popular assumption, however, the motivation to avoid failure tends to act as a brake on performance rather than a spur to greater achievement. The strength of the actual tendency to perform in an achievement-related situation is thus conceived as the *difference* between the respective levels of the motive to approach success and the motive to avoid failure—assuming, of course, that the former motive is in fact greater than the latter. More specifically, a person who is highly motivated to succeed but who is also strongly afraid of failure may not perform as well on an achievement-related task as one whose motivation to succeed is only at a moderate level of intensity, but whose fear of failure is relatively low.

It has also been found that the levels of the motive to approach success and the motive to avoid failure may be altered by varying the subjective probabilities of success and failure in a given situation (Atkinson, 1957). As long as the former motive is, in fact, greater than the latter, the strength of the tendency to perform is greatest when the subject is facing a task which he perceives to be of moderate difficulty. The "failure-threatened" individual, on the other hand, seeks to avoid challenge as much as possible. Thus, he tends to perform best when the subjective probability of success approaches 100% and the subjective probability of failure is virtually zero—or vice versa. That is, the person whose motivation to avoid failure is greater than his motivation to approach success will either tend to select tasks which are much too easy for him, and hence completely bereft of challenge, or he will tend to "gamble," preferring situations in which the outcome is primarily owing to chance rather than to his own efforts. Such individuals can be induced to return to more appropriate challenges through the use of suggestions which are aimed at modifying the perceived probabilities of success and failure—or at what is frequently referred to in popular writing as "overcoming mental blocks." Postinduction suggestions may be given as follows:

Please extend both arms straight out in front of you, palms facing inward, about four inches apart. Now I would like you to imagine that there is a large rubber band stretched around your wrists holding them close together, as they are now. This rubber band represents all the negative thoughts and feelings which have been holding you back and preventing you from attaining your true potential; and as I continue speaking, you will begin to notice a force pulling your hands apart, until the rubber band will suddenly snap and you will be free of all these negative thoughts and feelings once and for all. Feel the force beginning to pull at your outstretched hands now—tugging and tugging as it slowly draws your hands apart. Feel your wrists drawing farther and farther apart, and feel the rubber band stretching tighter and tighter between them. Soon the band will snap, and you will finally be free of these negative influences. It's ready to break; ready to break. *Now!* You are *free!*

Now you can rest your hands comfortably in your lap, as you continue listening to my voice. Let yourself relax completely now and think back to a time in the past when you were in a totally positive frame of mind, looking forward to a complete and certain success. This need not be a great success in the usual sense of the term—it's the positive feeling that counts. Everyone has experienced this type of feeling at one time or another, even if only in child-hood. So take your time, and when you have thought of the kind of situation I am describing, let your imagination focus on it clearly and capture the mood once more. And when you have caught this mood once again, you can signal me by raising the index finger of your right (or left) hand.

After the subject has responded:

All right. Now just hold this mood for a moment, and feel it growing even stronger.

Now, as the mood continues to grow ever clearer and stronger by the second, you are going to be able to carry it back with you and to call it up again whenever you wish. The mood will persist for a while after the trance is terminated, and whenever you need to, you are going to be able to act and feel in just this manner once again. You are going to be able to act and feel as if you were going toward a predetermined and certain success. You are going to be able to *act as if it were impossible to fail.* For this is the key which will enable you to continue to tap into your true potential and to employ your abilities to the fullest in pursuit of the goal you have chosen.

ARTISTIC EXPRESSION

Hypnography and hypnoplasty, or suggestion-induced drawing and sculpture, have been used in clinical settings as a method of encouraging the subject to express his innermost thoughts and feel-ings, thereby facilitating the development of self-affirmation and self-understanding (Meares, 1950). But such procedures need not be limited to solely therapeutic functions. Many artists find it difficult to paint unless they happen to be in just the proper mood for creative work, and unless they are able to visualize clearly the setting they wish to portray. Such mood changes and visualizations may be considera-bly facilitated by the appropriate use of suggestion.

The following technique is usually effective with only the best subjects; for the ability to respond to suggested visualizations with one's eyes open is at the high end of most suggestibility scales (Hil-gard, 1965). Many artists may fall into this category, however, because of their highly developed imaginations and their adeptness at han-dling visual imagery. Subjects who cannot open their eyes without disturbing their ongoing experience of trance may visualize the suggested imagery with their eyes closed and begin to paint after the trance is completed, often with similar results. With the artist seated and ready to paint, an induction and suggestions such as the following may be given, either by another person or, with slight modifications in wording, by the artist himself, if he has been properly trained in the use of autosuggestion and self-induced trances:

I'm going to count backward from five to one, and by the time I get to one you will no longer be here in the present setting; but instead, you will be seated in the middle of a lovely forest glade with your easel, paint, and brushes still before you. By the time I get to the count of one, you will be able to open your eyes and look around, and you will be able to paint what you see in rapid, steady strokes.

You will always be able to hear and to respond to my voice, and I will return you to the present setting in a while; but until I do so, every aspect of the situation to which I guide you will be completely real, and you will experience it all just as if you were actually there. And even though the experience may actually last for only a few moments, it will seem to be going on for a much longer time, so that your ability to respond to it artistically will be correspondingly enhanced. Just continue to listen to my voice now, as I begin to count backward from five to one.

Five. Your awareness of the present scene is beginning to grow dim, as you feel yourself and your equipment being transported to that lovely forest glade. Four. Your awareness of the present is dimming more and more, and you can begin to be aware of yourself seated in that lovely forest glade, with your easel and brushes before you, ready to commence painting in a few moments. And as soon as I get to the count of one, you will be able to open your eyes and look around, catching the mood perfectly as you do, and you will be able to paint as you have never painted before. Three. You can feel yourself becoming more and more aware of the forest glade around you, but keep your eyes closed until I get to the count of one and the transition has been completed. Two. Your anticipation and excitement are increasing with each passing second; for soon you will be able to open your eyes and gaze upon one of the most beautiful landscapes you have ever seen. One. Now you can open your eyes and take in all the breathtaking beauty before you, and in just a few seconds you will have caught the mood and you can begin to paint.

After a few moments have elapsed, it may be suggested to the subject that he will be able to retain the same mood, and the same ability to express what he has seen, after the trance is terminated. He may then be requested to close his eyes once more while the suggestor counts forward from one to five.

One. Your awareness of the forest glade is beginning to grow dim, as I return you to the scene from which you left. Two. Coming back more and more now, as your awareness of the forest glade begins to leave completely and you start to become aware of yourself back in the original setting. Three. Almost back now. And by the time I get to the count of five, the transition to the original setting will be complete. Four. Almost back. But you will remain in trance for a while, until I bring you out. Five. Now you are back in the original setting, still very much in trance, but feeling thrilled and delighted at all that you have seen and done and retaining the mood and the memory perfectly. And when the trance is over, you will be able to paint from memory just as clearly and just as well as if you were still there in the forest.

After the foregoing suggestions for painting from memory and for retention of the desired creative mood have been given, the trance may be terminated in the usual manner.

It is usually best to limit such visualizations to a few moments at a time; for if longer periods are employed, the visualization may begin to fade prematurely—although the time can be extended somewhat if another person is administering the suggestions; for as the subject is painting, the suggestor may continue to provide comments and suggestions concerning the beauty of the scene and the qualities of the creative mood which the subject is feeling. If the visualization should ever happen to fade prematurely, the suggestions for reorienting the subject to the original setting and for terminating the trance should still be presented, to eliminate the possibility of any residual effects of the earlier suggestions which might still interfere with the subject's normal here-and-now orientation.

Other topics for suggested visualization may include a human model, or a scene which the subject has experienced previously and would like to recapture. It may also be suggested that the subject reexperience a particular mood from the past in which he felt particularly inspired or productive (Watkins, 1971). The procedures outlined in the suggestions to facilitate creative writing and musical expression contained on pages 192 and 184, respectively, may also be adapted for the enhancement of artistic creativity.

EGO STRENGTHENING

In contrast to the approach favored by Hartland (1971a, b), which stresses the use of suggestions for ego strengthening combined with direct symptom removal, my position is that relatively permanent change is the result of learning new ways to behave which are more adaptive than the old. "Ego strengthening" suggestions can be of great assistance, however, in providing the subject with the necessary encouragement, confidence, and reassurance to enable him to try out a wider range of new behaviors and to persevere in them for a somewhat longer time, thereby increasing the likelihood that more adaptive responses will indeed be discovered and learned. The following suggestions are aimed at strengthening such assurances, provided these assurances are also properly instilled and nurtured in the context of the subject's total relationship with the suggestor. A similar approach using symbolic assertive training has been developed by Yarnell (1972).

Now I would like you to picture yourself standing at the top of a tall, snow-covered mountain, looking down into the valley below. Continue to hold this image in your mind and to focus on it, and soon it will become so vivid and so real to you that it will be just as if you were really there.

Down in the valley below, at the very foot of the mountain, you can see the place you have been trying to get to. Your journey has brought you as far as this mountaintop; but all along the mountainside, standing between you and your objective, are barriers and obstacles of many kinds, which represent all the things which have been standing between you and the attainment of your goal.

Bending down, you pick up a handful of snow and begin to examine it. Notice how soft and powdery it feels in your hands. In a way, it is comparable to how your resolve has sometimes been—soft and powdery, when it ought to have been firm and strong.

See yourself packing the snow together in your hand now and compressing it into a snowball as you add still more snow and pack it down, firm and round and hard. And as you do, you can feel your own courage and resolution becoming stronger and firmer too, as hard and as firm as the snowball you are preparing for its trip down the mountainside.

Now you walk over to a very steep incline at the side of the mountain and you gently begin to roll the snowball down it, straight at the obstacles below. Slowly, slowly the snowball begins to roll down the mountainside; and slowly, slowly it begins to grow. It's growing and growing and increasing in size with every foot it travels.

And as the snowball continues on, it grows to the size of a boulder, and then it becomes an avalanche, sweeping everything before it as it continues on all the way to the bottom.

Now you see that the way is clear before you. The obstacles have all been swept away, and you begin your descent down the mountainside, where your courage has gone before to clear a path for you.

And as you stride purposefully down the mountainside, you know that in your own mind, your resolution is continuing to grow, just like that snowball.

It is going to continue growing and getting stronger by itself, just as the snowball did. And soon it will become so strong that it, too, will sweep away every obstacle in its path, and you will easily be able to attain whatever goals in life you have set for yourself, just as easily as you now see yourself walking down the mountainside.

Now the scene is fading, and you are becoming aware of yourself back here with me once more, still in trance for a while, until I bring you out. But you will find in the coming days and weeks that the processes we have begun on the mountainside will continue of themselves: that your resolution will continue growing and getting stronger by itself; that each new day will find you stronger than the day before, until you are easily able to accomplish everything you have set out to do.

EMOTIONAL ENRICHMENT

Many people consistently go at life with such an air of grim determination that they eventually lose, or at least severely blunt, their capacity to experience joy and a zest for living—not merely abandoning their sense of childlike wonder, but also the deeper, richer experiences of fulfillment which are characteristic of the fully functioning adult (Schutz, 1967). Indeed, there are many individuals (and perhaps this includes most of us in the present culture) who have never fully developed such potentials in the first place (Maslow, 1964).

The following postinduction suggestions are not designed to induce excessive or inappropriate affect, nor are they intended to elicit strong emotion merely for its own sake. Rather, they are designed for use as a set of "toning up" exercises for sufficiently suggestible subjects who are familiar with their aims and purposes: as a means of strengthening and heightening the capacity for positive emotional response, and as a method of counteracting occasional tendencies toward depression when such tendencies are primarily the result of habit or of failure to maintain a sufficiently optimistic outlook on life. When combined with appropriate suggestions of time expansion, these suggestions may also be useful as a means of providing a temporary substitute for persons who are presently addicted to mood-altering drugs. They may also be used as a method of pain control by allowing the subject to experience the opposite emotions. A similar approach has been employed for this purpose by Sacerdote (1977).

Now, as you continue to listen to my words, you find yourself being mentally transported to the center of a large, green meadow which lies at the foot of a tall mountain. But this is no ordinary mountain looming up before you; for this is a mountain of pure joy, and you are about to climb all the way to the top of it.

Now you are beginning to climb the mountain of joy. And as you climb, you can feel this joy coursing through every fiber of your being, as the level of joy within you continues to rise.

> Now,
> you are about to be transported
> to greater heights of pleasure
> than you ever dreamed possible.
> As you continue soaring
> farther and farther into trance,
> you are already beginning
> to breathe more rapidly
> in anticipation
> of the joys which will soon be yours;
> for soon your entire body
> will be quivering with pleasure
> and tingling with delight.
> As you continue soaring
> farther and farther into trance,
> your ability to respond
> to experience of every kind
> is becoming infinitely keener.
> Your entire body
> is becoming exquisitely more sensitive
> and more responsive
> with every breath you take.
>
> You are beginning to breathe
> even faster now,
> as your capacity for experience
> multiplies itself over and over.
> And the higher you climb,
> the higher you want to climb
> and the stronger the effects of my words become.
>
> And as your entire body
> continues to grow more sensitive
> and more responsive
> with every breath you take,
> you are also becoming more free,
> more open,
> and more accepting
> of every type of experience.
> You are becoming totally and completely *free*,

as your responsiveness continues to grow
and your breathing comes still faster
in anticipation of the joys
which will soon be yours.
And the higher you go,
the higher you want to go
and the stronger the effects of my words become.

And now,
as your responsiveness and sensitivity
continue to increase
within an atmosphere of total freedom,
we are beginning to release
all of the vast, untapped resources
of feeling and emotion
which lie within you.
Probing the depths of your innermost self,
and releasing
every wonderful, positive emotion
for your exquisitely tuned body
to savor and experience to the fullest.

And the higher you go,
the higher you want to go
and the stronger the effects of my words become.

Great waves of pleasure, ecstasy, and delight
are gushing forth
from the innermost depths of your being
like water
from behind a bursting dam,
overwhelming you completely
as your breathing comes still faster
and your heart begins to pound.

But there is never any sense
of strain or fatigue;
for the heights
which you are able to achieve in trance
are truly without limit.
And the higher you go,
the higher you want to go
and the stronger the effects of my words become.

You are being guided
all the way to the peak of the mountain
by the sound of my words alone;
and as I continue,

you will feel wave after wave of ecstasy
building up
from the depths of your being
and rolling endlessly forth
like breakers upon an ocean shore.
Each successive wave,
as it comes crashing forth,
will carry you still higher,
leaving you ever more sensitive
and more responsive
to the one which is to follow.

And the higher you climb,
the higher you want to climb
and the stronger the effects of my words become.

The waves of joy
will come faster and faster
until they finally blend together
into one vast tide.
And when they finally fuse together
and become one,
they will carry you up to an ultimate peak of joy
which is the fulfillment of all existence.
And then you can sink back,
happy and fulfilled,
and able to experience joy more fully
in your everyday life.

And each time this exercise is repeated,
your capacity to experience joy will become greater,
and your ability to *live* joyfully
will be correspondingly enhanced.

Now, as you continue climbing on and on, you begin to sprint; for you are determined to reach the peak as soon as you can. And with every step, your speed increases. Running and running, breathing faster and faster, nearly bursting with delight as the level of joy within you continues to rise. And when you finally sink down upon the peak, a final burst of joy will explode within you like a rocket. Now you are very near the peak. Almost there. *Now!*

And as you sink down upon the peak and the joy begins to subside, it is followed by a boundless feeling of peace and tranquility, confidence and calm. You feel just as secure as a little baby nestled in its mother's arms. And as a result of having tapped into this vast potential for experiencing joy, you will be much more able to respond joyfully in everyday life situations; and each new day will contain new treasures of joy for you to discover and to experience.

Each time you climb this mountain of joy, you will be able to tap into more of this vast potential, and the joy which you are able to experience in your everyday life will be correspondingly enhanced.

Some individuals who possess the necessary training and skills have reported that the foregoing exercise may be facilitated by the simultaneous application of appropriate massage techniques.

AESTHETIC APPRECIATION AND ENJOYMENT

Although it has long been known that subjects are not capable of experiencing *genuine* hyperesthesias in response to suggestion (Hull, 1933), it is of course true that the *experiential* qualities of an event may be modified by such means. Thus, suggestion may be particularly useful in facilitating responsiveness to cultural products or works of art, as illustrated in the following procedure, which may be undertaken at the conclusion of an appropriate induction:

The next time you read a good novel, or see a quality motion picture, stage play, or television performance, what I am about to tell you will set in motion a number of changes in your artistic sensitivity and responsiveness; and these changes will greatly enhance your appreciation and understanding of what you experience, multiplying your enjoyment many times over.

You will find that all your senses will suddenly begin to feel much keener as the event begins, and that your emotional responsiveness is also considerably enhanced. These changes will enable you to become more and more deeply involved in the experience as it unfolds; for you will be able to follow it not merely with your senses alone, but with your entire being.

As time continues, the degree of your involvement in such cultural experiences will continue to increase, as this process repeats itself. And this enhancement of your artistic responsiveness will help you to discover new depths of appreciation in life itself, as you come to possess an ever-increasing ability to experience life in a richer and more rewarding manner.

FOREIGN LANGUAGE STUDY

For many persons having little contact with foreign language speaking people who are not themselves fluent in their newly adopted tongue, learning the vocabulary and syntax of a foreign language is of no immediate practical use, except perhaps for passing required examinations in the subject at school. Consequently, learning a foreign language is frequently experienced as about as tedious and devoid of meaning as learning a list of nonsense syllables. Thus, many students who may do well in other courses sometimes tend to "block" at language study, even when it is required, putting it off until the last possible moment and finally, after a disproportionate amount of effort, performing in a marginally satisfactory manner at best. Such a pattern may be encountered at any level, from the primary grades through advanced doctoral programs. However, most of the people who experience difficulty in the study of a foreign language probably took great delight in learning new words and phrases in their own native tongue when they were children. Indeed, the acquisition of language in normal young children is almost universally experienced as an enjoyable and a virtually effortless process.

Regardless of whether or not children may have more aptitude for language acquisition than adults, there is enough "child" remaining in all of us to continue learning in this relatively effortless manner long after childhood is past. Because of this tendency to continue to develop mastery over one's native tongue in a relatively effortless manner, most people have a "recognition" vocabulary which is considerably larger than the vocabulary they actually use in everyday communication. Thus, the apparent lack of relevance to everyday life of a basic vocabulary of foreign words and phrases can easily be overcome if one is able to view the new vocabulary as an extension of previous language-learning situations. Instead of blocking, a student will then be able to approach these tasks with the same attitude which has already enabled him to learn tens of thousands of rarely used words in his native tongue with little or no apparent effort.

The following suggestions are designed to further the development of such an identification of new language-learning tasks with those which have been undertaken previously. At the conclusion of an appropriate induction, one may proceed in the following manner:

Now I would like you to think of a particular nursery rhyme, bedtime story, or fairy tale which was your favorite when you were a child; or if you prefer, you can think of a motion picture or a television program which you particularly enjoyed when you were very young. I would like you to picture yourself as a young child again, listening to the story, or watching the program or the movie, and feeling completely enthralled by the performance, just as you did then. Just let your imagination go, and soon you will be able to recapture the mood completely, feeling now just as you felt then. And when you have fully caught the mood, you can signal me by raising the index finger of your right (or left) hand.

After the subject has raised his hand:

That's fine. Now just hold the mood for a moment and continue to listen to my voice, and as you do, you will notice the feeling growing even stronger. Notice how enthralled you feel, and how easy it is to concentrate and to absorb new information, almost without any deliberate effort.

From now on, whenever you wish, you will be able to call up this mood yourself, just by thinking of a situation like the one you have chosen and letting your imagination drift backward in time until you have recaptured the feeling completely. And the more often you practice doing this, the easier it will become, and the more strongly you will be able to feel such a mood once you have captured it again.

Now the mood is beginning to go away, but whenever you want to, you will be able to call it back and experience it once more, practicing and strengthening your ability to feel it ever more strongly and more intensely each time you do.

Now the mood is completely gone, but as a result of this experience, you are going to be able to transfer to your present language study more and more of the wonder and excitement which learning and using your own language used to hold for you as a child. When you are ready to begin your language homework, you will be able to call forth this same mood once again, just as I have shown you; and if the mood should start to "wear off" before you finish studying, you can take a break for a few moments and call it back again. For the more often you practice recalling and reexperiencing these feelings, the stronger your ability to reexperience them will become, and the more easily you will be able to do so.

And as a result of this change in mood and in attitude, you will find a great improvement taking place in your ability to acquire and to use foreign words and phrases; for they will not seem "foreign" to you at all, but rather, a continuation of the language learning you have always enjoyed. These new words and phrases will come to possess the same interest, the same fascination and appeal, and the same power to arouse your curiosity and to capture and hold your attention as did your own native language when you were first acquiring it. You will spend a great deal of time turning the new information over in your mind and making up games with it in order to amuse yourself, just as children often do. And consequently, you will be able to learn, to retain, and to use the new language with the same ease, the same naturalness of expression, and the same inherent grammatical sense which characterized the learning of your mother tongue as a child.

The entire process of language learning will become a natural, an enjoyable, and a spontaneous process once again, and you are going to be absolutely delighted at your progress.

INTERPERSONAL EFFECTIVENESS

Subjects occasionally ask to be given suggestions to enable them to be "more trusting," and "more accepting of others." I then feel obliged to point out that if there is something about another person which the subject might find difficult to accept, or which makes it hard for him to trust this person, then perhaps things are best left as they are, lest the subject run the risk of being hurt. However, suggestions may be administered to improve social skills and facilitate interpersonal effectiveness, which may often accomplish the same general purpose, leaving the degree of trust and acceptance in individual relationships to be determined by the nature of the particular relationship in question.

The following procedure also includes specific suggestions to facilitate the appropriate use of assertiveness, which many people—especially women—find particularly difficult to exhibit without such permission. After a hypnotic or a hyperempiric induction has been given, the following suggestions may be provided:

This experience will provide you with a great deal more confidence in yourself, which will be reflected in the greater ease and skill with which you will be able to deal with others. You will be a great deal less aware of yourself, and a great deal more attentive to those around you. You will be much more interested in what other people have to say, and much more able to lose yourself in the topic of conversation.

As you come to derive more and more enjoyment out of talking to others, you will find yourself constantly alert for qualities, attributes, and achievements which are justly deserving of praise, and you will be able and willing to unstintingly provide it. At the same time, you will be able to exercise a great deal of restraint over any anger or impatience you may have over the shortcomings of other people. And if you should happen to feel that another person is unfairly taking advantage of you in some way, you will be able to phrase your objections kindly and tactfully, in a manner which will enable you to speak up for your own rights without becoming unduly emotional, and without the other party unnecessarily taking offense.

As your confidence and skills improve, you will become vastly more sensitive to the emotional needs of those around you, and you will be able to find new sources of wisdom and understanding which will help you to meet those needs. There will be many people who will be able to look upon you as a friend to whom they can turn for comfort, for reassurance, and for advice, and there will be many whom you will be able to look upon as a friend in return. Your own life will consequently take on a great deal more meaning, and you will be able to enrich the lives of those around you considerably.

MUSICAL PERFORMANCE

The following postinduction suggestions are intended to facilitate musical performance by encouraging a close identification with musicians whose performance the student has previously come to admire. A similar approach has been reported by Raikov (1976):

Now I would like you to think of some musician who plays the same instrument you do, whose playing you are especially fond of—or, if you wish, you can think of one of the great virtuosos on this instrument from the past. I'm going to count backwards from five to one; and by the time I get to one, you will be able to feel just as if you were this person, feeling as he feels and playing as he plays.

You will always be able to hear and to respond to my voice, and I will return you to your own identity in a while; but until I do so, every aspect of the situation to which I guide you will seem completely real, and you will be able to experience it all just as if you were really there. So just continue listening to my voice now, as I begin to count backward from five to one.

Five. Your awareness of the present is beginning to grow dim as you feel yourself being mentally transported into a new situation and into a new identity. And by the time I get to the count of one, the transition will be complete. Four. You are beginning to lose awareness of the present completely now, as my words transport you on to the identity of the person you have chosen. Three. You are becoming aware of yourself as this other person now, as the musician you have selected. Feel yourself entering this other body, and feel your identities beginning to merge. Two. You can feel great wellsprings of talent and ability flowing through every muscle and every fiber and every nerve of this new body as your identities merge completely now; and you can see yourself playing as you have never played before. One. Your identities have merged completely now, and you can see and feel yourself playing as you have never played before. Live the experience, and enjoy it fully for a moment, and then it will be time to return.

(After a moment's pause:)

Now I am going to return you to your original identity. But you will be able to carry back with you the feelings which you have experienced, and your own playing and your own confidence will be greatly enhanced as a result. By the time I get to the count of five, you will be back to your normal identity; but you will remain in trance for a while, until I bring you out.

One. Beginning to lose your awareness of yourself as the other person, and beginning to become aware of your original identity once more, here in trance, with me once again. Two. Coming back now, coming all the way back, but remaining in trance for just a while longer. Three. Beginning to be fully aware of your true identity now. Four. Almost back. Five. Now you have fully resumed your own identity, but you will still remain in trance for a while, until I bring you out.

As a result of the experience you have just undergone, you will notice a great many improvements taking place in your own musical performance. Whenever you begin to play for others, you will become completely absorbed in the music with the very first note. You will become so absorbed in the piece you are playing that all sense of self is lost, and all traces of fear and doubt are lost as well. Your timing and your concentration will be perfect, and as you and the music merge together, you will be able to tap into the feelings you have experienced just now and feel the same wonderful sense of power and ability flowing out from the innermost depths of your being and flowing on to touch the hearts of everyone who hears you play.

When the performance is ended, you will realize just how deeply you have been able to tap into the boundless wellsprings of talent and ability which lie within you, and you will experience a great surge of exaltation and a deep sense of personal fulfillment and satisfaction at the realization that you have been able to perform so well. It will always be a source of deep personal satisfaction to you that you are able to use your own vast talents so fully and so well, and you will come to look forward to each performance supremely confident that you are honing your talent to its finest possible edge, looking forward to the inevitable moment of triumph which this awareness will bring to you when the performance is completed.

A specific situation may also be suggested which represents a special moment of triumph in the career of the artist chosen, or in the future career of the artist himself. Moreover, if the subject is able to open his eyes without disturbing his ongoing experience of trance, he may actually perform for a few moments while imagining himself in the identity of another. With the subject seated before his instrument and ready to play, an induction may be administered in the usual manner and the preceding suggestions may be administered as far as the count of two, at which time the following verbalizations may be substituted:

You can feel great wellsprings of power and ability flowing through every muscle and every fiber and every nerve of your body as your identities begin to merge completely. One. Your identities have completely merged together now, and you can open your eyes and begin to play. Live the experience fully and play as you have never played before.

After a moment or two has elapsed, the subject may be requested to close his eyes and the suggestions for canceling the identification may be administered as previously indicated.

PROBLEM SOLVING

Wallas (1926) has postulated that creative thinking tends to occur in four distinct phases: *preparation,* during which time one becomes familiar with the relevant aspects of a problem; *incubation,* when the solution is forming—even though one's conscious attention may be temporarily occupied with other matters; *illumination,* when the solution finally emerges into awareness; and *verification,* when the new idea is scrutinized to determine whether or not it does indeed constitute a valid solution to the problem at hand. Whatever its other merits, such a fourfold classification is useful in pointing to the fact that many problems do seem to be easier to resolve if one lays them aside temporarily after becoming sufficiently familiar with their content; and that the solution, when it does occur, often seems to come to mind spontaneously while one is consciously engaged in some other type of activity.

Bowers (1978) has recently found a strong relationship between the ability to solve problems in an apparently effortless manner and the ability to experience a suggested trance. It is my own belief that the process of incubation may be facilitated by direct suggestion—if only because the subject is thereby made more confident that an effective solution will be forthcoming. At the conclusion of an induction, the following suggestions may be given:

In the coming days and weeks, your thoughts will often turn to the consideration of important decisions you have to make, and important problems for which you have as yet found no solution. Even when you are not consciously thinking about these topics, your mind will continue to deal with them so that, when your attention returns to them once more, you are going to be surprised and delighted at how many potentially useful ideas you are able to come up with; and some of these ideas are even likely to catch you by surprise at times, emerging into your awareness while you are thinking of something else. They might even enter your dreams at night, or you might wake up with some of these new ideas in mind; but regardless of how they make their appearance, they are going to be very helpful and beneficial to you.

Of course, you will always try to make sure that you have sufficient information on which to base any final decisions, and you will always want to check out these new ideas to make sure that they are practical, just as you would check out information from any other source. You will also continue to be aware that sometimes the best decision is a decision to wait or to secure additional information before acting. But nevertheless, you are going to be surprised and pleased at how much more clearly and creatively you are going to be able to think, and at how much more confidently and effectively you will be able to deal with the issues and problems which lie before you.

PUBLIC SPEAKING

The following suggestions may be administered at the conclusion of an induction procedure as a means of providing the subject with an opportunity to displace his anxiety over speaking in public to a time before the talk actually begins, and to diminish his self-consciousness during the course of the speech itself by fostering an enhanced involvement with the material. As the subject begins to discover from direct personal experience how much more effectively he is able to speak in public without his fear to impede him, suggestions such as these may help to foster a permanent diminution in anxiety:

First of all, I would like you to allow yourself to express your fear of public speaking freely and openly for a moment, allowing it to escape like steam escaping from a safety valve, to relieve the pressure. So just picture yourself up there giving your talk, and let yourself feel all the anxiety for a moment, just as strongly as you can. Let your imagination go, and let yourself feel all the anxiety you have been holding back. Feel it surging to the surface. Let yourself feel it all and experience it all. *Now!*

And as I continue to speak, your fear is beginning to leave; for you have allowed most of it to escape by permitting yourself to express it openly. Your fear has been considerably weakened, and what little is left of it is going away completely. It's almost gone. Now your fear is completely gone, and you can feel a great sense of relief.

And whenever you are about to give any kind of public speech, you will be able to feel and experience all the anxiety that the speech may cause you; but this anxiety will always be felt *before* you are about to begin, so that by the time you actually start to speak, most of the anxiety will already have been released. And any remaining tension will be well within the range that is helpful—just enough to add liveliness and sparkle to your delivery, but not enough to detract from it or prevent you from doing your very best.

Because you are able to express all your unnecessary anxiety ahead of time, you will be able to concentrate completely on what you have to say as soon as your speech begins, without worrying about how you may look or sound to others. And as your talk progresses, you will soon become so engrossed in what you have to say that you will forget about yourself completely.

When your speech is concluded, you will be full of the warm feeling of accomplishment which comes from the certain knowledge that you have done well. And as time goes on, this realization of how well you are actually doing will cause your anxiety to become less and less, until it disappears completely.

SALESMANSHIP

Most of the commission income in selling appears to be earned by a small proportion of the total sales force. Thus, many sales organizations are organized around a small core of stellar performers, together with a rather large coterie of what is sometimes termed *revolving door people*—relative newcomers to the organization who will soon be leaving because they do not become proficient at the job quickly enough.

Selling on commission may be viewed as an example of variable ratio reinforcement (Ferster & Skinner, 1957). That is, the commission salesman is almost never certain whether a day's work is going to result in a large number of orders for his product, a relatively few orders, or perhaps even no orders at all. Consequently, his monthly income is subject to a considerable amount of fluctuation; and much more effort may be necessary for the fledgling salesman to earn a commission at the beginning of his employment than will be necessary later, as the ratio improves.

Because this type of reinforcement schedule is difficult for most people to adapt to—even though it does tend to result in optimum levels of performance for those who do—and because it is difficult to shape the appropriate selling skills on such a schedule if the newcomer is not proficient in selling already, turnover in such organizations tends to be quite high in spite of attempts to deal with the problem by the use of inspirational talks and other morale-building techniques.

The following exercise may be used to encourage persistence when present sources of reinforcement may not be entirely adequate. By means of a suggested temporal progression (Erickson, 1954), the subject is enabled to experience perceptions which normally are associated only with goal attainment, thereby enhancing the clarity and meaningfulness of the goal itself while at the same time inducing pleasant emotions which act to reinforce the subject's present efforts and sharpen his expectations of the satisfactions which are to come when the goal is finally achieved. After a hypnotic or a hyperempiric induction, suggestions may be administered as follows:

Now I would like you to think of some major incentive which you are working toward, and which you would like to achieve in the future. It might be taking an ocean cruise, or seeing a child graduate from college, or building your dream house—in fact, it could be almost anything. But whatever it is, this goal should be an important one, and one which is within your power to achieve as a result of your own efforts.

And when you have the goal firmly in mind, I would like you to picture yourself transported into the future, savoring the fruits of your achievement and enjoying the knowledge that the goal for which you have worked so long and so hard is finally yours. Continue to hold the image in your mind, and to focus on it, and soon it will be just as if you were really there.

Let yourself begin to live the experience now. You have achieved what you have set out to attain, and the fruits of your efforts are yours to enjoy. Live the fulfillment of your goal and allow yourself to experience all the joy and the satisfaction which come from knowing that your ambitions have at last been realized. Let yourself savor the thrill of achievement and bask in the warm, rewarding glow of a job well done.

And as you allow yourself to let go completely and experience this event fully, savoring your triumph and all its fruits, the feelings of satisfaction and achievement are becoming clearer and sharper and more intense with every passing moment.

In a little while, I'm going to return you to the present time. But until I do, let yourself continue to enjoy the fulfillment of the goal which you have worked so hard to attain, as the feelings of achievement and satisfaction continue to grow, and each passing second finds them stronger than they were before.

(After a two-minute interval of free fantasy:)

It's time to return to the present now, to the time from which you left. You are beginning to return to the present time, and the scene you have been experiencing in your mind is beginning to fade, but you will still remain in trance for a while, until I bring you out. You will feel renewed and recharged as a result of your experience, and you will possess a heightened resolve to succeed in the attainment of your goal.

And now the scene is fading more and more, almost gone. Now the scene is completely gone, and you are back with me in the present. You are feeling renewed and recharged, and more determined than ever to succeed in the attainment of the goal you have envisioned, for its benefits and attractions are now so much more clearly apparent than they were before.

Sales productivity may also be facilitated by a number of other techniques presented herein, such as the suggestions for ego strengthening and for achievement motivation.

The foregoing approach may be adapted to increasing work output in a wide variety of other situations in which present sources of reinforcement may not be sufficient to maintain performance at the necessary level—for example, in spurring the performance of graduate students who are experiencing "dissertation doldrums."

SPORTS PERFORMANCE

Since even the best players can occasionally encounter a losing streak, care should be taken to avoid suggesting specific targets which might lead to a loss of faith in the efficacy of the procedure if specific levels of athletic performance are not attained. By the same token, athletes should not be encouraged by means of suggestion to train or to compete so strenuously that they run the risk of possible injury or of diminishing their resources instead of continuing to improve. However, suggestion may be employed to maximize the enjoyment of playing well, while simultaneously decreasing the fear of possible failure, thus providing the subject with positive attitudes which are highly conducive to continued growth. The following suggestions may be administered at the conclusion of an appropriate induction:

As a result of what I am about to tell you now, you will find that any negative aspects of sports performance which might have troubled you in the past will have greatly diminished in importance, and as times goes on, their importance will continue to decrease. With each passing day, you will find yourself adopting a much brighter outlook, in which the positive aspects of playing and the lure of success have taken on a great deal more appeal. And in this more positive frame of mind, you will come to experience wonderful new feelings of strength and energy as you find yourself looking forward eagerly to each new challenge, wanting more than ever to play and to win.

Any psychological barriers or obstacles which might have been keeping you from performing well are being eliminated. You are able to look forward to each new game, secure in the knowledge of your own abilities and of the vast potential within you for further growth. Nothing is holding you back any longer. Every barrier, every obstacle, has been removed. You are completely free to develop all the vast potential within you to its fullest extent.

And as you proceed, the success of winning will be experienced as infinitely richer and more rewarding than it has ever been before; whereas the sting of any occasional setback you may still encounter will be so considerably diminished that you will scarcely notice it. You will be able to accept any occasional reversal calmly and philosophically, as the small price which must be paid to experience the rich joys of playing and of winning. And even an occasional losing streak will no longer be of any undue concern to you. Since playing itself has become so enjoyable, you will be able to derive satisfaction from *any* game, regardless of the outcome.

All these changes will naturally result in marked improvements in your training, your preparation, and in everything which contributes to your actual performance. You will make sure that you get all the rest that you require, and you will be able to sleep soundly and well. You will be able to do whatever else is necessary as part of your training and preparation.

You will not waste time and energy worrying about your past or future performance; for each time you play, you will feel yourself improving. Each time you play, regardless of whether you win or lose, you will take continuing pride in your strategy and skill, and in your timing and coordination. And each time you play, you will find that you are advancing closer and closer to the goal of becoming the player that you want to be.

THEATRICAL PERFORMANCE

Shaw (1978) has recently reported that students enrolled in an acting school appeared to perform their stage roles more effectively after being administered a hypnotic induction, although enunciation seemed to be somewhat less distinct and concern for the audience slightly diminished. I have observed a similar apparent increase in effectiveness, without any discernible negative effects, by employing suggestions such as the following, which are administered after a hyperempiric or hypnotic induction:

Whenever you are rehearsing a part, you will be able to identify so closely with the character you portray that you will come to experience the part in just the same way that the character is supposed to have lived it. You will be able to feel the character's own emotions and think the character's own thoughts, as you submerge yourself in the part completely; and when the rehearsal is over, or whenever you should need to before then, it will be just as easy to slip back into your own identity once again.

You will also be pleased to find how much easier it is going to be to learn your lines; for identifying so closely with the part will make it seem as if the words were your very own.

By the time of the performance, you will have become able to submerge yourself so completely in the role that every trace of self-consciousness will have vanished, and every trace of stage fright along with it.

For as long as you need to while the performance is going on, you will be able to feel as if you have actually become the character you are to portray, laughing his laughter and crying his tears. You will be able to live the part so intensely that you will project this personality clearly and vividly to every member of the audience. And you are going to be absolutely delighted at the extent to which your heightened involvement with the part will result in a steady and continuing improvement in your acting abilities.

WRITING ABILITY

Many established writers have come to experience their work as necessarily involving a considerable amount of stress. Indeed, it is often said that good writing is inevitably the product of personal pain and trauma on the part of the writer. This association of creativity with pain and struggle may often be the result of one's having initially turned to writing as a means of catharsis or escape, or as the principal source of earning one's livelihood at a time when the income which could be derived from such endeavors was fairly meagre. In addition to the difficulty often associated with writing itself, many writers, particularly those who are just getting started, are often subject ot prolonged periods of inactivity referred to as *writer's block.*

Many psychologists are agreed, however, that creativity is intrinsically a natural, joyful process (Rogers, 1959; Wertheimer, 1945). Although many writers have apparently been impelled by a "personal demon," in the form of early traumatic experiences which drove them to write, much as a grain of sand beneath the shell of any oyster may compel the oyster to produce a pearl, writing itself need not be experienced as distressing or painful. Not only does the net effect of such a pattern tend to be counterproductive—like attempting to drive a car by applying pressure to the brake and gas pedals simultaneously—but it is also a pattern few writers would consciously wish to emulate if they were given a choice.

Probably the two most fundamental principles of psychology are that learned behavior will not long persist unless it leads to consequences which are in some way rewarding or reinforcing for the individual concerned, and that the immediate consequences of an action are usually much more important determinants of such desirability than are its long-range consequences. A person who is engaged in writing—whether it be a novel, a newspaper article, or a doctoral dissertation—is frequently in a position to take full advantage of these all-important principles; for a writer is often able to exercise a great amount of choice and flexibility in regard to the specific times and locations in which the writing is to be carried out. Instead of becoming unduly concerned with a series of artificially imposed deadlines, if one takes as one's primary obligation to insure genuinely that each period spent in writing is experienced as pleasurable, regardless of how much or how little is actually accomplished, one need give little thought to the eventual conclusion of the project; for with each such time period pleasurably spent, the desire to write will become stronger and the pace of the work will tend to accelerate. As writing comes to be experienced as ever more enjoyable, the process will also tend to become a great deal more efficient as one's ideational processes become more fully committed to the task, even when one is not consciously engaged in it.

The following suggestions for the enhancement of writing ability may also be presented, in conjunction with suggestions for ego strengthening and for achievement motivation, to assist the subject to replace recurring fantasies of failure with positive expectations of success:

Whenever you are engaged in creative writing, you will find that during your spare moments your thoughts will tend to turn to whatever you are writing about. These frequent moments of extra attention will keep new ideas constantly forming in your mind, even when you are consciously preoccupied with other matters.

Because of this extra attention, new ideas and associations will frequently emerge into your awareness as though unbidden; and when you begin to write, these new ideas and associations will flow even more freely, providing you with a steady stream of inspiration.

As you write, you will be able to maintain continuous contact with these vast resources of creativity which lie within you. You will be able to carry out any revisions which may be necessary as the work progresses, without any undue reluctance on your part to change what you have already written, and without striving for perfection for its own sake in those instances wherein it is more important to finish what you have begun.

You will be able to break your writing down into small segments which can be comfortably fitted into the time you have at your disposal, enabling you to maintain a pace which is both productive and enjoyable, without feeling unduly rushed or under pressure. And when each writing period is over, or each segment of the work is completed, you will experience strong feelings of pride, achievement, and accomplishment, which stem from an ever-growing realization that you are employing your abilities fully and well. Writing will thus be experienced as a spontaneous, natural, and joyful process, which will enable you to make the fullest use of your creative potential.

References

Allport, G. W. *Pattern and growth in personality*. New York: Holt, Rhinehart & Winston, 1961.

Anderson, M., & Savary, L. *Passages: A guide for pilgrims of the mind*. New York: Harper & Row, 1972.

Andreychuk, T., & Skriver, C. Hypnosis and biofeedback in the treatment of migraine headaches. *International Journal of Clinical and Experimental Hypnosis*, 1975, 23, 172–183.

Araoz, D. L. *Clinical hypnosis in treating sexual abulia*. Paper presented at the meetings of the American Psychological Association, Toronto, August, 1978.

Arluck, E. W. *Hypnoanalysis: A case study*. New York: Random House, 1964.

Atkinson, J. W. Motivational determinants of risk-taking behavior. *Psychological Review*, 1957, 64, 359–372.

Atkinson, J. W., & Litwin, G. Achievement motive and test anxiety conceived as motive to approach success and motive to avoid failure. *Journal of Abnormal and Social Psychology*, 1960, 60, 52–63.

Bakan, P. Hypnotizability, laterality of eye movements and functional brain asymmetry. *Perceptual and Motor Skills*, 1969, 28, 927–932.

Barber, T. X. *Hypnosis: A scientific approach*. New York: Van Nostrand Reinhold, 1969.

Barber, T. X. Suggested "hypnotic" behavior: The trance paradigm versus an alternate paradigm. In E. Fromm & R. E. Shor (Eds.), *Hypnosis: Research developments and perspectives*. Chicago: Aldine-Atherton, 1972.

Barber, T. X. Responding to "hypnotic" suggestions: An introspective report. *American Journal of Clinical Hypnosis*, 1975, 18, 6–22.

Barber, T. X. Hypnosis, suggestions, and psychosomatic phenomena: A new look from the standpoint of recent experimental studies. *American Journal of Clinical Hypnosis*, 1978, 21, 13–27.

Barber, T. X., & Calverley, D. S. "Hypnotic-like" suggestibility in children and adults. *Journal of Abnormal and Social Psychology*, 1963, 66, 589–597.

Barber, T. X. & Calverley, D. S. Toward a theory of hypnotic behavior: Experimental evaluation of Hull's postulate that hypnotic susceptibility is a habit phenomenon. *Journal of Personality*, 1966, 34, 416–433.

Barber, T. X., & De Moor, W. A theory of hypnotic induction procedures. *American Journal of Clinical Hypnosis*, 1972, 15, 112–135.

195

Barber, T. X., & Wilson, S. C. Hypnosis, suggestion, and altered states of consciousness: Experimental evaluation of the new cognitive-behavioral theory and the traditional trance-state theory of "hypnosis." In W. E. Edmonston (Ed.), *Conceptual and investigative approaches to hypnotic phenomena. Annals of the New York Academy of Sciences*, 1977, *296*, 34–45.

Barber, T. X., Ascher, L. M., & Mavroides, M. Effects of practice on hypnotic suggestibility: A re-evaluation of Hull's postulates. *American Journal of Clinical Hypnosis*, 1971, *14*, 48–53.

Baumann, F. Hypnosis and the adolescent drug user. *American Journal of Clinical Hypnosis*, 1970, *13*, 17–21.

Bernstein, M. *The search for Bridey Murphy.* Garden City, N.Y.: Doubleday, 1956.

Bonny, H. *Music and your mind.* New York: Harper & Row, 1973.

Boring, E. G. *A history of experimental psychology* (2nd ed.). New York: Appleton-Century-Crofts, 1950.

Bowers, P. Hypnotizability, creativity, and the role of effortless experiencing. *International Journal of Clinical and Experimental Hypnosis*, 1978, *26*, 184–202.

Bristol, C. *The magic of believing.* New York: Prentice-Hall, 1957.

Cannon, W. B. *Bodily changes in pain, hunger, fear, and rage* (2nd ed.). New York: D. Appleton, 1929.

Chaves, J., & Brown, J. *Self-generated strategies for control of pain and stress.* Paper presented at the meetings of the American Psychological Association, Toronto, August, 1978.

Cheek, D. B., & LeCron, L. M. *Clinical hypnotherapy.* New York: Grune & Stratton, 1968.

Coe, W. C., & Sarbin, T. R. Hypnosis from the standpoint of a contextualist. In W. E. Edmonston (Ed.), *Conceptual and investigative approaches to hypnotic phenomena. Annals of the New York Academy of Sciences*, 1977, *296*, 2–13.

Coleman, J. C. *Abnormal psychology and modern life* (5th ed.). Glenview, Ill.: Scott, Foresman, 1976.

Conn, J. Is hypnosis really dangerous? *International Journal of Clinical and Experimental Hypnosis*, 1972, *20*, 61–79.

Cooper, L. Time distortion in hypnosis. In L. Le Cron (Ed.), *Experimental hypnosis.* New York: Macmillan, 1956, pp. 217–228.

Cooper, L., & Erickson, M. *Time distortion in hypnosis: An experimental and clinical investigation.* Baltimore: Williams & Wilkins, 1954.

Coué, E. *Self-mastery through conscious autosuggestion.* London: Allen & Unwin, 1932.

Crasilneck, H. B., & Hall, J. A. *Clinical hypnosis: Problems and applications.* New York: Grune & Stratton, 1975.

Crawford, H. J. *Hypnotic pain reduction: Relationship to measured hypnotic susceptibility.* Paper presented at the meetings of the American Psychological Association, Toronto, August, 1978.

Deabler, H. Fidel, E., Dillenkoffer, R., & Elder, S. The use of relaxation and hypnosis in lowering high blood pressure. *American Journal of Clinical Hypnosis*, 1973, *16*, 75–83.

Deibert, A., & Harmon, A. *New tools for changing behavioror.* Champaign, Ill.: Research Press, 1977.

de Ropp, R. *The master game: Pathways to higher consciousness beyond the drug experience.* New York: Dell, 1968.

Diamond, J. J. Hypnotizability is modifiable: An alternative approach. *International Journal of Clinical and Experimental Hypnosis*, 1977, *25*, 147–166.

Dollard, J., & Miller, N. *Personality and psychotherapy.* New York: McGraw-Hill, 1950.

Donk, L. J., Vingoe, F. J., Hall, R. A., & Doty, R. The comparison of three suggestion techniques for increasing reading efficiency in a counterbalanced research paradigm. *International Journal of Clinical and Experimental Hypnosis*, 1970, *18*, 126–133.

Erickson, M. Pseudo-orientation in time as a hypnotherapeutic procedure. *Journal of Clinical and Experimental Hypnosis*, 1954, *2*, 261–283.

Erickson, M., & Rossi, E. Varieties of double bind. *American Journal of Clinical Hypnosis*, 1975, *17*, 143–157.

Erickson, M., Rossi, E., & Rossi, S. *Hypnotic realities*. New York: Wiley, 1976.

Evans, F. J. Comment at meetings of the American Psychological Association, Toronto, August, 1978.

Ferster, C. B., & Skinner, B. F. *Schedules of reinforcement*. New York: Appleton-Century-Crofts, 1957.

Festinger, L. *A theory of cognitive dissonance*. New York: Harper & Row, 1957.

Fischer, R. A cartography of ecstatic and meditative states. *Science*, 1971, *174*, 897–904.

Frank, J. D. *Persuasion and healing: A comparative study of psychotherapy*. Baltimore: The Johns Hopkins University Press, 1974.

Friedman, H., & Taub, H. The use of hypnosis and biofeedback procedures for essential hypertension. *International Journal of Clinical and Experimental Hypnosis*, 1977, *25*, 335–347.

Fromm-Reichmann, F. *Principles of intensive psychotherapy*. Chicago: University of Chicago Press, 1950.

Gardner, M. *Fads and fallacies in the name of science*. New York: Dover, 1957.

Gaunitz, S. C., Unestahl, L., & Bergland, B. A posthypnotically released emotion as a modifier of behavior. *International Journal of Clinical and Experimental Hypnosis*, 1975, *23*, 120–129.

Gibbons, D. Directed experience hypnosis: A one-year follow-up investigation. *American Journal of Clinical Hypnosis*, 1971, *13*, 101–103.

Gibbons, D. *Beyond hypnosis: Explorations in hyperempiria*. South Orange, N.J.: Power Publishers, 1973.

Gibbons, D. Hyperempiria: A new "altered state of consciousness" induced by suggestion. *Perceptual and Motor Skills*, 1974, *39*, 47–53.

Gibbons, D. Hypnotic vs. hyperempiric induction: An experimental comparison. *Perceptual and Motor Skills*, 1976, *42*, 834.

Gibbons, D., & Glenn, R. Hypnotic vs. hyperempiric induction with institutionalized delinquents. Paper presented at the meetings of the American Psychological Association, Toronto, August, 1978.

Gibbons, D., Kilbourne, L., Saunders, A., & Castles, C. The cognitive control of behavior: A comparison of systematic desensitization and hypnotically induced "directed experience" techniques. *American Journal of Clinical Hypnosis*, 1970, *12*, 141–145.

Gibson, H. B. *Hypnosis: Its nature and therapeutic uses*. New York: Taplinger, 1977.

Gill, M., & Brenman, M. *Hypnosis and related states*. New York: International Universities Press, 1959.

Goddard, H. H. *Two souls in one body? A case of dual personality*. New York: Dodd, Mead, 1927.

Graham, G. W. Hypnotic treatment for migraine headaches. *International Journal of Clinical and Experimental Hypnosis*, 1975, *23*, 165–171.

Greenberg, I. *Psychodrama and audience attitude change*. Beverly Hills, Calif.: Behavioral Studies Press, 1968.

Haley, J. *Strategies of psychotherapy*. New York: W. W. Norton, 1973.

Hartland, J. Further observations on the use of "ego strengthening" techniques. *American Journal of Clinical Hypnosis*, 1971, *14*, 1–8. (a)

Hartland, J. *Medical and dental hypnosis and its clinical applications* (2nd ed.). London: Baillière Tindall, 1971. (b)

Hilgard, E. R. *Hypnotic susceptibility*. New York: Harcourt, Brace & World, 1965.

Hilgard, E. R. A neo-dissociation interpretation of pain reduction in hypnosis. *Psychological Review*, 1973, *80*, 396–411.

Hilgard, E. R. Toward a neo-dissociation theory: Multiple cognitive controls in human functioning. *Perspectives in Biology and Medicine*, 1974, *17*, 301–316.

Hilgard, E. R. *Divided consciousness: Multiple controls in human thought and action*. Somerset, N.J.: Wiley Interscience, 1977. (a)

Hilgard, E. R. The problem of divided consciousness: A neodissociation interpretation. In W. E. Edmonston (Ed.), *Conceptual and investigative approaches to hypnotic phenomena. Annals of the New York Academy of Sciences*, 1977, *247*, 48–59. (b)

Hilgard, E. R., & Hilgard, J. R. *Hypnosis in the relief of pain*. Los Altos, Calif.: William Kaufmann, 1975.

Hilgard, J. R. *Personality and hypnosis: A study of imaginative involvement*. Chicago: University of Chicago Press, 1970.

Hilgard, J. R. Sequelae to hypnosis. *International Journal of Clinical and Experimental Hypnosis*, 1974, *32*, 281–298. (a)

Hilgard, J. R. Imaginative involvement: Some characteristics of the highly hypnotizable and the non-hypnotizable. *International Journal of Clinical and Experimental Hypnosis*, 1974, *22*, 138–156. (b)

Hilgard, J. R., Hilgard, E. R., & Newman, M. Sequelae to hypnotic induction with special reference to earlier chemical anesthesia. *Journal of Nervous and Mental Disease*, 1961, *133*, 461–478.

Hull, C. L. Quantitative methods of investigating waking suggestion. *Journal of Abnormal and Social Psychology*, 1929, *24*, 153–169.

Hull, C. L. *Hypnosis and suggestibility: An experimental approach*. New York: Appleton-Century, 1933.

Huxley, A. *Brave New World*. New York: Harper & Row, 1932.

Johnson, R. F., Maher, B. A., & Barber, T. X. Artifact in the "essence of hypnosis:" An evaluation of trance logic. *Journal of Abnormal Psychology*, 1972, *79*, 212–220.

Johnson, R. F. Q., & Barber, T. X. Hypnosis, suggestions, and warts: An experimental investigation indicating the importance of "believed-in efficacy." *American Journal of Clinical Hypnosis*, 1978, *20*, 165–174.

Jones, R. A. *Self-fulfilling prophecies*. New York: Wiley, 1977.

Kampman, R. Hypnotically induced multiple personality: An experimental study. *International Journal of Clinical and Experimental Hypnosis*, 1976, *24*, 215–227.

Katz, N. W. *Comparative efficacy of sleep/trance instructions and behavior modification instructions in enhancing hypnotic suggestibility*. Doctoral dissertation, Washington University, 1975.

Kidder, L. E. On becoming hypnotized: How skeptics become convinced: A case of attitude change? *Journal of Abnormal Psychology*, 1972, *80*, 317–322.

Kline, M. V. *Freud and hypnosis*. New York: Julian Press, 1950.

Kline, M. V. The production of antisocial behavior through hypnosis: New clinical data. *International Journal of Clinical and Experimental Hypnosis*, 1972, *20*, 80–94.

Knox, V. J., Morgan, A. H., & Hilgard, E. R. Pain and suffering in ischemia: The paradox of hypnotically suggested analgesia as contradicted by reports from the "Hidden Observer." *Archives of General Psychiatry*, 1974, *30*, 840–847.

Kroger, W. S. *Clinical and experimental hypnosis in medicine, dentistry, and psychology* (2nd ed.). Philadelphia: Lippincott, 1977.

Krogger, W. S., & Fezler, W. D. *Hypnosis and behavior modification: Imagery conditioning.* Philadelphia: Lippincott, 1976.

Lawlor, E. Hypnotic intervention with "school phobic" children. *International Journal of Clinical and Experimental Hypnosis,* 1976, *24,* 74–86.

Lecky, P. *Self-consistency: A theory of personality.* New York: Island Press, 1945.

Lee, W. *Formulating and reaching goals.* Champaign, Ill.: Research Press, 1978.

Levitt, E. Comment at the meetings of the American Psychological Association, Toronto, August, 1978.

Levitt, E. Research strategies in evaluating the coercive power of hypnosis. In W. E. Edmonston (Ed.), *Conceptual and investigative approaches to hypnotic phenomena. Annals of the New York Academy of Sciences,* 1977, *296,* 86–99.

Lindner, R. *The fifty-minute hour.* Des Plaines, Ill.: Bantam, 1976.

London, P. Hypnosis in children: An experimental approach. *International Journal of Clinical and Experimental Hypnosis,* 1962, *10,* 79–91.

Maier, N. R. F., Glaser, N. M., & Klee, J. B. Studies of abnormal behavior in the rat: III. The development of behavior fixations through frustration. *Journal of Experimental Psychology,* 1940, *26,* 521–546.

Maltz, M. *Psycho-cybernetics.* New York: Prentice-Hall, 1960.

Marks, R. W. The story of hypnotism. New York: Prentice-Hall, 1947.

McDonald, R. D., & Smith, J. R. Trance logic in tranceable and simulating subjects. *International Journal of Clinical and Experimental Hypnosis,* 1975, *23,* 80–89.

Maslow, A. *Religion, values, and peak experiences.* Columbus: Ohio State University Press, 1964.

Masters, R., & Houston, J. *Mind games: The guide to inner space.* New York: Viking, 1972.

Meares, A. *A system of medical hypnosis.* Philadelphia: Saunders, 1950.

Miller, G., Galanter, E., & Pribram, L. *Plans and the structure of behavior.* New York: Holt, Rinehart, & Winston, 1960.

Morban-Lancer, F. A. Sucking habits in the child and their origins in psychological traumas. *American Journal of Clinical Hypnosis,* 1961, *4,* 128–132.

Moss, A. Hypnodontics: Hypnosis in dentistry. In W. S. Kroger (Ed.), *Clinical and experimental hypnosis* (2nd ed.). Philadelphia: Lippincott, 1977.

Moss, C. *The hypnotic investigation of dreams.* New York: Wiley, 1967.

Murphy, G. *Personality.* New York: Harper & Row, 1947.

Nisbett, R. E. Hunger, obesity, and the ventromedial hypothalamus. *Psychological Review,* 1972, *79,* 433–453.

Orne, M. T. The nature of hypnosis: Artifact and essence. *Journal of Abnormal and Social Psychology,* 1959, *58,* 277–299.

Orne, M. T. On the social psychology of the psychological experiment: With particular reference to demand characteristics and their implications. *American Psychologist,* 1962, *17,* 776–783.

Orne, M. T. Can a hypnotized subject be compelled to carry out otherwise unacceptable behavior? *International Journal of Clinical and Experimental Hypnosis,* 1972, *20,* 101–117. (a)

Orne, M. T. On the simulating subject as a quasi-control group in hypnosis research: What, how, and why. In E. Fromm & R. E. Shor (Eds.), *Hypnosis: Research developments and persepectives.* Chicago: Aldine-Atherton, 1972, pp. 399–443. (b)

Orne, M. T. The construct of hypnosis: Implications of the definition for research and practice. In W. E. Edmonston (Ed.), *Conceptual and investigative approaches to hypnotic phenomena. Annals of the New York Academy of Sciences,* 1977, *296,* 14–33.

Owens, H. E. Hypnosis by phone. *American Journal of Clinical Hypnosis*, 1970, *12*, 57–60.

Paskewitz, D. A. EEG alpha activity and its relationship to altered states of consciousness. In W. E. Edmonston (Ed.), *Conceptual and investigative approaches to hypnotic phenomena. Annals of the New York Academy of Sciences*, 1977, *296*, 154–161.

Pearson, R. E., Thompson, K. F., & Edmonston, W. E. Clinical and experimental trance: What's the difference? A symposium. *American Journal of Clinical Hypnosis*, 1970, *13*, 1–16.

Perls, F. S. *In and out of the garbage pail.* New York: Bantam, 1972.

Perry, C. Variables influencing the posthypnotic persistence of an uncanceled hypnotic suggestion. In W. E. Edmonston (Ed.), *Conceptual and investigative approaches to hypnotic phenomena. Annals of the New York Academy of Sciences*, 1977, *296*, 264–273.

Raikov, V. The possibility of creativity in the active stages of hypnosis. *International Journal of Clinical and Experimental Hypnosis*, 1976, *25*, 258–268.

Reik, T. *Listening with the third ear.* New York: Farrar, Straus, 1948.

Richardson, E. H. *Hypnosis as a means of overcoming impotency.* Paper presented at the meetings of the American Psychological Association, Toronto, August, 1978.

Rogers, C. Toward a theory of creativity. In H. H. Anderson (Ed.), *Creativity and its cultivation.* New York: Harper & Brothers, 1959, pp. 69–82.

Rogers, C. *On becoming a person: A therapist's view of psychotherapy.* Boston: Houghton-Mifflin, 1961.

Rosen, G. History of medical hypnosis: From animal magnetism to medical hypnosis. In J. M. Schneck (Ed.), *Hypnosis in modern medicine* (3rd ed.). Springfield, Ill.: Charles C Thomas, 1963.

Sacerdote, P. Applications of hypnotically elicited mystical states to the treatment of physical and emotional pain. *International Journal of Clinical and Experimental Hypnosis*, 1977, *25*, 309–324.

Sarbin, T. R. Contributions to role-taking theory: I. Hypnotic behavior. *Psychological Review*, 1950, *57*, 255–270.

Sarbin, T. R., & Andersen, M. L. Role-theoretical analysis of hypnotic behavior. In J. E. Gordon (Ed.), *Handbook of clinical and experimental hypnosis.* New York: Crowell-Collier, 1967, pp. 319–344.

Sarbin, T. R., & Coe, W. C. *Hypnosis: A social psychological analysis of influence communication.* New York: Irvington, 1972.

Sarbin, T. R., & Lim, D. Some evidence in support of the role-taking hypothesis in hypnosis. *International Journal of Clinical and Experimental Hypnosis*, 1963, *9*, 98–103.

Schmidt, J. *Help yourself: A guide to self-change.* Champaign, Ill: Research Press, 1976.

Schneck, J. M. *Hypnosis in modern medicine* (3rd ed.). Springfield, Ill.: Charles C Thomas, 1962.

Schofield, W. *Psychotherapy: The purchase of friendship.* Englewood Cliffs, N. J.: Prentice-Hall, 1964.

Schutz, W. C. *Joy: Expanding human awareness.* New York: Grove Press, 1967.

Selye, H. *The stress of life.* New York: McGraw-Hill, 1956.

Severson, R. A., & Hurlbut, R. W. *Hypnosis, hyperempiria, and the ability to learn: A new look.* Paper presented at the meetings of the American Society of Clinical Hypnosis, Altanta, Georgia, October, 1977.

Shaw, H. L. Hypnosis and drama: A note on a novel use of self-hypnosis. *International Journal of Clinical and Experimental Hypnosis*, 1978, *26*, 154–157.

Sheehan, P. W. Incongruity in trance behavior: A defining property of hypnosis? In W. E. Edmonston (Ed.), *Conceptual and investigative approaches to hypnotic phenomena. Annals of the New York Academy of Sciences*, 1977, *296*, 194–207.

Sheehan, P. W., & Perry, C. *Methodologies of hypnosis: A critical appraisal of contemporary paradigms of hypnosis.* Hillsdale, N.J.: Erlbaum, 1976.

Shor, R. Hypnosis and the concept of generalized reality orientation. *American Journal of Psychotherapy,* 1959, *13,* 582–602.

Silva, J., & Miele, P. *The Silva mind control method.* New York: Simon & Schuster, 1977.

Spanos, N. P., & Barber, T. X. Toward a convergence in hypnosis research. *American Psychologist,* 1974, *29,* 500–511.

Spanos, N. P., & Barber, T. X. Behavior modification and hypnosis. In M. Hersen, R. M. Eisler, & P. M. Miller (Eds.), *Progress in behavior modification* (Vol. 3). New York: Academic Press, 1976.

Spanos, N. P., Rivers, S. M., & Ross, S. Experienced involuntariness and response to hypnotic suggestions. In W. E. Edmonston (Ed.), *Conceptual and investigative approaches to hypnotic phenomena. Annals of the New York Academy of Sciences,* 1977, *296,* 208–221.

Spiegel, H. The Hypnotic Induction Profile (HIP): A review of its development. In W. E. Edmonston (Ed.), *Conceptual and investigative approaches to hypnotic phenomena. Annals of the New York Academy of Sciences,* 1977, *296,* 119–128.

Spock, B. *Baby and child care.* New York: Affiliated Publishers, 1957.

Stanton, H. E. Hypnotherapy at a distance through the use of the telephone. *American Journal of Clinical Hypnosis,* 1978, *20,* 278–281.

Starker, S. Persistence of a hypnotic dissociative reaction. *International Journal of Clinical and Experimental Hypnosis,* 1974, *22,* 131–137.

Stevens, J. (Ed.). *Gestalt therapy verbatim.* New York: Bantam, 1971.

Swiercinsky, D., & Coe, W. C. The effect of "alert" hypnosis and hypnotic responsiveness on reading comprehension. *International Journal of Clinical and Experimental Hypnosis,* 1971, *19,* 146–153.

Tart, C. The hypnotic dream: Methodological considerations and a review of the literature. *Psychological Bulletin,* 1965, *63,* 87–99. (a)

Tart, C. Toward the experimental control of dreaming: A review of the literature. *Pyschological Bulletin,* 1965, *64,* 81–92. (b)

Tart, C. J. Psychedelic experiences associated with a novel hypnotic procedure, mutual hypnosis. In C. J. Tart (Ed.), *Altered states of consciousness.* New York: Wiley, 1969.

Thigpen, C. H., & Cleckley, H. M. *The three faces of Eve.* New York: McGraw-Hill, 1957.

Tinkler, S. The use of hypnosis in dental surgery. In J. Hartland (Ed.), *Medical and dental hypnosis and its clinical applications* (2nd ed.). London: Baillière Tindall, 1971.

Ulett, G., & Peterson, D. *Applied hypnosis and positive suggestion in medicine, dentistry, and patient care.* St. Louis, Mo: Mosby, 1965.

Vingoe, F. J. Comparison of the Harvard Group Scale of Hypnotic Susceptibility, Form A, and the Group Alert Trance Scale in a university population. *International Journal of Clinical and Experimental Hypnosis,* 1973, *21,* 169–179.

Walch, S. L. The red balloon technique of hypnotherapy: A clinical note. *International Journal of Clinical and Experimental Hypnosis,* 1976, *24,* 10–12.

Wallas, G. *The art of thought.* New York: Harcourt, Brace, 1926.

Watkins, J. The affect bridge: A hypnoanalytic technique. *International Journal of Clinical and Experimental Hypnosis,* 1971, *19,* 21–27.

Watkins, J. Antisocial behavior and hypnosis: Possible or impossible? *International Journal of Clinical and Experimental Hypnosis,* 1972, *20,* 61–79.

Weitzenhoffer, A. Open-ended distance hypnotherapy. *American Journal of Clinical Hypnosis,* 1972, *14,* 236–248.

Wertheimer, M. *Productive thinking.* New York: Harper, 1945.

Wickramasekera, J. On attempts to modify hypnotic susceptibility: Some physiological procedures and promising directions. In W. E. Edmonston (Ed.), *Conceptual and investigative approaches to hypnotic phenomena. Annals of the New York Academy of Sciences,* 1977, *296,* 143–153.

Wilson, S. C., & Barber, T. X. The Creative Imagination Scale as a measure of hypnotic responsiveness: Applications to clinical and experimental hypnosis. *American Journal of Clinical Hypnosis,* 1978, *20,* 235–249.

Wolberg, L. R. *Hypnoanalysis.* New York: Grune & Stratton, 1945.

Wolpe, J. The systematic desensitization treatment of neurosis. *Journal of Nervous and Mental Disease* 1961, *132,* 189–203.

Yarnell, T. Symbolic assertive training through guided affective imagery in hypnosis. *American Journal of Clinical Hypnosis,* 1972, *14,* 194–196.

Index